KORE

FROM ZERO!

George Trombley

Reed Bullen

Sunhee Bong

Myunghee Ham

Jiyoon Kim

Korean From Zero! Book 1
Proven Methods to Learn Korean with integrated Workbook

PREFACE

Korean From Zero! is a Korean language book series built on Korean grammar that makes sense! Each book is crafted page by page and lesson by lesson to have relevant (and sometimes fun) Korean conversation and sentence structure patterns that enhance the Korean learner's ability to speak Korean faster and understand the small nuances of Hangul and everyday Korean speech.

DEDICATION

This book is dedicated and made for people who truly want to learn Korean but also:

Korean culture lovers, Korean drama watchers, Korean beginners, KPOP music fans, people of Korean heritage connecting to their history, and anyone planning travel to Korea!

This began as a project for myself (George). This is the book I wanted when I started learning Korean, but it's also for anyone like me who loves Korea and the Korean language and want to have a closer connection to Korea itself.

All of us on the *Korean From Zero!* team wish you success on your road to Korean fluency.

DISTRIBUTION

Distributed in the UK & Europe by:
Bay Language Books Ltd.
Unit 4, Kingsmead, Park Farm, Folkestone,
Kent. CT19 5EU, Great Britain
sales@baylanguagebooks.co.uk

Distributed in the USA & Canada by:
From Zero LLC.
10624 S. Eastern Ave. #A769
Henderson, NV 89052, USA
sales@fromzero.com

COPYRIGHT

Printed in USA / England / Australia
ISBN-10: 0989654524
ISBN-13: 978-0-9896545-2-4

1st edition, May 2014
5th edition, (corrections) September 2020

Thanks for the nice comments! We love feedback!

I have already learned so much. I am excited for book 2 and 3!
Lauren C. – facebook

I'm not starting from zero but I had a ton of "now I get it moments" thanks to Korean From Zero!
Karen D. – twitter

I just finished reading Vol. 1 of this series and it was awesome! Basically under two months, I was able to get a deep understanding of the language. Some books would rely on heavy technically arranged jargon! I don't mean to say those books are awful, but they're really not handy for total beginners like me.
Andrei C. – via email

Excellent teaching. I understand so much better now. Having a native speaker present also gives me confidence that it is correct.
Permacore – youtube

I have tried other language books and software and nothing has had the affect on me that Korean From Zero has.
Josh F. – email

I tried many Korean books and found yours to be the best by far! Thanks again for such a great learning tool!
Christopher C. – email

I am from Morocco, I began to learn Korean 7 months ago and because of your book I can read, write and understand the Korean language.
I really enjoyed.
Zineb B. – email

I'm so glad I've found you, you're really helping me out and I appreciate it ❤ Kamsahamnida ❤ Hwaiting!!
Bella C. – facebook

I am a Russian guy, who admires your study book. It is really perfect, I understand everything fast and easily! My Korean becomes better day by day due to you!
Mikhail S. – email

안녕하세요!! I really looove this book! It teaches really clear and I understand easily, you guys did an amazing great job!
An L. – email

feedback@fromzero.com

Korean From Zero! – Book 1

You can help with a book review!

Reviews help! Please visit any of the major book seller websites and post a review of *Korean From Zero!* We are fanatical about making the best books for students who don't have access to a Korean teacher. Your book reviews help make new books possible!

You can help with feedback!

If you love, hate, or are confused about any concept in this book please email as at **feedback@fromzero.com** with your feedback so we can improve future versions.

VISIT **KoreanFromZero.com!**

Support for your Korean Learning!

- PDF copy of the book
- Mobile and Browser Audio Anytime Streaming
- FULL AUDIO sound pack for PC and WINDOWS

Thank you and enjoy your Korean journey,

The entire KFZ! team

How this book works:

Welcome!

Getting Started

❑ Play the sounds on mobile and in the browser!

To listen to the audio files on your mobile device or in any browser visit:
koreanfromzero.com/sounds

❑ Download the sound pack!

Visit **koreanfromzero.com** and download the100% Free Audio Files.

STEP 1: Download the zipped audio file to your WINDOWS or MAC computer. The direct link to the audio is **koreanfromzero.com/audio**

STEP 2: Unzip (uncompress) the zipped file.

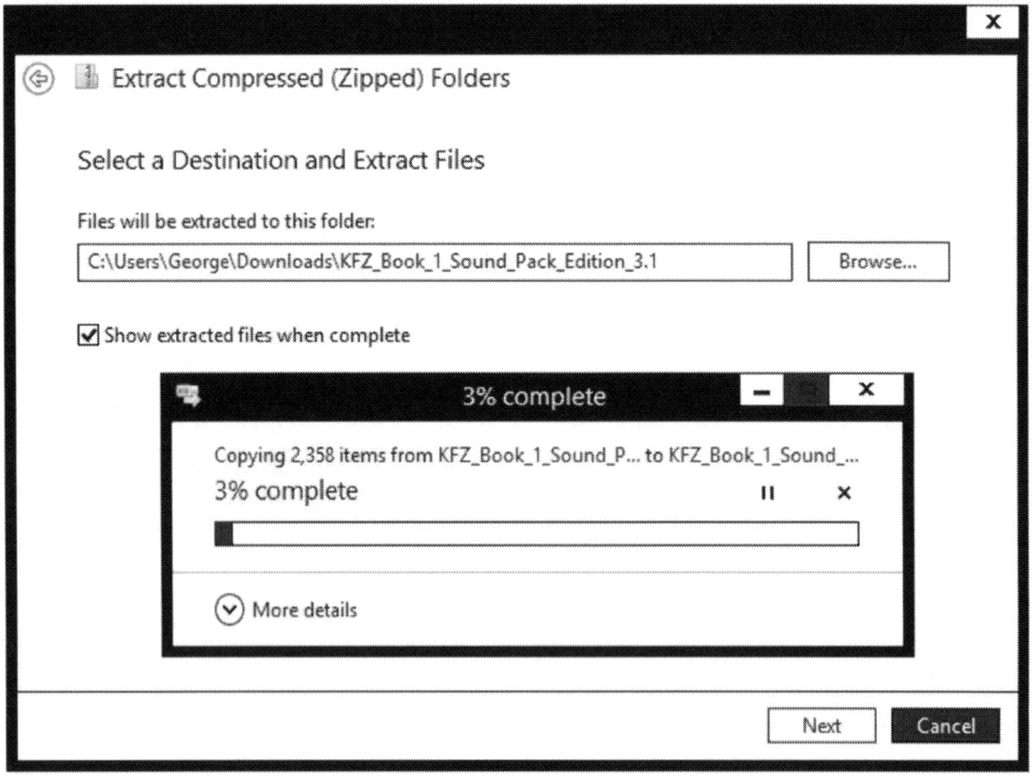

STEP 3: Each lesson will have its own folder.

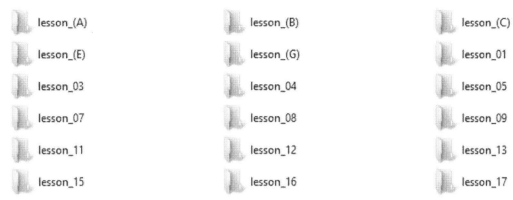

lesson_(A)	lesson_(B)	lesson_(C)
lesson_(E)	lesson_(G)	lesson_01
lesson_03	lesson_04	lesson_05
lesson_07	lesson_08	lesson_09
lesson_11	lesson_12	lesson_13
lesson_15	lesson_16	lesson_17

STEP 4: Open any lesson to view the sections of that lesson.

Action_Verb_Usage_Examples	Additional_Vocabulary	Conversation_E-K
Descriptive_Verb_Usage_Examples	Grammar_Examples	New_Action_Verbs
New_Words	Question_and_Answer	

STEP 5: In each section folder, you will find the sounds for that section in the order that they appear in the book.

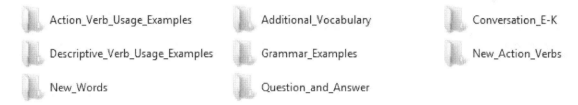

0001-What-...	1	What color do you like? 무슨 색깔을 좋아해요?
0002-What-f...	2	What foods do you dislike? 무슨 음식을 싫어해요?
0003-What-...	3	What kind of animals do you like? 어떤 동물을 좋아해요?
0004-What-t...	4	What type of things did you buy? 어떤 것을 샀어요?
0005-Which...	5	Which restaurant did you go to? 어느 식당에 갔어요?
0006-Which...	6	Which one is cheap? 어느 것이 싸요?
0007-There-...	7	There are a lot of red cars in front of my college. 제 대학교 ...
0008-I-boug...	8	I bought a black computer this Saturday. 이번주 토요일에 ...
0009-There-...	9	There are a lot of white things in hospitals. 병원에 하얀 것...
0010-Today-...	10	Today isn't so cold. 오늘은 별로 춥지 않아요.
0011-I-dont-...	11	I don't like apples that much. 나는 사과를 별로 좋아하지 않...
0012-I-dont-...	12	I don't go to America that much. 미국에는 별로 안 가요.
0013-I-dont-...	13	I don't watch basketball matches much. 농구시합을 별로 ...
0014-I-didnt...	14	I didn't get so many presents at the party. 파티에서 선물을 ...
0015-More-...	15	More water please. 물 더 주세요.
0016-I-boug...	16	I bought more fruits. 과일 더 샀어요.
0017-More-f...	17	More friends came. 친구들이 더 왔어요.

❑ Determine where to start!

If you can read and write the Korean writing system, HANGUL, then skip to lesson 1 on page 49. If not complete all the Hangul lessons first. This book does NOT use Romanized Korean after this section.

Introduction

❑ Welcome to KOREAN FROM ZERO!

LEARNING KOREAN can be intimidating at first, but don't worry! Our method is designed to guide you step-by-step through the basics of Korean grammar. You will be surprised how much easier a language is if you learn the basics. This book is dedicated to hammering the basics into your head.

Whether you're learning Korean for business, travel, or to make new friends, we've created these lessons to make sure you feel confident in your ability to SPEAK, READ, and WRITE what you've learned.

❑ Korean characters

WHAT ARE THESE CIRCLES, LINES, AND SQUARES? The Korean language uses a set of symbols called *Hangul* (한글, pronounced hangool), to spell all words in the Korean language. In the past, *hanja,* Chinese characters, were heavily used in Korea, but in modern Korea you can get by without ever learning very much - if any - *hanja*. In the first book, we will give you a crash course in *Hangul*. It is said that *Hangul* can be learned in a day but takes years to master. Throughout the lessons we will reinforce what is taught in the *Hangul* lessons and teach you exceptions to the rules, such as specific sound changes, as needed. NOTE: Hangul is sometimes spelled “hangeul” because it matches western spelling expectation, however the official Korean Romanization is “Hangul".

❑ Korean punctuation facts

HERE ARE SOME QUICK FACTS about Korean writing to help you get started.

UPPERCASE/LOWERCASE
In English, we learn to write both *A* and *a*, but in Korean there are no upper and lower cases. In other words, 아 is always 아 no matter where you find it in a sentence.

SENTENCE ENDING PUNCTUATION
Written Korean uses question marks, exclamation points, commas, and periods just like English. You will see their usage throughout the book.

❑ Before grammar…

Lessons A-G are dedicated to *Hangul* characters. After that a few lessons are dedicated to teaching numbers, key phrases, and how to introduce yourself. It's VERY important that you don't stress over the phrases and numbers lessons. Those sections are just for easy access to some things you will need before you know how to make your own sentences. The real power comes in knowing how the patterns work. Patterns will set your mind free of mindlessly memorizing phrases.
The best thing you can do, for your Korean, is learn how to read Korean well.
This is not a choice. You MUST learn *Hangul*. Once you know how to read, you will learn many key Korean grammar concepts that will set you firmly on the path to fluency.

❑ About the authors

George Trombley
Author George Trombley is a professional Japanese interpreter and author of the "Japanese From Zero!" book series. For over 20+ years he has interpreted at corporations such as Microsoft, IBM, NTT DoCoMo, Lucent Technologies, Varian Medical and in countries throughout North America, Europe, Asia and the Middle East. For "Korean From Zero!" book 1, George has teamed up his co-authors to create a book that is accessible for beginners, yet deep enough to help students of Korean at any level.

Reed Bullen
Author Reed Bullen, fluent in Korean, initially learned Korean through an intense immersion prior to his 2 year Mormon mission in the Korean countryside. During his mission he met thousands of Koreans and honed his skills teaching English as a free service of his church. After completing his mission, Reed continued mastering Korean. Reed befriended George at the bi-weekly Korean language meetup in Las Vegas. After working as a teacher at a private school in Korea, Reed married his Korean wife, Seah and now has a beautiful daughter. He is currently attending graduate school.

Myunghee Ham
Myunghee Ham attended college at Myongji university and has a degree in Korean literature and is also fluent in Japanese. She has been teaching Korean to foreigners for over 13 years, and currently works as a Korean teacher in Seoul.

Sunhee Bong
Native Korean Sunhee Bong grew up just south of Seoul in the city of Cheonan. Sunhee spent hundreds of hours working together with George and Reed to create natural Korean sentences and conversations. As a native Korean speaker, her contributions to the sometimes intense debate on Korean grammar have been invaluable to the book. Sunhee is currently ghosting Reed and George OR she has changed her number and all other forms of social media. Either way, we really want her to contact us since we miss her.

❑ WRITE IN THIS BOOK!

This book is your tool to learning in a way that will stick! Learning Korean is hard work so we want your knowledge to last forever. *Korean From Zero!* is designed to be an interactive workbook where you can take personal notes, add new words or phrases of your own, and develop your writing skills from hopeless/crazy/illegible (we all start that way!) to expert-level.

Every time you write in this book, you're making your connection to Korean a little bit stronger - we guarantee it!

화이팅! (hwaiting!)

*Koreans say this to mean, "persevere". It comes from the English word "fighting".

George Trombley
Reed Bullen
Sunhee Bong
Myunghee Ham

한글을 읽을 수 있어요?

Already know how to read Hangul?

Skip this section and move to Lesson 1 on page 49!

Korean Reading and Writing:
Introduction to Hangul

Why Learn Hangul?

Hangul is the main writing system of Korea. It's famous for being easy to learn and in many linguistic circles is considered genius. Prior to its invention in the 15th century, Korean used the same Chinese characters as China and Japan. Japanese and Chinese children spend a significant part of the school years devoted to learning the often complicated Chinese characters, but hangul can be learned in a few days for an average adult.

漢字 **Hanja**
Over 5000 characters for Chinese and 2000 for Japanese are used commonly.

한글 **Korean Hangul**
Just 24 unique symbols combine to make 12,000+ Hangul combinations.

If you aren't convinced yet as to how cool hangul is, here are the top five reasons you should learn hangul:

1. **It's easy. WAY easier than you imagine!**
   Some people say you can learn it in just two hours.

2. **It's cool. Seriously… none of your friends can write it!**
   Unless your friends are all studying Korean or ARE Korean you will be the coolest person around when you say, and show them, that you can read and write Korean!

3. **Your accent improves.**
   You have spent much of your life reading Roman letters (ABC) in a certain way. If you learn Korean with those letters you will often still read them the same way and not have a great Korean accent. If you learn hangul, you won't have to fight your English speaking habits!

4. **Korean Romanization can be a bit confusing. It's just easier to learn hangul.** With combinations like "SEO" and "SAE" and "SEU" it's pretty easy to screw up the Romanization of Korean. Hangul fixes this problem. Besides… imagine if a Korean person decided to learn English only using hangul characters!

5. **There is no choice!** Because hangul is so easy, It's rare that a book teaching Korean teaches using Roman letters. Even this book teaches 100% in hangul after the hangul lesson section.

Hangul Consonants and Vowels

Hangul characters are "built" using consonant and vowel parts. Using these individual parts over 12,000 characters can be constructed.

Don't worry about memorizing the chart on this page, it is mainly to be used as a reference. The next few lessons will gradually teach you how to read and write hangul.

In the "Korean From Zero!" series, hangul is taught using the most common input interface in the modern world, the keyboard. In the last writing lesson you will learn the basics of typing in Korean. **NOTE:** It's helpful if you know what each of the symbols are called in Korean. Check the "Hangul Character Name Chart" in the back of this book.

Consonants: single key on keyboard

ㄱ	ㄴ	ㄷ	ㄹ	ㅁ	ㅂ	ㅅ	ㅇ	ㅈ	ㅊ	ㅋ	ㅌ	ㅍ	ㅎ
G	N	D	R/L	M	B	S	null/NG	J	CH	K	T	P	H

Consonants: double key on keyboard (shift + consonant)

ㅃ	ㅉ	ㄸ	ㄲ	ㅆ
PP	JJ	DD	KK	SS

Vowels: single key on keyboard

ㅏ	ㅑ	ㅓ	ㅕ	ㅗ	ㅛ	ㅜ	ㅠ	ㅡ	ㅣ	ㅐ	ㅔ
a	ya	eo	yeo	o	yo	u	yu	eu	i	ae	e

Vowels: double key on keyboard (shift OR vowel + vowel)

ㅒ	ㅖ	ㅘ	ㅙ	ㅚ	ㅝ	ㅞ	ㅟ	ㅢ
yae	ye	wa	wae	woe	wo	we	wi	ui

A Korean Reading and Writing: Creating Simple Hangul

A New Hangul

In this lesson we will focus on the first five consonants and five vowels only to get used to creating the characters. Writing with the correct stroke order will make your writing neater.

Consonants

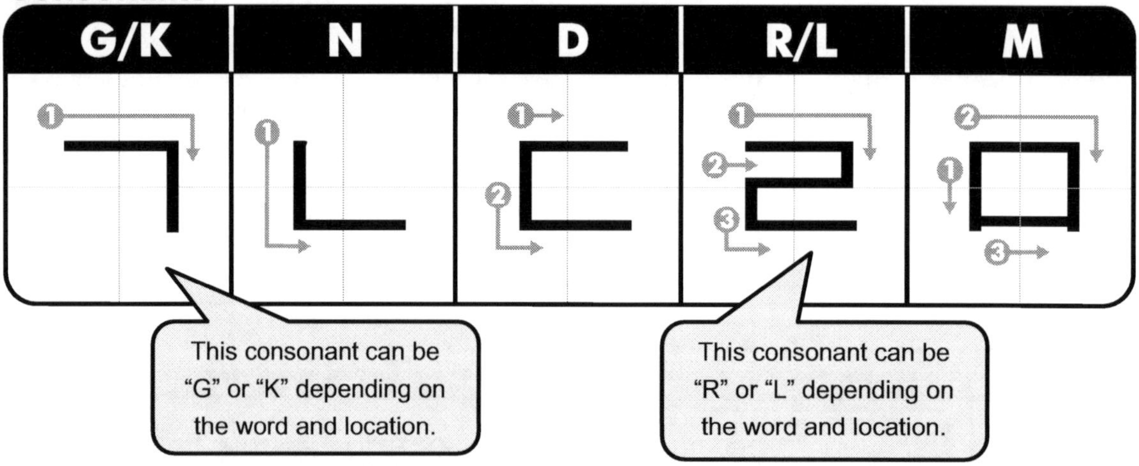

Vowels

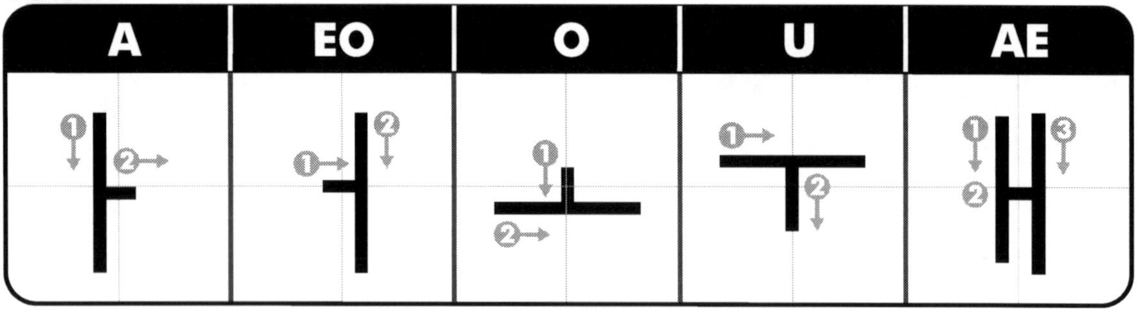

as in father   as in awe   as in boat   as in zoo   as in men

NOTE: You will never just write a consonant or vowel alone. They are always combined. In the next section we will combine them to make a variety of sounds.

A Hangul Points

❑ A-1. Using consonants and vowels to create simple hangul

When creating a hangul character you will always start with a consonant, and then follow it with a vowel. Let's look at some simple consonant + vowel combinations:

g		a		ga
ㄱ	+	ㅏ	=	가

d		a		da
ㄷ	+	ㅏ	=	다

n		a		na
ㄴ	+	ㅏ	=	나

r		a		ra
ㄹ	+	ㅏ	=	라

❑ A-2. Writing order and orientation

There are standing (vertical) and laying (horizontal) vowels. Standing vowels always "stand" to the right of the consonant. Laying vowels always "lay" below the consonant.

C = consonant V = vowel

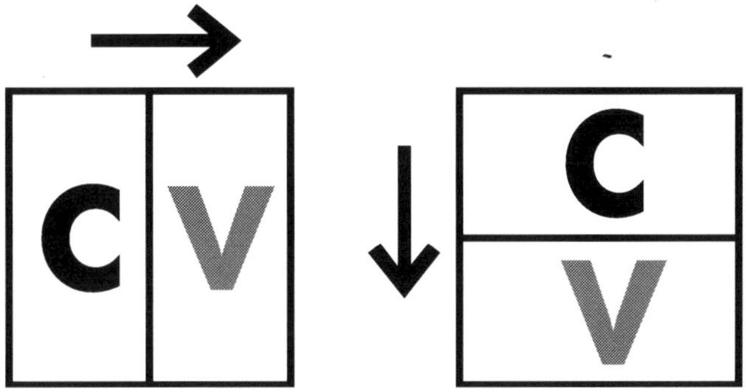

left / right combinations

ga	ge	na	ne	da	de	ra	re	ma	me
가	개	나	내	다	대	라	래	마	매

top / bottom combinations

go	gu	no	nu	do	du	ro	ru	mo	mu
고	구	노	누	도	두	로	루	모	무

❑ A-3. The different sounds of ㄱ, ㄹ

ㄱ can be pronounced like a G or a K. Typically at the beginning of a sentence or word you will hear ㄱ like a K, and if it is in the middle of a word it's closer to a G.

고구마 koguma
(sweet potato)

ㄹ can be pronounced like an R or an L. Typically at the beginning of a sentence you will hear ㄹ like a R and in the middle more like L.

레벨 rebel
(level)

As you learn Korean you will find that, depending on the word, the sound of ㄱ and ㄹ will shift. In many cases you just have to learn how that particular word is pronounced.

❑ A-4. The sound difference between ㅓ and ㅗ

The sound for ㅓ doesn't really exist in English so it might be hard to master.
One technique to getting closer to the right sound is this trick:

1. Shape your mouth as if you are going to say "AH"
2. Now say "OH". It should feel as if the sound is coming from the back of your throat.

A Writing Practice

To practice stroke order, first trace the light gray characters, then write each character 5 times.

ga	가						ru	루					
na	나						mae	매					
no	노						mo	모					
da	다						meo	머					
do	도						ma	마					
reo	러						go	고					

A Words You Can Write

Using just the hangul from this lesson, we can already write many Korean words.

개
dog

다
everything, all

가구
furniture

나라
country

노래
song

누구
who

도마
cutting board

모래
sand

매너
manners

모두
everyone

누나 | 누 | 나 | | | | | | | | | |
older sister (when said by males)

고구마 | 고 | 구 | 마 | | | | | | | | |
sweet potato

A Hangul Matching

Connect the dots between each hangul and the correct Romanization. You can check your answers in the Answer Key at the back of the book.

매 ·	· reo
다 ·	· do
도 ·	· gu
루 ·	· ma
마 ·	· mae
내 ·	· ru
러 ·	· da
고 ·	· go
구 ·	· nae

B Korean Reading and Writing: Pure Vowel Sounds

B New Hangul

In this lesson we learn five more consonants and five more vowels.

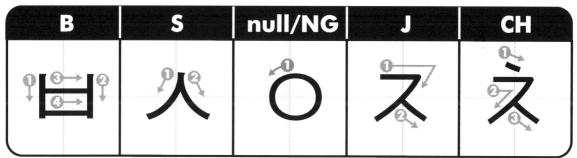

Consonants

B	S	null/NG	J	CH
ㅂ	ㅅ	ㅇ	ㅈ	ㅊ

Vowels

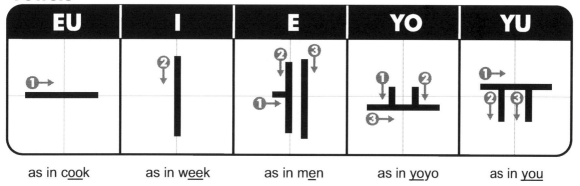

EU	I	E	YO	YU
ㅡ	ㅣ	ㅔ	ㅛ	ㅠ
as in cook	as in week	as in men	as in yoyo	as in you

B Hangul Points

❑ B-1. Creating pure vowels with ㅇ

In this lesson we introduce the hangul character ㅇ. In order to say a pure vowel, meaning a vowel all by itself, you must use ㅇ in the consonant spot. Here are some examples:

아 (a) 이 (i) 오 (o) 애 (ae)

You MUST start a pure vowel hangul with ㅇ. In other words, you can never have a vowel by itself. When ㅇ is the first character then it is silent and makes no sound. Notice how the orientation of the ㅇ changes depending on the vowel it's used with. The shape of the ㅇ doesn't have to change, but many Korean fonts change the shape for balance reasons.

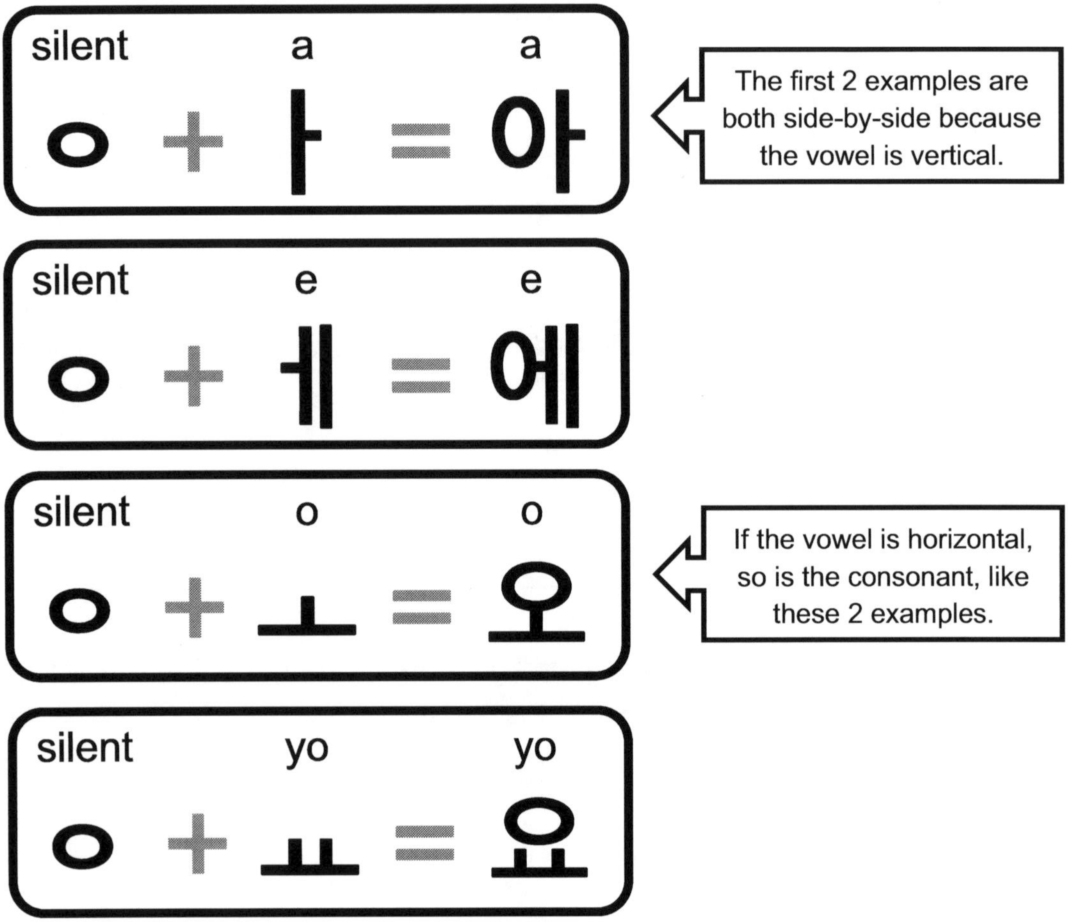
silent a a
ㅇ + ㅏ = 아
The first 2 examples are both side-by-side because the vowel is vertical.
silent e e
ㅇ + ㅔ = 에
silent o o
ㅇ + ㅗ = 오
If the vowel is horizontal, so is the consonant, like these 2 examples.
silent yo yo
ㅇ + ㅛ = 요

Here are some example words using the hangul you have already learned. See if you can read them.

Example words

아이 child
우유 milk
이유 reason
오다 to come
요리 cooking
어디 where
아기 baby
이 teeth

❑ B-2. Written versions versus font versions of hangul

When you first learn hangul you might be confused as to how some characters change when written versus when typed. Let's look at how ㅈ and ㅊ change when written.

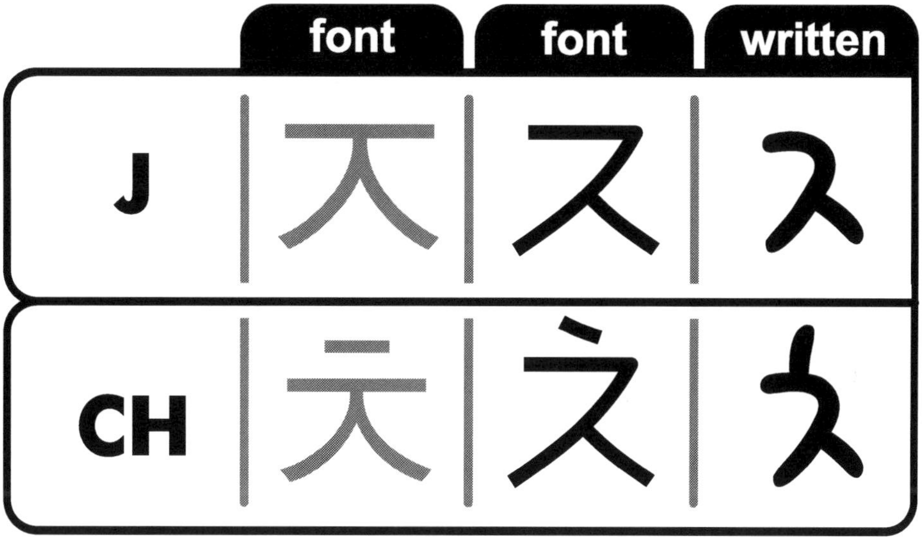

❑ B-3. The different sounds of ㅅ

ㅅ normally sounds like an "S" sound, however when combined with certain hangul it will sound like an "SH" sound. We cover this rule in Lesson G in more depth.
NOTE: When ㅛ (yo) and ㅠ (yu) are combined the "y" is discarded in the Romanization.

said as "S"	사 (sa)	서 (seo)	소 (so)
새 (sae)	세 (se)	수 (su)	스 (seu)

said as "SH"	시 (shi)	쇼 (sho)	슈 (shu)
셔 (sheo)	샤 (sha)		

ㅓ and ㅑ vowels are introduced in the next lesson.

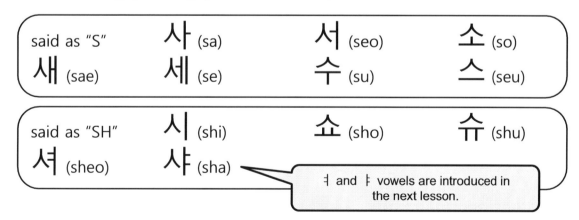

❑ B-4. The difference between ㅐ and ㅔ

In modern Korea, there is no sound difference between ㅐ and ㅔ. Some words will use one or the other based on the roots of the word. You simply just need to learn how to "spell" some words in Korean, just like in English.

❑ B-5. The difference between ㅜ and ㅡ

To the untrained ear these will both sound the same. But the mouth makes a different shape for ㅜ and ㅡ.

ㅜ is said with the lips pushed out like you're trying to kiss someone and saying "oo" as in "moon".

ㅡ is said by pulling the lips back almost as far as you can and saying the same "oo" sound.

B Writing Practice

To practice stroke order, first trace the light gray characters, then write each character 5 times.

beu	브						a	아					
bi	비						shi	시					
se	세						shu	슈					
ji	지						chae	채					
byo	뵤						jeo	저					
yo	요						eu	으					

B Words You Can Write

Using just the hangul from this lesson, we can already write many Korean words.

비
rain

시
poem

차
car

버스
bus

세대
generation

아기
baby, infant

주스
juice

자유
freedom, liberty

개미
ant

베개
pillow

다시	다	시										

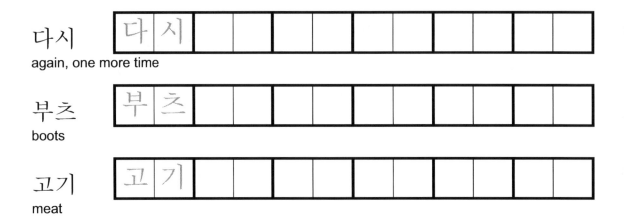

again, one more time

부츠	부	츠										

boots

고기	고	기										

meat

B Hangul Matching

Connect the dots between each hangul and the correct Romanization.

시 ·	· jeo
슈 ·	· shi
오 ·	· che
체 ·	· ja
브 ·	· se
요 ·	· shu
자 ·	· beu
저 ·	· o
세 ·	· yo

C Korean Reading and Writing: Hard Hangul Sounds

C New Hangul

In this lesson we learn four more consonants and five more vowels.

Consonants

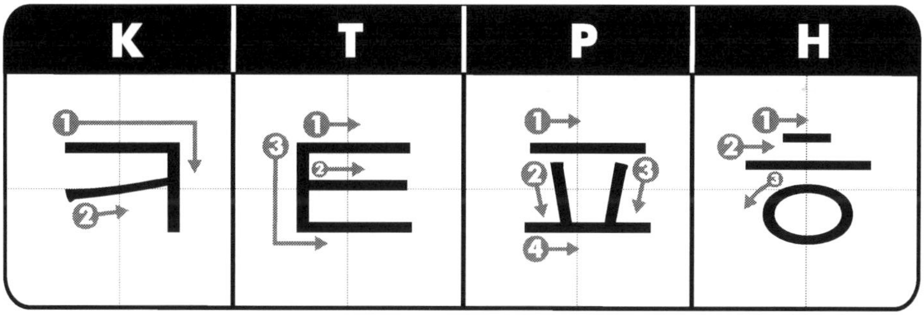

Vowels

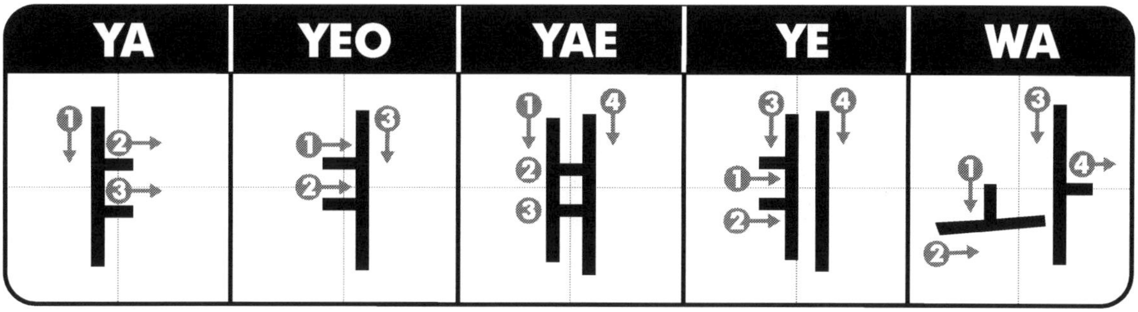

as in yarn | as in awe | as in yen | as in yen | as in wash

C Hangul Points

❑ C-1. Hard and soft sounds with Hangeul

If you are like me, you may be a bit frustrated with how ㅂ, ㄷ, ㅈ, and ㄱ seem to shift sounds in Korean. Koreans also have a hard time explaining the exact timing of the shift of these sounds. ㅂ is a “B” sound, but there are cases where it also sounds like a “P”. ㄷ is “D”, but in some cases it will be “T”. ㅈ is “J” but sometimes it’s “CH”. And finally, ㄱ is “G”, but in some cases it will sound like “K”.

You will find that in the beginning of a word ㅂ, ㄷ, ㅈ, and ㄱ will tend to be the "stronger" sounds like P, T, CH, and K. But they will be softer in the middle and end of words.

ㅍ (P), ㅌ (T), ㅊ (CH), ㅋ (K) on the other hand are ALWAYS pronounced with hard sounds.

❑ C-2. The difference between ㅒ and ㅖ

ㅒ and ㅖ are both pronounced like the "ye" in "yen". In modern Korean there is no change in sound. You will see both symbols used in Korean words. Consider them just different ways of spelling. Just like in English you will have to learn the correct spelling.

❑ C-3. Written and typed versions of ㅎ

ㅎ (H), looks different depending on the font and penmanship. Look at how it can change.

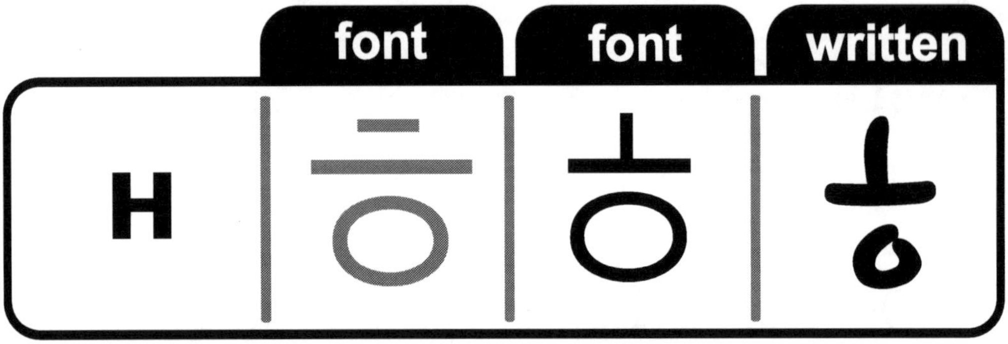

C Writing Practice

To practice stroke order, first trace the light gray characters, then write each character 5 times.

ko	코						wa	와					
teu	트						gye	계					
pa	파						teo	터					
ha	하						gwa	과					
sha	샤						ryeo	려					
gyeo	겨						hye	혜					

C Words You Can Write

Using just the hangul from this lesson, we can already write many Korean words.

코 nose	코
화 anger	화
타다 to ride	타 다
피 blood	피
세계 the world	세 계
파티 party	파 티
피자 pizza	피 자
노트 notebook	노 트
얘기 story, talk	얘 기
그녀 her, she	그 녀

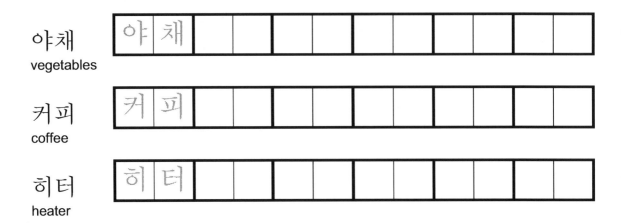

야채
vegetables

야	채										

커피
coffee

커	피										

히터
heater

히	터										

C Hangul Matching

Connect the dots between each hangul and the correct Romanization.

히 ·	· teu
파 ·	· pa
와 ·	· hi
커 ·	· yae
트 ·	· gye
얘 ·	· keo
랴 ·	· rya
계 ·	· hwa
화 ·	· wa

D Korean Reading and Writing: Double Consonants

D New Hangul

In this lesson we learn the final five consonants and six more vowels.

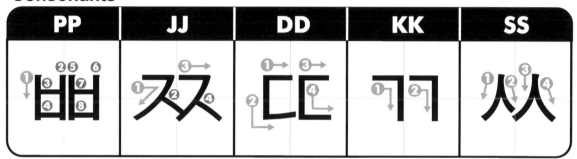

Consonants

PP	JJ	DD	KK	SS
ㅃ	ㅉ	ㄸ	ㄲ	ㅆ

Vowels

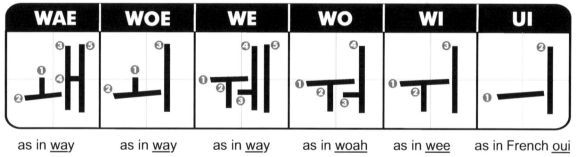

WAE	WOE	WE	WO	WI	UI
ㅙ	ㅚ	ㅞ	ㅝ	ㅟ	ㅢ
as in <u>way</u>	as in <u>way</u>	as in <u>way</u>	as in <u>woah</u>	as in <u>wee</u>	as in French <u>oui</u>

D Hangul Points

❑ D-1. Double vowels

Double vowels are made by writing, or typing two of the vowels you have already learned together. They are written and input from the left vowel to right. Just like the single vowels when they are used alone they still require the "null" character.

왜 (wae) 외 (woe) 워 (wo) 의 (ui)

❑ D-2. 위 vs 외 sound differences

These two double vowel types are commonly used in Korean. Despite looking similar in style, 외 is pronounced like the English word “WAY” and 위 is pronounced like the English word “WE”. Perhaps this guy below will help you remember which is which.

❑ D-3. The double vowels

ㅙ ,ㅚ, and ㅞ, despite having different parts, all sound like the “WE” in “wet”. When said slowly by your Korean friends they might sound out the first part of the double vowel, but in spoken Korean you might not hear the sound difference.

❑ D-4. ㅟ and ㅢ sound differences

ㅟ and ㅢ might be tricky to pronounce since they are so close in sound. The sound change of these characters is similar to the sound change for ㅜ and ㅡ. For each sound, start with the “oo” part of “moon”, then transition into the “ee” (like clean). The only difference is the shape of your mouth when you say the “oo” part.

❑ D-5. Double consonant sounds versus other sounds

ㅂ (b / p), ㅈ (j / ch), ㄷ (d / t), ㄱ (g / k) have a “hard” and “soft” sound. The double consonants ㅃ,ㅉ,ㄸ,ㄲ, and ㅆ are sounded out with more energy than single consonants. You push air into your mouth that is held back, you PAUSE slightly to let the pressure build. Then you release to make the sound. Try not to spit on anyone.

D Writing Practice

To practice stroke order, first trace the light gray characters, then write each character 5 times.

sshi	씨						dwae	돼					
we	웨						gwi	귀					
ddo	또						noe	뇌					
ggeu	끄						wo	워					
ui	의						ppa	빠					
jja	짜						wi	위					

D Words You Can Write

Using just the hangul from this lesson, we can already write many Korean words.

귀 ear	귀											
또 again, once	또											
씨 family, clan (Mr., Mrs. etc)	씨											
뒤 back, rear	뒤											
뇌 brain	뇌											

뭐
what? huh?

뭐											

짜다
salty

짜	다										

외부
the outside

외	부										

빼기
subtraction

빼	기										

꼬리
tail

꼬	리										

의미
meaning

의	미										

위치
position, location

위	치										

궤도
orbit

궤	도										

돼지
pig

돼	지										

지뢰
land mine (explosive)

지	뢰										

쓰레기
garbage, trash

쓰	레	기									

D Hangul Matching

Connect the dots between each hangul and the correct Romanization.

돼 ·	· sshi
짜 ·	· wi
빠 ·	· mwo
씨 ·	· dwae
꼬 ·	· dwi
위 ·	· ppa
뭐 ·	· jja
뒤 ·	· gwi
귀 ·	· kko

E Korean Reading and Writing: Final Consonants

There will be no new hangul vowels or consonants taught in this lesson, because you have learned all of them!

This lesson introduces the most important concept when learning hangul. Understanding the ideas taught in this lesson will allow you to conjugate verbs, adjectives and create even basic sentence structure.

E Hangul Points

❑ E-1. Hangul with a "final consonant"

So far all of the hangul characters in prior lessons have ended with a vowel and only had two parts. Now we will add consonants to the bottom of the character. These "final" consonants are called 받침 (batchim).

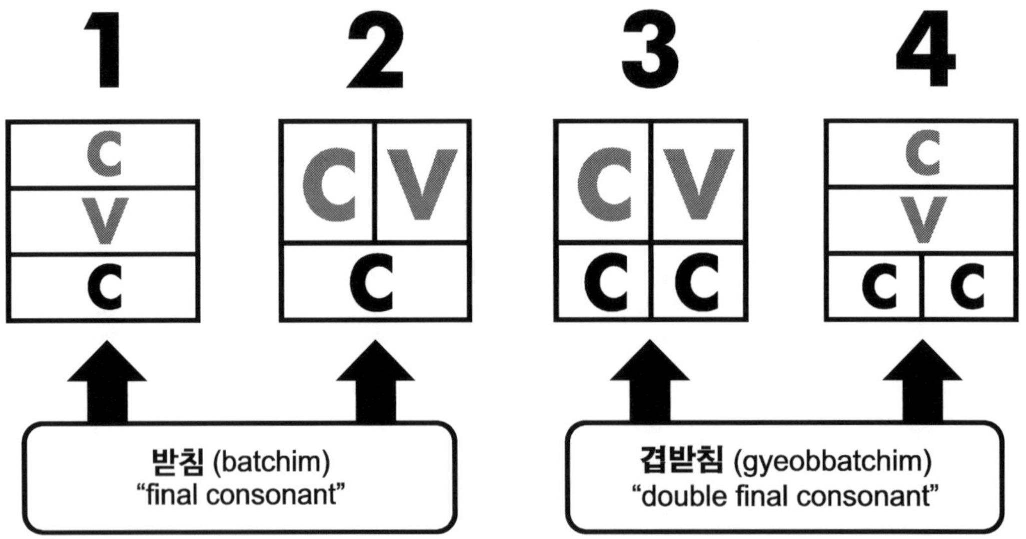

1 – This shows the first consonant with a horizontal vowel and final consonant.
2 – This shows the first consonant and a vertical vowel and final consonant.
3 – This shows the first consonant with a vertical vowel and double final consonant.
4 – This shows the first consonant with a horizontal vowel and double final consonant.

Now let's look at some actual complete hangul that have final consonants.

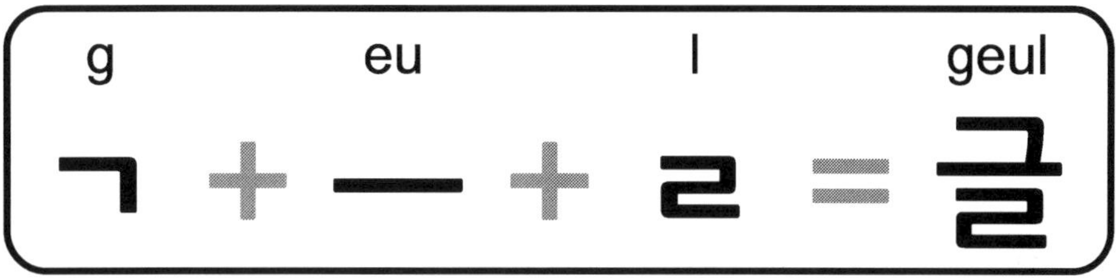

The following hangul characters are all built using the same initial consonant and vowel combination. The final consonant, 받침 (batchim), is the only thing that is different. The black portion is the 받침 (batchim).

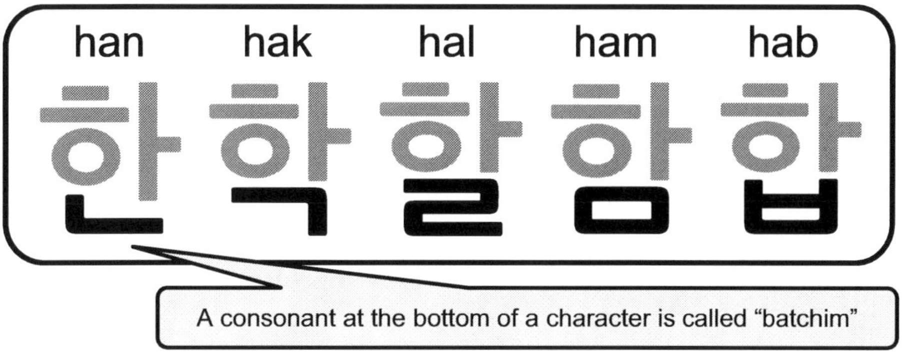

Here are some words that contain 한글 (hangul) that have 받침 (final consonant).

Example Words

한국 (Korea)	책 (book)	눈 (eye, snow)	손 (hand)
지갑 (wallet)	택시 (taxi)	감자 (potato)	발 (foot)
남자 (man)	친구 (friend)	사람 (person)	돈 (money)

❑ E-2. Answers to common questions

1. A vowel is never called *batchim*. There is no *batchim* if the character ends with a vowel.
2. ㅃㅉㄸㄲㅆ can be in the final position as a final consonant, but they aren't considered "double final consonants".

Example Words (with 겹받침, double batchim)

많다 (to be many)
넓다 (to be wide)
닭갈비 (chicken ribs)
읽다 (to read)

Example Words (with ㅃ,ㅉ,ㄸ,ㄲ,ㅆ)

바쁘다 (to be busy)
짜다 (to be salty)
닦다 (to wipe)
가깝다 (to be close)
떡 (rice cakes)
있다 (to have)

❑ E-3. Double vowels

Some words have “double vowels”.

Example Words (with double vowels)

사과 (apple)
의미 (meaning)
귀 (ear)
위치 (position)

❑ E-4. The “ng” sound when ㅇ is the final consonant

When ㅇ is used as the final consonant, then it is no longer silent and instead makes an “ng” sound.

g		a		ng		gang
ㄱ	+	ㅏ	+	ㅇ	=	강

j		eo		ng		jeong
ㅈ	+	ㅓ	+	ㅇ	=	정

The following words will contain a standalone vowel and / or a sound with ㅇ as the batchim.

Example Words

안녕 (goodbye)
이야기 (a story)
우산 (umbrella)
방 (room)
농담 (a joke)
동물 (animal)
아이 (child)
이유 (reason)
등 (etc)
요가 (yoga)
오염 (pollution)
공항 (airport)

Ready for more fun? Here are words that have 2 ㅇ in some of their characters. The first ㅇ allows the vowel to stand alone without a consonant, and the second ㅇ is the "ng" sound as the batchim.

Example Words

응급 (emergency)
영국 (United Kingdom)
양말 (socks)
용 (dragon)
고양이 (cat)
엉덩이 (buttocks)
옹알이 (babbling)
앵두 (cherry)

F Korean Reading and Writing: Typing Hangul

In your life, you will probably type Korean a lot more than you will write it. Of course, when you are learning Korean, you will write it a lot, but when you are talking to your friends using chat programs on your phone or computer, you will be typing.

In order to type Korean on your computer you will need to first make sure you have installed the proper programs. You can go here for a tutorial on how to install Korean on your device.

http://www.KoreanFromZero.com/install-korean
(it's 100% free)

You can also purchase stickers for just a few dollars to place hangul on your own keyboard. Search Amazon.com or your favorite online store to see what is available.

F Hangul Typing Points

❑ F-1. Typing your first and second characters

The Korean keyboard is designed to make it easy to type Korean. All the consonants (black) are on the left, and all the vowels (white) on are the right.

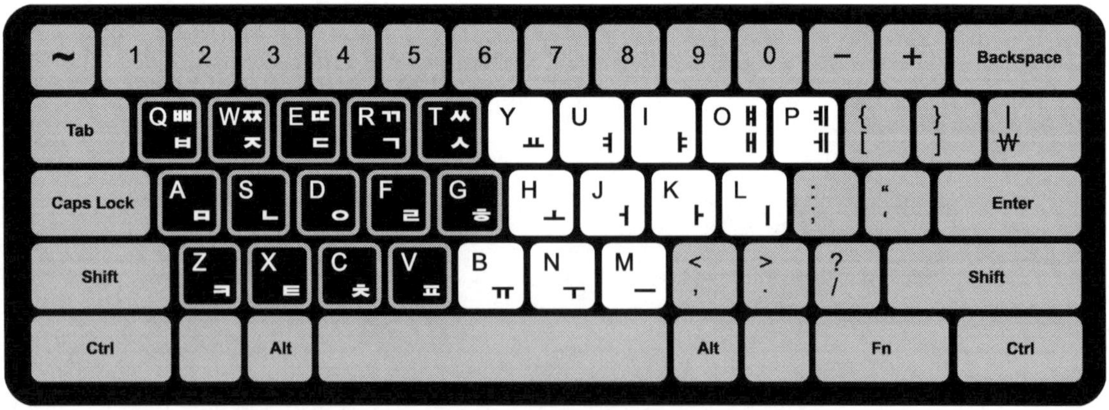

In order to make one character, we need at least two keystrokes. Even the most basic and the most complicated Korean character will start with a consonant (black key) followed by a vowel (white key). You can cut out the keyboard in the back of the book for easy reference.

As you type, the character will "build" on the screen. It might be confusing at first, but just keep typing. You do not have to "finish" a character. The keyboard input software knows when to end your character as long as you have correctly typed it.

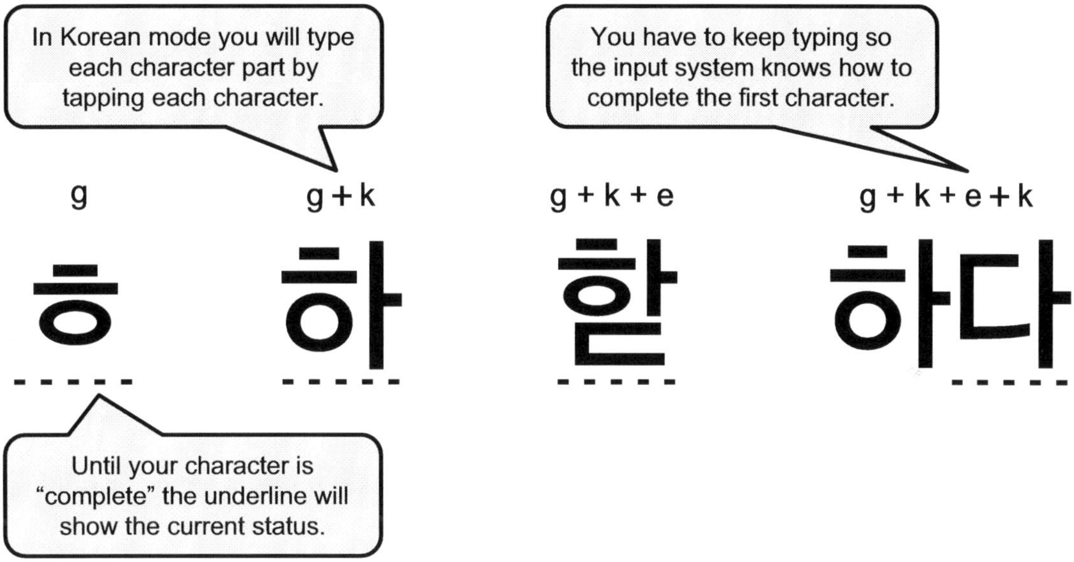

As you are typing, sometimes the 3rd key stroke gets added to the bottom of the first character, EVEN though you want this to be the 1st stroke of the 2nd character. DO NOT PANIC! Once you type the next vowel the 2nd character will be created. This is because NO Korean character can have a CVCV combination. Once the software sees CVCV it knows to make two characters. If it doesn't type what you want it to… YOU have made a mistake. You can always use backspace to erase just the last input.

❑ F-2. Shift characters

The "double consonants" require the shift key to be pressed first. Or, in the case of "double vowels", two vowels in a row will be required to complete the vowel.

Double Key Examples	**Example Word**
shift + ㄷ = ㄸ	또 (again, once more)
shift + ㅈ = ㅉ	짜다 (salty)
ㅗ + ㅏ = ㅘ	화요일 (Tuesday)
ㅜ + ㅓ = ㅝ	월요일 (Monday)

❑ F-3. Shortcuts and the spacebar (Windows)

On a Windows PC, you can cycle installed language input methods by pressing "ALT" key and "SHIFT" at the same time. When in Korean mode you can toggle to English input by hitting the RIGHT "ALT" key. The left one does NOT toggle. When you hit the space bar, the character you are working on will immediately complete and a space will be added.

❑ F-4. Hangul typing exercise

If you don't have stickers or a Korean keyboard, you can print a copy of the keyboard from the back of this book.

Now you should practice typing Korean. Here are some practice words along with the actual keys pressed to make them display. As you type each key, watch how the characters build on the screen.

The letters on top of each example are what you ACTUALLY type on your keyboard when you are in Korean mode.

rla	cl
김	치

Kimchee

gks	rnr	tk	fka
한	국	사	람

Korean person

dks	sud	gk	tp	dy
안	녕	하	세	요

Good Afternoon / Hello

dl rjt dms shift+wk dy

이것은 짜요

This is salty.

dh smf dms cn dnj dy

오늘은 추워요

Today is cold.

rhos cksg dk dy

괜찮아요

It's okay.

G Korean Reading and Writing: Sound Change Rules

Why is this lesson is important?
When certain hangul are combined, their sounds can change in unexpected ways. You will eventually learn some words with spellings that don't match their pronunciation.

Check this lesson later!
As you learn more Korean, this lesson should be reviewed to make sure you aren't missing any common sound change rules.

❑ G-1. T-stops

When certain characters are used as a 받침 they are converted to "T" sound. The "T Stop" characters are ㅅ,ㅈ, ㅊ, ㅎ. ㄷ and ㅌ are also T sounds but since they are normally T sounding they are left out of the examples.

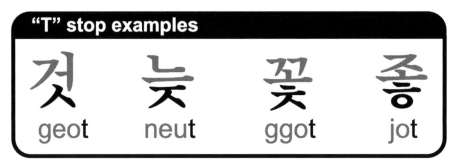

"T" stop examples

것	늦	꽃	좋
geot	neut	ggot	jot

Example with T-stops

1. 이것 (pronounced 이걷) — this one
2. 늦게 (pronounced 늗게) — late
3. 몇 개 (pronounced 멷개) — how many?
4. 좋다 (pronounced 조타) — to be good (see section G-9)

When any T stop consonant is followed by ㅇ(이응) then the T stop is cancelled.

"T" stop cancels when followed by 이응

것이	받아	늦어	꽃이
geoshi	bada	neujeo	ggochi

❑ G-2. ㅅ followed by ㅎ

When ㅅ is followed by a ㅎ in the next hangul character the sound moves into the ㅎ position and is pronounced as ㅌ.

ㅅ is a ㅌ sound when before ㅎ

못하다 → 모타다

sounds like

못해요 → 모태요

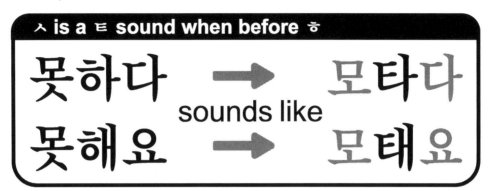

❑ G-3. "S" to "SH" sound with ㅅ

When ㅅ is combined with ㅣ, ㅕ, ㅑ, ㅛ, ㅠ the "S" changes to an "SH" sound.
The sound REMAINS as "S" when combined with ㅏ, ㅓ, ㅜ, ㅗ, ㅡ, ㅐ, ㅔ.

"SH" sounds for ㅅ

시	쇼	셔	샤	슈
shi	sho	sheo	sha	shu

"S" sounds for ㅅ

사	소	서	스	수
sa	so	seo	seu	su

Example of S and SH sound for ㅅ

1. 소시지 sausage
2. 셔츠 shirt
3. 쇼핑 shopping
4. 샴푸 shampoo
5. 슈퍼마켓 super market
6. 사서 librarian

❑ G-4. "L" and "R" sound for ㄹ (리을)

When there are two ㄹ back to back the sound is always "L". When ㄹ is at the end of a word it's always an "L" sound. When ㄹ is at the beginning of a word it's an "R" sound.

2 ㄹ in a row is "L" sound

빨라	멜론	몰라
ppalla	mellon	molla

Last ㄹ in a word is "L"

한글	과일	이발
hangeul	gwail	ibal

❑ G-5. ㄹ(리을) and ㄴ (니은) combinations

When a ㄹ is followed by a ㄴ OR the ㄴ is followed by ㄹ the combined sound changes to a double "L" sound.

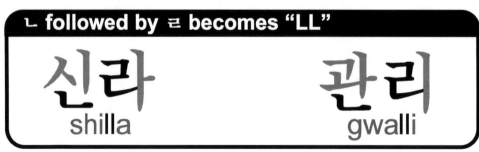

ㄹ followed by ㄴ becomes "LL"

설날	줄넘기
seollal	chulleomgi

ㄴ followed by ㄹ becomes "LL"

신라	관리
shilla	gwalli

❑ G-6. Silent 겹받침 (double consonant)

As discussed in a prior lesson, sometimes one of the double consonants in a double consonant is silent.

Some double 받침 have silent parts

삶 → 삼
sounds like
싫어 → 시러

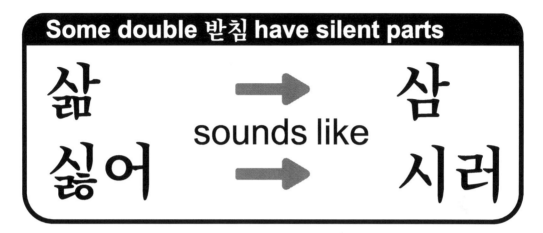

The double consonants you might see are ㄺ, ㄻ, ㄿ, ㅀ, and ㅄ.

❑ G-7. Random CH sound when not expected

When ㄷ is followed by ㅎ the resulting sound is "CH".
Similarly when ㅌ is followed by 이 the ㅌ changes to a "CH" sound.

Example CH sounds

1. 끝이 (pronounced 끄치) — tip, end
2. 같이 (pronounced 가치) — together
3. 닫히다 (pronounced 다치다) — to shut

❑ G-8. The various sounds for 하다

After lesson 6 you will learn about 하다 verbs, and this sound change will be important then. 하다 tends to blend into the hangul character before it.

1. Soft 하다

After you begin learning the 하다 verbs you might feel that it's RARE to hear 하다 actually as HADA. It often sounds like 아다 instead of 하다, or the H sound is weak.

Examples

1. 공부**하**다 (sounds like 공부**아**다) — to study
2. 말**하**다 (sounds like 마**라**다) — to tell, to talk
3. 단순**하**다 (pronounced 단수**나**다) — to be simple

2. Harder sound before 하다

When consonants like ㄱ, ㅂ are followed by 하다 they blend into a harder sound. See section G-9 also.

Examples

1. 대답하다 (sounds like 대다**파**다)	to reply, to answer
2. 착하다 (sounds like 차**카**다)	to be kind

특별 정보 Special Information

SUMMARY: Learning VS actual speaking is different.
When you are learning Korean, and you have a friend or teacher helping you they might actually say 하다 as “HADA” because they are saying it slow.

The 하다 sound change is actually common with other words that start with ㅎ.

Examples

1. 천천**히** (sounds like 천천**이**)	slowly
2. 안녕**하**세요 (sounds like 안녕**아**세요)	hello

❑ G-9. Shift to hard sound after and before ㅎ

When ㄱ,ㄷ,ㅂ, or ㅈ are before or after ㅎ their sound shifts to their harder sound counterparts ㅋ,ㅌ,ㅍ, and ㅊ.

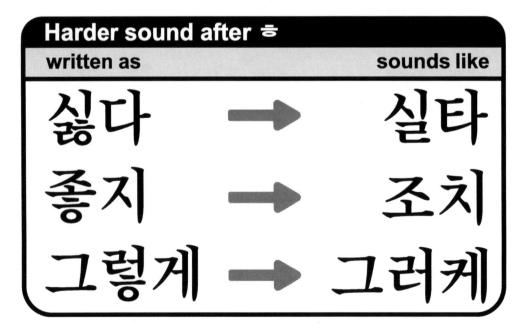

Harder sound after ㅎ

written as		sounds like
싫다	→	실타
좋지	→	조치
그렇게	→	그러케

Harder sound prior to ㅎ

written as		sounds like
축하	→	추카
대답해	→	대다패

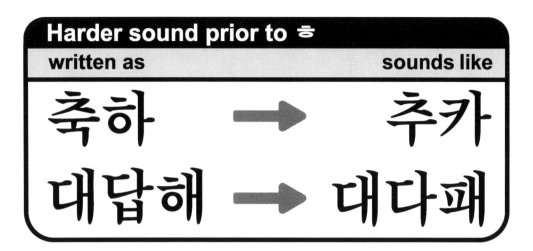

G Hangul Practice Boxes

Use these boxes to practice writing any of the hangul you learned in lessons A-G.

Lesson 1:

20 Starter Phrases

1

Before This Lesson

1. Make sure you know, or have an understanding of, how to read hangul. From this point on there will be no Roman letters.

Lesson Goals

1. Learn some of the basic phrases that you will need right away when speaking Korean.

From The Teachers

1. Don't worry too much about the grammar behind any of the phrases. As you learn more, the grammar in these phrases will start to make sense. Right now your goal should be to memorize and use these phrases.

2. If you can't read the hangul just go back to the hangul charts and lessons to refresh your memory.

As a language teacher, I am never happy when students focus on phrases instead of grammar. It's like the saying, "Give a man a fish and you feed him for a day. Teach a man to fish and you feed him for a lifetime."

Memorizing phrases is nowhere near as effective as learning how to build your OWN sentences. These phrases will help you communicate when your Korean still… sucks.

1 Communication

These phrases are handy when you begin using the Korean you have learned.

1. **천천히 말해 주세요.**
   Please speak slowly.

2. **다시 한 번 말해 주세요.**
   Please say it again once more.

3. **영어로 뭐예요?**
   What is it in English?

4. **한국어로 뭐예요?**
   What is it in Korean?

5. **한국어 잘 못 해요.**
   I can't understand Korean well.

> 못 해요 is pronounced like 모 태요. There is no "S" sound.

1 Coming and Going

6. **안녕하세요.**
   Hello, Good morning, Good afternoon, Good evening

7. **잘 지냈어요?**
   How have you been?

8. **오래간만이에요!**
   Long time no see!

9. **안녕히 가세요.**
   Goodbye (said to the person going)

10. 안녕히 계세요.
Goodbye (said to the person staying)

11. 안녕.
Goodbye / Hello (used with friends only)

1 Quick Answers

These are some quick answers you can give when questions are asked to you in Korean.

12. 네.
Yes.

13. 아니요.
No.

14. 아마도. (아마 can also be used as part of a sentence.)
Maybe.

15. 괜찮아요.
It's okay. / I'm okay.

16. 안돼요.
No! (strong) / I can't!

1 Manners

17. 감사합니다.
Thank you.

18. 고맙습니다.
Thank you.

19. 고마워.
Thanks. (used only with friends)

20. 천만에요.
You're welcome. (not very commonly used)

1 Additional Phrases

Use this area to write in other phrases you have learned outside of this book. Put the Korean phrase first.

K: ______________________ E: ______________________

K: ______________________ E: ______________________

K: ______________________ E: ______________________

K: ______________________ E: ______________________

K: ______________________ E: ______________________

K: ______________________ E: ______________________

K: ______________________ E: ______________________

K: ______________________ E: ______________________

K: ______________________ E: ______________________

K: ______________________ E: ______________________

K: ______________________ E: ______________________

K: ______________________ E: ______________________

Lesson 2:

Korean Numbers

2

Before This Lesson

1. Review hangul.
2. Practice writing or typing the phrases you learned in the last lesson.

Lesson Goals

1. Learn the two types of Korean counting systems.

From The Teachers

1. It will take some effort to learn the two counting systems. Don't worry too much if you are slow to memorize them. The first 10 numbers of both systems are most important.

   These systems are repeated in several lessons throughout the book so eventually you will memorize them.

Lesson Highlights

2-7.
Differences between the Korean and Chinese number systems

2-12.
100 and above

2 Korean Number System 한국의 숫자

❑ 2-1. Different Korean Number Systems

Korean has two number systems. They are the "Korean numbers" and "Chinese numbers". Each one has its specific uses that you will learn as we progress through the lessons.

The two systems are typically never mixed, with the exception of telling time.

You must know both systems to survive in Korea. Both systems will be taught in this lesson and reinforced in following lessons.

❑ 2-2. The singles 1-10 (Korean Number System)

The Korean numbers only go up to 99. Let's look at 1-10.

the singles (1–10)		
Number	Korean Number	Sounds Like
1	하나	
2	둘	
3	셋	섿
4	넷	넫
5	다섯	다섣
6	여섯	여섣
7	일곱	
8	여덟	여덜
9	아홉	
10	열	

Some typical things that use the Korean numbers are: age, time (hours), and a variety of counters. We will learn these in later lessons. For now just learn how to count 1-10.

❑ 2-3. The teens (Korean Numbers)

The teens (11-19) are very easy. Just add 열 (10) in front of the single numbers 1-9.

the teens (11-19)		
Number	Korean Number	Sounds Like
11	열하나	
12	열둘	
13	열셋	열셋
14	열넷	열넷
15	열다섯	열다섣
16	열여섯	열여섣
17	열일곱	
18	열여덟	열여덜
19	열아홉	

❑ 2-4. The tens (Korean Numbers)

The Korean number system has unique words for the 10's.

the tens (20-90)	
Number	Korean Number
20	스물
30	서른
40	마흔
50	쉰
60	예순
70	일흔
80	여든
90	아흔

❑ 2-5. Combining the tens and singles to make 11-99 (Korean Numbers)

Now you know every word required to count from 1-99 with the Korean numbers. You can make all the other numbers simply by stringing them together.

For example if you want to make 22 you just say 20 then 2.

Examples

22 is	스물 (20)	+	둘 (2)	=	스물둘
45 is	마흔 (40)	+	다섯 (5)	=	마흔다섯
76 is	일흔 (70)	+	여섯 (6)	=	일흔여섯
99 is	아흔 (99)	+	아홉 (9)	=	아흔아홉

tens + singles 21-29

Number	Korean Number
21	스물하나
22	스물둘
23	스물셋
24	스물넷
25	스물다섯
26	스물여섯
27	스물일곱
28	스물여덟
29	스물아홉

❑ 2-6. 100 and above (Korean Numbers)

The Korean counting system stops at 99. Above 99 you must jump to the “Chinese system” also called “Sino-Korean numbers”. All numbers 100 and above will be taught in section 9-11. Before you get there, let the first 99 absorb!

2 Chinese Number System 한국의 숫자

❑ 2-7. Differences between the Korean and Chinese numbers

The Chinese number system is completely unique from the Korean system. The Korean system stops at 99, but with the Chinese system, numbers from 1 to 1,000,000,000 and beyond can be made. Depending on the usage, one number system will be used over the other. We will discuss when each system is used as we learn counters and other Korean concepts in this book and other books in the series.

It's important to note that even though it's called the "Chinese" system, these numbers are considered part of the Korean language and not part of Chinese. In other texts you may see the Chinese numbers referred to as "Sino-Korean". "Sino" just means "Chinese". We feel that calling them "Chinese" is more comfortable.

❑ 2-8. The singles 1-10 (Chinese System)

Let's look at the first 10 numbers in the Chinese counting system.

the singles 1–9	
Number	Chinese Number
1	일
2	이
3	삼
4	사
5	오
6	육
7	칠
8	팔
9	구
10	십

❑ 2-9. The teens (Chinese Numbers)

The teens (11-19) are just as easy as the Korean system. Just add 십 (10) in front of the single numbers 1-9.

the teens 11–19		
Number	Korean Number	Sounds Like
11	십일	시빌
12	십이	시비
13	십삼	십쌈
14	십사	십싸
15	십오	시보
16	십육	심뉵
17	십칠	
18	십팔	십팔
19	십구	십꾸

The 십 sound in this chart should sound like an abruptly ending "B" sound. It isn't as hard as a "P".

The 십 changes to the "M" sound 심.

NOTE! The word 씨팔 in Korean is the same as the "F" word in English. So don't put too much emphasis on the first ㅅ sound!

❑ 2-10. The tens (Chinese Numbers)

The Chinese number system doesn't have unique words for the 10's. Instead you simply say 2 in front of 10 to say 20. The pattern is very easy!

Examples

20 is	이 (2)	+	십 (10)	=	이십
40 is	사 (4)	+	십 (10)	=	사십

the tens (20–90)			
Number	Chinese Number	Number	Chinese Number
20	이십	60	육십
30	삼십	70	칠십
40	사십	80	팔십
50	오십	90	구십

❑ 2-11. Combining tens and singles for 11-99 (Chinese Numbers)

In order to make 11-99 you can just string the numbers together to create them.

Examples

25 is	이 (2)	+	십 (10)	+	오 (5)	=	이십오 (25)
38 is	삼 (3)	+	십 (10)	+	팔 (8)	=	삼십팔 (38)
59 is	오 (5)	+	십 (10)	+	구 (9)	=	오십구 (59)
82 is	팔 (8)	+	십 (10)	+	이 (2)	=	팔십이 (82)

tens + singles (21–29)	
Number	Chinese Number
21	이십일
22	이십이
23	이십삼
24	이십사
25	이십오
26	이십육
27	이십칠
28	이십팔
29	이십구

❑ 2-12. 100 and above (Chinese Numbers)

It's not hard to do numbers above 100, but you shouldn't overwhelm yourself this early! We will teach higher numbers in section 9-11. Right now you should focus on 1-99 in both number systems.

2 Workbook Area

❑ A2-1. Korean VS Chinese number practice

Look at the following numbers and try to say both versions. Write in the numbers as best as you can with the *hangul* you know. You can check your answers in the Answer Key in the back of the book.

1. 12

   Korean: ______________________________

   Chinese: ______________________________

2. 43

   Korean: ______________________________

   Chinese: ______________________________

3. 29

   Korean: ______________________________

   Chinese: ______________________________

4. 55

   Korean: ______________________________

   Chinese: ______________________________

5. 16

   Korean: ______________________________

   Chinese: ______________________________

6. 20

   Korean: ______________________________

   Chinese: ______________________________

Lesson 3:

Self Introduction / Age

3

Before This Lesson

1. Learn the Korean numbers, since saying your age in Korean requires them.

Lesson Goals

1. Learn the key phrases to say to people you are meeting for the first time.

2. Learn how to say your age in Korean.

From The Teachers

1. This is the last lesson where phrases are taught in such quantity. After this lesson we will begin teaching grammar patterns. However, introducing yourself is a key part of speaking Korean, so the only option at this point is to memorize the key phrases.

3 First Meeting 첫인사

When you first meet new Koreans you will hear a variation of the first or second phrase. If you are meeting in a more formal situation then the first phrase will be used. In more casual situations such as language meetups, the classroom, or among friends you will most likely hear the second sentence.

1. 만나서 반갑습니다.

Nice to meet you. (very polite)

습니다 despite written with a "B" sound (ㅂ) is pronounced like 슴니다 with an "M" sound. (ㅁ)

Pronunciation Note

As needed we will remind you of some of the pronunciation rules.

Simple Rule

When ㅂ (B) is followed by ㄴ (N) the sound always changes to ㅁ (M).

Longer Explanation

In Korean words, when the 받침, also called "the final consonant", is ㅂ, the final sound of the character would be a "b" sound. However, when ㅂ is immediately followed by ㄴ (n sound) the sound changes to an "m" sound as if the ㅂ was actually ㅁ.

seub ni da
습니다

sounds like →

seum ni da
슴니다

2. 반가워요.

Nice to meet you. (Casual Polite)

This phrase is used when you are meeting new people in a casual situation. Perhaps a friend introduced you to their friends, or you are at one of the many language meetups around Korea. NOTE: If you want a quick way to make Korean friends in Korea, you should travel to a language meetup. Many major cities throughout the world have meetups. Visit Meetup.com and search for "Korean Language Exchange".

3 Asking Names 이름 묻기

This simple phrase also has a few variations depending on the formality of the situation. In formal situations, such as talking to someone above you in status, (bosses, someone older than you, teachers) the first two can be used, but in more casual situations the third one is fine.

3. 성함이 어떻게 되세요?
What is your name? (formal)

4. 성함이 어떻게 되십니까?
What is your name? (formal)

5. 이름이 뭐예요?
What is your name? (when talking to equals or people below you)

How to answer

When answering, there are a few ways to do it.

The reality is that, since you are not Korean, any way will be fine. Koreans will be tougher on native Koreans in regard to formality than a foreigner learning the language. So if you get this wrong, you will not be summarily killed. Even Koreans will answer a formal question with a more casual / polite response depending on the situation.

Typically, you are safe to match formal to formal and casual to casual. But if the person is older than you, your response should show them the respect they "deserve" as an elder, even if they ask in a casual manner.

6. ________ 입니다.
I am ______________________________.

This is very standard, yet formal and polite. Nothing bad can happen if you are polite.

7. ________ (이) 라고 합니다.
I am called ________________________.

This is used if your name and what you are called are different. If you are "Joseph" but everyone calls you "Joe" this is the phrase you use. If the Korean version of your name ends with a 받침 then use the 이 in the parenthesis.

8. 제 이름은 ______________________ 입니다.
My name is ___________________.

This is the polite way to tell someone your name if you haven't been asked.

3 Asking Age 나이 묻기

9. 나이가 어떻게 되세요?

How old are you?
This literally means "What does your age become?" and is polite.

10. 몇 살이에요?

(sounds like 며쌀)
How old are you?
This is polite, but is much closer to casual than formal. It can be asked to children.

11. ______________________ 입니다.
(sounds like 임니다) (always use Korean numbers)

I am ___________ years old.
This is the polite way to say how old you are, either way you are asked your age.

ages (1-100 years old)					
Age	Korean	Age	Korean	Age	Korean
1	한 살	18	열여덟 살	35	서른다섯 살
2	두 살	19	열아홉 살	36	서른여섯 살
3	세 살	20	스무 살	37	서른일곱 살
4	네 살	21	스물한 살	38	서른여덟 살
5	다섯 살	22	스물두 살	39	서른아홉 살
6	여섯 살	23	스물세 살	40	마흔 살
7	일곱 살	24	스물네 살	41	마흔한 살
8	여덟 살	25	스물다섯 살	42	마흔두 살
9	아홉 살	26	스물여섯 살	43	마흔세 살
10	열 살	27	스물일곱 살	44	마흔네 살
11	열한 살	28	스물여덟 살	45	마흔다섯 살
12	열두 살	29	스물아홉 살	50	쉰 살
13	열세 살	30	서른 살	60	예순 살
14	열네 살	31	서른한 살	70	일흔 살
15	열다섯 살	32	서른두 살	80	여든 살
16	열여섯 살	33	서른세 살	90	아흔 살
17	열일곱 살	34	서른네 살	100	백 살

❑ 3-1. Korean age VS International age

In Korea you might be surprised that even a baby can be born and in one month be 2 years old. Koreans use the Chinese New Year to count their age. So everyone in Korean age is always 1-2 years older than their international age. It all depends on when they were born.

So when you ask a Korean person who hasn't travelled abroad their age, they will most likely give you their "Korean age". So that "18" year old girl might actually be 16… you have been warned!

Example conversation

A: 몇 살이에요?
B: 열여덟 살이에요.
A: 몇 살이에요?
B: 스무 살입니다.

A: How old are you?
B: I am 18 years old.
A: How old are you?
B: I am 20 years old.

3 Workbook Area

❑ A3-1. Korean Ages

Write the Korean ages in the blanks provided. Remember to only use the Korean counting system. Write in the answers as best as you can with the Hangul you know. You can check your answers in the Answer Key in the back of the book.

1. 19 years old ______________________
2. 41 years old ______________________
3. 22 years old ______________________
4. 20 years old ______________________
5. 36 years old ______________________
6. 28 years old ______________________
7. 5 years old ______________________
8. 67 years old ______________________

3 Vocabulary Builder

During your studies you will soon realize that grammar points aren't so easily forgotten. But you need more than grammar to speak effectively – you need a lot of vocabulary too!

Throughout this book we will introduce groups of words that are important for everyday Korean speaking. You don't have to try to memorize them all at once. Just familiarize yourself with each group since they will be showing up in subsequent lessons.

■ Group A: the body 몸

몸	body
입	mouth
눈	eye
귀	ear
코	nose
얼굴	face
손	hand
발	foot
팔	arm
다리	leg
손가락	finger
발가락	toes
머리	head, hair
이	tooth

Lesson 4:

Creating Simple Sentences

Before This Lesson

1. Know vocabulary group: A words (the body).

Lesson Goals

1. Learn how to make simple questions and answer them in Korean.

From The Teachers

1. This is the first lesson where we begin to work on learning grammar structures. From this lesson forward we will build more and more on what we already know.

4

Lesson Highlights

4-1.
Creating simple sentences with 이다

4-2.
Making questions with 이다

4 New Words 새로운 단어

책	book
펜	pen
잡지	magazine
사과	apple
바나나	banana
고양이	cat
개	dog
차	car
버스	bus
친구	friend
박민수	Minsu Park (man's name)
김준호	Junho Kim (man's name)

4 New Phrases 새로운 어구

1. 뭐예요?
What is it?

2. 몰라요.
I don't know.

4 Korean Culture 한국 문화

Korean names are often just three characters long. The last name is one character, and the first name is two characters. The family name, (last name) is actually said first. 씨 follows the name, to mean "Mr.", "Mrs.", etc. There is always a space before the 씨.

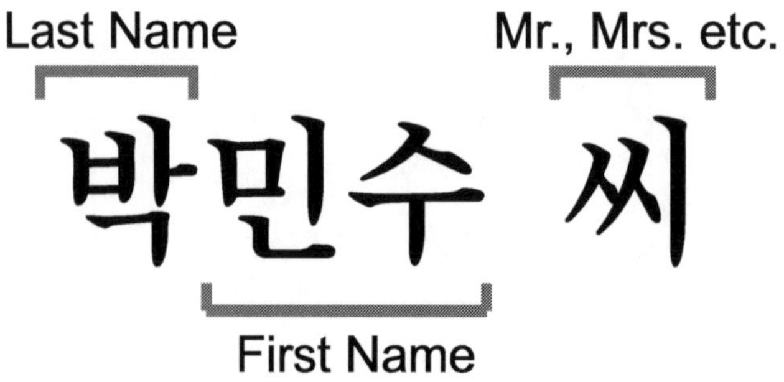

4 Grammar 문법

4-1. Creating simple sentences with 이다

이다, depending on the context, can mean: "it is", "this is", "they are", "these are", "I am", "you are", "he is", "she is", and "we are". It's always placed at the end of a sentence. As discussed in prior lessons we know that Korean has several levels of politeness. Let's look at how to conjugate 이다 into a few forms.

The most polite form of 이다 is:
입니다 (pronounced like 임니다)

> Whenever ㅂ is the 받침 followed by ㄴ the ㅂ sound changes to ㅁ

[noun]입니다. (no space after the noun)
It's a [noun].

Example sentences

1. 책입니다. It's a book.
2. 펜입니다. It's a pen.
3. 사과입니다. It's an apple.
4. 고양이입니다. It's a cat.

Among friends it's more common to change 입니다 to 이에요 which is the 요 form conjugation of 입니다. The 요 form is still considered polite, so if you accidentally use it with someone you don't know it isn't a problem.

Example sentences

1. 책이에요. It's a book.
2. 펜이에요. It's a pen.

Notice that the sentences above each have objects where the final sound is a consonant. In this case you will always use 이에요. However, if the final sound is a vowel, 이에요 can't be used. Instead, you MUST use 예요.

Example sentences

1. 차예요. It's a car.
2. 코예요. It's a nose.
3. 사과예요. It's an apple.
4. 고양이예요. It's a cat.

> 이 in 고양이 is part of the word. 예요 is used since 이 has no 받침.

NOTE: It doesn't matter if the final sound is a vowel or consonant when using 입니다. Either way you will use 입니다.

❍ 4-2. Making questions with 이다

The way you create a question is different, depending on which version of 이다 you use. If you use the 요 form (이에요) then you simply add a question mark and make it sound like a question.

[noun]이에요? (no space after the noun)
Is it a [noun]?

1. Example conversation between friends.

A: 뭐예요?	A: What is it?
B: 발이에요.	B: It's a foot.

2. Example conversation between friends.

A: 고양이예요?	A: Is it a cat?
B: 아니요. 개예요.	B: No, it's a dog.

The more polite form of 이다 (입니다) has a special question form.

[noun] 입니까?
Is it a [noun]?

Example conversation

1. Conversation between friends.

A: 뭐입니까?	A: What is it?
B: 발입니다.	B: It's a foot.

2. Conversation between friends.

A: 고양이입니까?	A: Is it a cat?
B: 아니요. 개입니다.	B: No, it's a dog.

❍ 4-3. Remember that 이다 is neutral

In English we use a lot of pronouns like "he", "she", etc. in our sentences. Korean also has pronouns that will be taught in lesson 7, but pronouns are typically not expressed directly. The context of the conversation decides if 이다 means "it is", "he is", "she is", etc.

Example conversation

1. Conversation between friends at a party full of people.

A: (pointing) 친구예요? — A: Is she a friend?
B: 네. 친구예요. — B: Yes, she is a friend.

2. Conversation between Mr. Kim and a person he doesn't know.

A: 박민수 씨입니까? — A: Are you Minsu Park?
B: 아니요. 김준호입니다. — B: No, I am Junho Kim.

4 Question and Answer 질문과 대답

1. **책이에요?** — **Is it a book?**
   네. 책이에요. — Yes. It's a book.
   아니요. 잡지예요. — No. It's a magazine.

2. **뭐예요?** — **What is it?**
   차예요. — It's a car.
   버스예요. — It's a bus.
   몰라요. — I don't know.

3. **귀예요?** — **Is it an ear?**
   아니요. 코예요. — No. It's a nose.
   아니요. 입이에요. — No. It's a mouth.
   네. 귀입니다. — Yes. It's an ear.

4. **다리입니까?** — **Is it a leg?**
   아니요. 발입니다. — No. It's a foot.
   아니요. 머리예요. — No. It's a head.
   네. 다리예요. — Yes. It's a leg.

5. **버스예요?** — **Is it a bus?**
   네. 버스예요. — Yes. It's a bus.
   아니요. 차예요. — No. It's a car.
   아니요. — No.

6. **사과예요?** — **Is it an apple?**
   아니요. 바나나예요. — No. It's a banana.
   네. 사과예요. — Yes, it's an apple.
   네. 사과입니다. — Yes, it's an apple.

7. **개입니까?** — **Is it a dog?**
아니요. 고양이입니다. — No. It's a cat.
아니요. 고양이예요. — No. It's a cat.
네. 개입니다. — Yes, it's a dog.
네. 개예요. — Yes, it's a dog.

4 Workbook Area

❑ A4-1. Questions to you

Answer the following question as if it was asked to you.

1. 박민수입니까?

____

❑ A4-2. Sentence Jumble

Using ONLY the words and particles provided, create Korean sentences that match the English translation. Conjugate verbs and reuse items as needed.

1. 이다, 차, 책, 버스, 개, 네, 아니요

____
It's a dog.

____
Is it a book?

____
No. It's a car.

2. 바나나, 사과, 이다, 버스, 네, 아니요

____
It's an apple.

____
Is it a banana?

____
No. It's a bus.

❑ A4-3. Picture question and answer

Answer the following questions by looking at the pictures. You can check your answers in the answer key for this lesson.

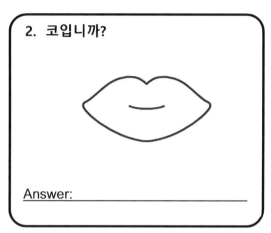

1. 뭐예요?

Answer: ______________________

2. 코입니까?

Answer: ______________________

3. 박민수 씨예요?

Answer: ______________________

4. 뭐예요?

Answer: ______________________

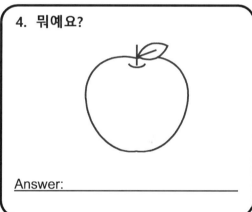

4 Sentence Building 문장 만들기

In each lesson we will build on a previous sentence. Watch it grow and transform each time new concepts are introduced.

뭐예요?
What is it?

4 Vocabulary Builder

Here are some more words that will be helpful when you are speaking Korean. Many of these words will be used in the following lesson, so make sure to learn them.

■ Group B: foods 음식

과일	fruit
야채	vegetable
고기	meat
귤	tangerine/mandarin orange
오이	cucumber
버섯 (버섣)	mushroom
멜론	melon

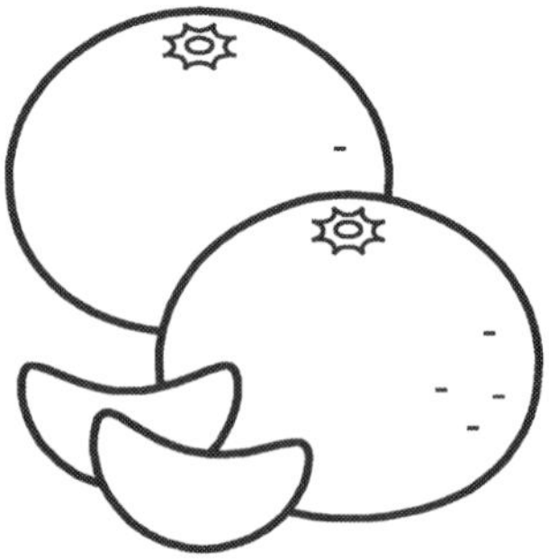

■ Group C: countries 나라

미국	America
한국	Korea
영국	United Kingdom
호주	Australia
캐나다	Canada
중국	China
태국	Thailand
일본	Japan
독일	Germany
프랑스	France
멕시코	Mexico
필리핀	Philippines
인도	India

Lesson 5:

This, That, and Negatives

5

Before This Lesson

1. Know vocabulary groups: B (foods) and C (countries).
2. Know how to say basic Korean sentences and questions.

Lesson Goals

1. Learn how 받침 affect Korean pronunciation and particle choice.
2. Learn how to ask someone their nationality.

From The Teachers

1. It is very important that you understand the section on sound blending. This will heavily effect how understandable your Korean is.

Lesson Highlights

5-2.
The topic marker
은 / 는

5-4.
Sound blending

5-5.
This, that, and that over there

5 New Words 새로운 단어

이것	this / this one
그것	that / that one
저것	that / that one over there
사람	person
나라	country
어느 나라 사람	which nationality?
자전거	bicycle

5 New Phrases 새로운 어구

1. **어느 나라 사람입니까?**
   What nationality are you?

2. **이것은 뭐예요?**
   What is this?

> 입니까 is the question form of 이다. The answer to this question can have 예요 or 입니다 in it depending on politeness level.

5 Grammar 문법

❍ 5-1. Nationalities in Korean

In this lesson we learn how to say some countries. You can add the word 사람 (person, people) to the end of any country to say the nationality of that country.

Examples

미국 사람	American person
한국 사람	Korean person
영국 사람	English person
호주 사람	Australian person
캐나다 사람	Canadian person
필리핀 사람	Filipino person
태국 사람	Thai person
중국 사람	Chinese person

Example Q&A

1. **어느 나라 사람입니까?**
   What nationality are you?

   미국 사람입니다.
   I am American.

   영국 사람입니다.
   I am English.

2. **미국 사람이에요?**
   Are you American?

   네. 미국 사람이에요.
   Yes. I am American.

   아니요. 캐나다 사람이에요.
   No. I am Canadian.

❍ 5-2. The topic marker 은 / 는

Korean uses a variety of "markers", also referred to as "particles". These markers always come after a word. The first marker we will learn is the topic marker 은 / 는.

If the topic word ends with a 받침 then it is followed by 은 and if it doesn't then 는 is used.

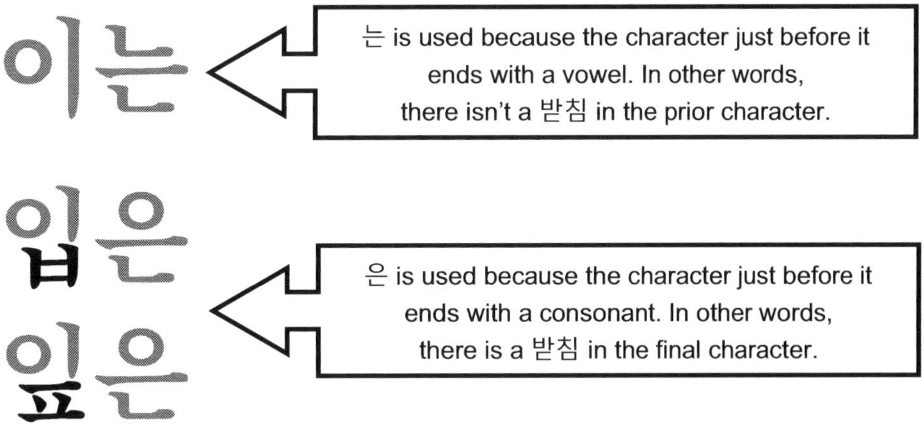

이는
는 is used because the character just before it ends with a vowel. In other words, there isn't a 받침 in the prior character.
입은
잎은
은 is used because the character just before it ends with a consonant. In other words, there is a 받침 in the final character.

In the following sentences pay attention to which version of the topic marker is used.

Example sentences

1. 바나나는 과일이에요.
   Bananas are fruit.
2. 귤은 과일이에요.
   Tangerines are fruit.
3. 오이는 야채예요.
   Cucumbers are vegetables.
4. 버섯은 야채예요. ★ (read 5-4)
   Mushrooms are vegetables.

❍ 5-3. Sound changes for ㅅ

ㅅ has a different sound depending on where it is in a word.

beginning a character ㅅ sounds like "S"	ending a character ㅅ sounds like "T"	depending on position ㅅ sounds both like "S" and "T"
sa ram	i geot	beo seot
사람	이것	버섯
(people)	(this one)	(mushroom)

❍ 5-4. Sound blending

When ㅅ (시옷) or other final consonants are followed by any character that begins with ㅇ (이응) the sound of that character moves to the position of the ㅇ (이응).
You can imagine that the ㅇ (이응) is absorbing the sound of the prior 받침.
This happens EVERY time you have a 받침 followed by the topic marker 은.

gyul eun / gyu reun
귤은 sounds like 규른

sa ram eun / sa ra meun
사람은 sounds like 사라믄

beo seos eun / beo seo seun
버섯은 sounds like 버서슨

★ In section 5-3 we explained that ㅅ (시옷) is pronounced like a "T" when it's at the end of a character. However, when it is followed by ㅇ (이응) it is an "S" sound. Now go back and re-read sentence 4 in section 5-2.

❍ 5-5. This, that, and that over there

The usage of 이것 (this), 그것 (that), and 저것 (that over there) is similar to English. Since all three of the words end with 것 you just need to remember how to pronounce them when they are in a sentence followed by the topic marker 은. If necessary refer to the sound blending taught in section 5-3 and 5-4. The position of the object in relation to the speaker and listener affects the usage.

이것, 그것, 저것 position relationships

object is close to the speaker | object is far from the speaker but close to the listener | object is far from both the speaker and listener

Example sentences

1. **이것**은 과일이에요. — **This** is a fruit.
2. **저것**은 차입니다. — **That over there** is a car.
3. **그것**은 뭐예요? — What is **that**?
4. **이것**은 오이예요. — **This** is a cucumber.

⟨!⟩ 특별 정보 Special Information ⟨!⟩

When referring to an item someone is holding, or that is near them, then it doesn't matter how far they are from you, 그것 (that) and not 저것 (that over there) must be used.

Also, normally if you are talking to yourself, or are thinking you can freely use 그것 instead of 저것. But… since no one can hear you… it doesn't really matter!

❍ 5-6. Saying "it isn't" with 아닙니다 and 아니에요.

입니다 (it is) and 아닙니다 (it isn't) are opposite in meaning. However, when using 아닙니다, the "subject marker" 이 / 가 must be placed after the item being talked about. We will learn more about the 이 / 가 marker in lesson 8. For now just learn the following rules:

1. You must have a pattern of [item] 가 아닙니다
2. If the item ends with a 받침 (final consonant) then 이 is used instead of 가.
3. 입니다 will NEVER use 이 / 가.

It's a dog.
개입니다
개예요

It's a person.
사람입니다
사람이에요

It isn't a dog.
개**가** 아닙니다
개**가** 아니에요

It isn't a person.
사람**이** 아닙니다
사람**이** 아니에요

아니에요 is the negative version of 이에요 taught in the prior lesson. Both are polite but 아닙니다 is more polite than 아니에요.

Example sentences

1. 오이는 과일이 **아닙니다**.
   Cucumbers **are not** fruit.

2. 사과는 야채가 **아닙니다**.
   Apples **are not** vegetables.

3. 이것은 고기가 **아닙니까**?
   Isn't this meat?

   Asking a negative question is common just like in English. In this case the speaker thought the food was meat and is expecting that it is.

4. 고양이는 개가 **아니에요**.
   Cats **are not** dogs.

5. 친구는 한국 사람이 **아닙니다**.
   (My) friend **is not** a Korean person.

6. 그것은 얼굴이 **아닙니다**.
   That **is not** a face.

5 Question and Answer 질문과 대답

1. 이것은 뭐예요?	**What is this?**
귤이에요.	It's a tangerine.
고기예요.	It's meat.
몰라요.	I don't know.
2. 저것은 고기예요?	**Is that (over there) meat?**
네. 고기예요.	Yes. It's meat.
아니요. 그것은 버섯이에요.	No. That is a mushroom.
아니요. 오이예요.	No. It's a cucumber.
3. (당신은) 어느 나라 사람이에요?	**What nationality are you?**
저는 미국 사람이에요.	I'm American.
저는 한국 사람이에요.	I'm Korean.
4. 이것은 과일이에요?	**Is this a fruit?**
아니요. 그것은 오이예요.	No. That is a cucumber.
네. 과일입니다.	Yes. It's a fruit. (The person answering is being respectful.)
5. 버섯은 고기예요?	**Is a mushroom meat?**
아니요. 야채예요.	No. It's a vegetable.
몰라요.	I don't know.
6. 영국 사람이에요?	**Are you English?**
아니요. 저는 캐나다 사람이에요.	No. I am Canadian.
아니요. 저는 호주 사람이에요.	No. I am an Australian.
7. 한국 사람이에요?	**Are you Korean?**
네. 한국 사람이에요.	Yes. I am Korean.
아니요. 중국 사람이에요.	No. I am Chinese.

5 Conversation 대화 K-E

1. Conversation between a mother and her child at the supermarket.

A: 이것은 오이예요?	Is this a cucumber?
B: 아니요. 바나나예요.	No. It's a banana.
A: 저것은 멜론이에요?	Is that a melon?
B: 아니요. 사과예요.	No. It's an apple.

2. Conversation between a teacher and a student learning Korean.

A: 이것은 뭐예요?	What is this?
B: 그것은 다리입니다.	That's a leg.
A: 그것은 책이에요?	Is that a book?
B: 아니요. 잡지입니다.	No. It's a magazine.

3. Conversation between friends discussing various paintings of abstract art.

A: 그것은 버스예요?	Is that a bus?
B: 아니요. 이것은 자전거예요.	No. this is a bicycle.
A: 그것은 개입니까?	Is that a dog?
B: 아니요. 고양이입니다.	No. It's a cat.

5 Sentence Building 문장 만들기

In each lesson we will build on a previous sentence. Watch it grow and transform each time new concepts are introduced.

이것은 뭐예요?
What is this?

Compare how the sentence has changed from the prior lessons:

Lesson 4: 뭐예요?
What is it?

5 Workbook Area

❑ A5-1. Sentence Jumble

Using ONLY the words and particles provided, create Korean sentences that match the English translation. Conjugate verbs and reuse items as needed.

1. 야채, 그것, 이것, 뭐, 가, 예요, 이에요, 고기, 멜론, 아니에요, 이, 버섯, 은, 는

   ____

   Is this a mushroom?

   ____

   That is not meat.

   ____

   What is "vegetable"?

2. 사람, 미국, 이, 가, 입니다, 는, 은, 영국, 어느 나라, 한국, 일본, 저, 아닙니다

   ____

   What nationality are you?

   ____

   I am American.

   ____

   I am not Korean.

3. 오이, 가, 이, 는, 눈, 은, 이것, 그것, 다리, 발, 머리, 코, 이에요, 아니에요, 예요

   ____

   This is not a cucumber.

   ____

   Feet are not legs.

   ____

   That is a nose.

❑ A5-2. Picture question and answer

Answer the following questions by looking at the pictures. You can check your answers in the answer key for this lesson. Answer with the same style of sentence as the question.

1. 이것은 뭐예요?

Answer:

2. 고양이예요?

Answer:

3. 뭐예요?

Answer:

4. 코입니까?

Answer:

5. 고기예요?

Answer:

6. 뭐예요?

Answer:

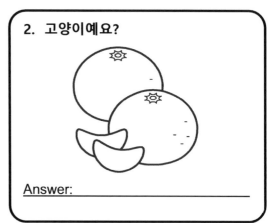

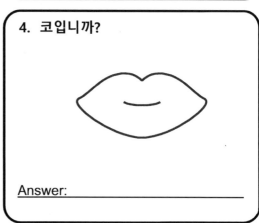

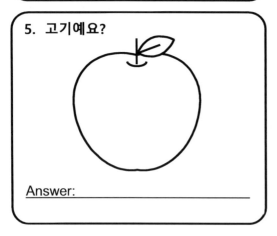

❑ A5-3. Korean translation

Translate the following conversation into English.

1.
A: 이것은 뭐예요? B: 그것은 고기예요. A: 저것은 차예요? B: 아니에요, 저것은 자전거예요.
A:
B:
A:
B:

❑ A5-4. English translation

Translate the following conversation into Korean.

1.
A: Is it a cat? B: No, it is a dog. A: Is he Min Su Park? B: No, he is Min Su Kim.
A:
B:
A:
B:

5 Vocabulary Builder

The words in this vocabulary group will be used in the next and following lessons.

■ Group D: people 사람

여자	girl, woman
남자	boy, man
여자친구	girlfriend
남자친구	boyfriend
학생	student
대학생	college student
선생님	teacher
아버지	father
어머니	mother
동생	younger sibling
여동생	younger sister
남동생	younger brother
누나 (only used by boys)	older sister
언니 (only used by girls)	older sister
형 (only used by boys)	older brother
오빠 (only used by girls)	older brother

Lesson 6:

Introduction to descriptive verbs

6

Before This Lesson

1. Know vocabulary group: D (people) words.

Lesson Goals

1. Learn how to conjugate Korean verbs into the BASIC form.

2. Understand the difference between the verb BASIC form and STEM.

3. Learn how to specify objects using this and that.

From The Teachers

1. As teachers we found it difficult to effectively teach the existing 아/어/여 verb rules without confusing the students. To solve this problem we created a form we call the "BASIC" form. We are confident this form will help you a great deal on your road to Korean fluency. LEARN IT WELL!

Lesson Highlights

6-1.
Descriptive verbs / Adjectives

6-2.
Korean verb stems

6-8.
This, that, and that over there

6 New Words 새로운 단어

날씨	weather
김밥	seaweed roll
국	soup
영화	movie
만화책	comic book
음식	food
주스	juice
요거트	yogurt
신발	shoes
양말	socks
피자	pizza
~씨	Mr., Mrs., Miss

6 New Descriptive Verbs 새로운 형용사

❑ 6-1. Descriptive verbs / Adjectives

Korean verbs are grouped into "action" and "descriptive" verbs. Action verbs include words like, "to swim", "to eat", and "to go". Descriptive verbs include words like , "cold", "spicy", and "nice". Action and descriptive verbs have slightly different usage rules, so it's important to know which verb type you are using. Let's start with some descriptive verbs.

다 form	BASIC form	English	Type
싸다	싸	cheap	regular
비싸다	비싸	expensive	regular
짜다	짜	salty	regular
달다	달아	sweet	regular
쓰다	써	bitter	regular
크다	커	big	regular
작다	작아	small	regular
좋다	좋아	good, nice	regular
나쁘다	나빠	bad	regular
재미있다	재미있어	interesting, fun	regular
맛있다	맛있어	tasty, delicious	regular

6 Grammar 문법

❍ 6-2. Korean verb stems

In section 6-1 we introduced 11 new descriptive verbs. Each verb has two forms listed. The 다 form is what will be in the dictionary.

When you remove the 다 from any verb you are left with what we will call the "stem". The black portion is the verb stem.

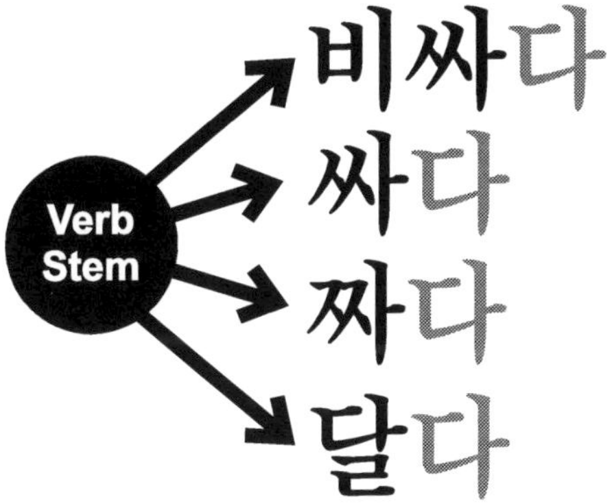

All verb "dictionary forms" end with **다**.

Without the **다** only the verb stem is left.

❍ 6-3. Korean verb BASIC form

The "BASIC" form is sometimes called the "fully conjugated stem", "vowel contraction", or very commonly the "아 / 어 / 여 form". But, these names don't give the form the recognition it deserves. For this reason, we choose to call it the BASIC form.

Why is BASIC form great?
The BASIC form can be casual, polite, present tense, future tense, or even a command. In fact, the BASIC form is a fundamental part of many Korean grammar patterns. It's one of the most important verb forms you will learn.

You will need to understand the difference between the stem, and the basic form. Many grammar patterns will be listed as: STEM + (something), or BASIC + (something)

	다 form	STEM	BASIC
to eat	먹다	먹	먹어
good	좋다	좋	좋아

❍ 6-4. Creating verb BASIC form

To make the BASIC form, 아 / 어 / 여 is added to the stem using the set of rules shown in the chart below.

The following rules are used to create the BASIC form for most verbs.
As needed, we will introduce irregular conjugations in other lessons. From the stem and the stem's LAST vowel you can create the BASIC form.

"BASIC" Form Rules 아/어/여

Rule	A Last Vowel	B HAS 받침	C NO 받침
1	하		change to 해
2	ㅏ ㅗ	add 아	overlay ㅏ
3	ㅣ	add 어	change to ㅕ
4	ㅓ ㅐ ㅔ ㅜ	add 어	overlay ㅓ
5	ㅡ	add 어	change final vowel to ㅓ EXCEPTION If prior character HAS ㅏ or ㅗ change final vowel to ㅏ

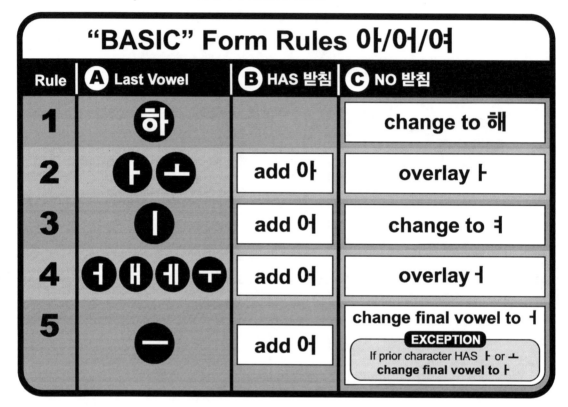

작다 (small)
A) Stem Last Vowel: ㅏ
HAS 받침
B) add **아**
BASIC Form: **작아**
Rule used: 2

쓰다 (bitter)
A) Stem Last Vowel: ㅡ
NO 받침, no prior character
C) change to ㅓ
BASIC Form: **써**
Rule used: 5

달다 (sweet)
A) Stem Last Vowel: ㅏ
HAS 받침
C) add **아**
BASIC Form: **달아**
Rule used: 2

맛있다 (tasty)
A) Stem Last Vowel: ㅣ
HAS 받침
B) add **어**
BASIC Form: **맛있어**
Rule used: 3

조용하다 (quiet)
A) Stem Last Hangul: **하**
NO 받침
B) change character to **해**
BASIC Form: **조용해**
Rule used: 1

멀다 (far)
A) Stem Last Vowel: ㅓ
HAS 받침
B) add **어**
BASIC Form: **멀어**
Rule used: 4

Here is a breakdown of how each rule applies. Note: Some of the verbs are new to better demonstrate the rules.

BASIC Rule 1

하다 (to do)	What happens?
A last hangul: 하 **C** change to 해 BASIC is 해	If the verb has 하 as the final hangul the 하 is changed to 해. 하 CHANGES TO 해

BASIC Rule 2

싸다 (to be cheap)	What happens?
A last vowel: ㅏ **C** overlay ㅏ BASIC is 싸	ㅏ is overlaid on the stem, but since ㅏ is already there, nothing changes. 싸 OVERLAY ㅏ = 싸

오다 (to come)	What happens? **Rule 2**
A last vowel: ㅗ **C** overlay ㅏ BASIC is 와	ㅏ is overlaid on the existing stem. The vowel is converted to ㅘ. 오 OVERLAY ㅏ = 와

BASIC Rule 3

마시다 (to drink)	What happens?
A last vowel: ㅣ **C** changes to ㅕ BASIC is 마셔	ㅣ changes to ㅕ This changes the sound. 마시 OVERLAY 마셔

BASIC Rule 4

주다 (to give)	What happens?
A last vowel: ㅜ **B** overlay ㅓ BASIC is 줘	ㅓ is overlaid on the existing stem. The vowel is converted to ㅝ. 주 OVERLAY ㅓ = 줘

내다 (to pay)	What happens?
A last vowel: ㅐ **C** no changes BASIC is 내	ㅓ is overlaid on the existing stem. It fits perfect! Nothing changes. 내 OVERLAY ㅓ = 내

BASIC Rule 5

나쁘다 (to be bad)	What happens?
A last vowel: ㅡ **C** change to ㅏ BASIC is 나빠	Because the prior hangul character has ㅏ the ㅡ changes to ㅏ. 나쁘 CHANGES TO 나빠

슬프다 (to be sad)	What happens?
A last vowel: ㅡ **C** change to ㅓ BASIC is 슬퍼	Because the prior hangul has ㅡ the ㅡ in the final hangul changes to ㅓ. 슬프 CHANGES TO 슬퍼

특별 정보 Special Information

Some verbs have a double vowel as the last vowel in their stem. We have not defined BASIC rules for double vowel verbs. For example when you have ㅚ in the stem then you overlay ㅓ to make ㅙ to make the BASIC form.

The BASIC form of 되다 (to become) is 돼

Verbs with double vowels ㅢ ㅝ ㅟ etc. are not very common. They are too rare to expand the rules to include them. For double vowel stems just add 어 after them. This example demonstrates one such verb.

The BASIC form of 사귀다 (to date) is 사귀어

6-5. Simple sentences using descriptive verbs

One of the most common uses of the BASIC form is "present tense".
If you use the BASIC form "as is" what you are saying will be very informal / casual, and possibly rude Korean depending on who you are speaking with. In order to make the BASIC form polite you add 요. 요 form is one of the most common polite forms used.

(BASIC descriptive verb) + 요
It's (BASIC descriptive verb)

Example sentences

1. 비싸요. — It's expensive.
2. 작아요. — It's small.
3. 나빠요. — It's bad.
4. 맛있어요. — It's delicious.

5. 싸요. — It's cheap.
6. 짜요. — It's salty.
7. 커요. — It's big.
8. 써요. — It's bitter.

9. 좋아요. — It's good.
10. 달아요. — It's sweet.
11. 재미있어요. — It's interesting.

❍ 6-6. Using descriptive verbs with subjects

Instead of 은/는 use the subject marker 이/가 to mark the item being talked about. If the item ends in a vowel use 가 and if it ends with a 받침 use 이.

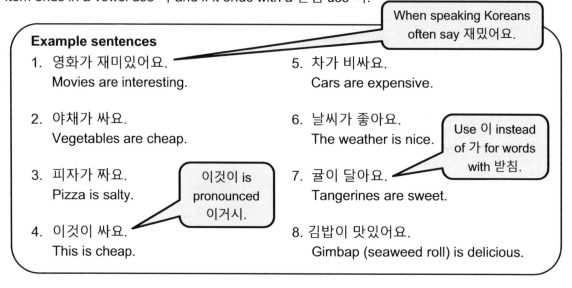

Example sentences

1. 영화가 재미있어요.
   Movies are interesting.

   (When speaking Koreans often say 재밌어요.)

2. 야채가 싸요.
   Vegetables are cheap.

3. 피자가 짜요.
   Pizza is salty.

4. 이것이 싸요.
   This is cheap.

   (이것이 is pronounced 이거시.)

5. 차가 비싸요.
   Cars are expensive.

6. 날씨가 좋아요.
   The weather is nice.

7. 귤이 달아요.
   Tangerines are sweet.

   (Use 이 instead of 가 for words with 받침.)

8. 김밥이 맛있어요.
   Gimbap (seaweed roll) is delicious.

❍ 6-7. Korean consonants eat cookies

If you imagine the ㅇ (이응) as a cookie that 받침 LOVE to eat, than you can easily visualize what happens during the sound blending learned in section 5-4.

❍ 6-8. This, that, and that over there + NOUN

If you want to specify "this dog" or "that person" you will not use 이것 (this one) etc. Instead you use the prefix 이, 그, and 저 + noun.

이~, 그~, 저~ position relationships

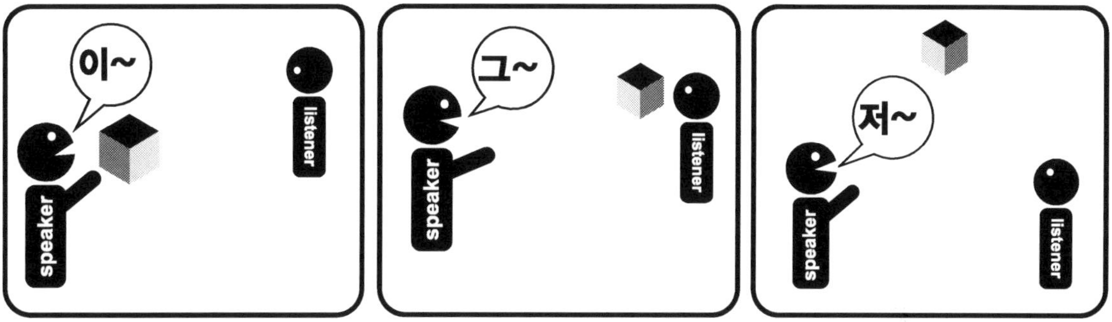

object is close to the speaker | object is far from the speaker but close to the listener | object is far from both the speaker and listener

이 (noun) / 그 (noun)
this (noun) / that (noun)

When using 이, 그, 저, the speaker is typically pointing at something, or talking about something specific. Topic marker 은/는 sounds more natural but 이/가 can still be used.

Example sentences

1. 이 책은 싸요.	This book is cheap.
2. 그 사람은 한국 사람이에요.	That person is Korean.
3. 이 피자가 짜요.	This pizza is salty.
4. 저 과일이 비싸요.	That fruit over there is expensive.
5. 이 국은 뭐예요?	What is this soup?
6. 이 영화가 재미있어요.	This movie is interesting.
7. 저 차는 커요.	That car over there is big.
8. 그 요거트는 달아요.	That yogurt is sweet.
9. 그 사람은 대학생입니다.	That person is a college student.
10. 그 김밥이 맛있어요?	Is that gimbap tasty?
11. 이 만화책이 좋아요?	Is this comic book good?
12. 이 주스는 써요.	This juice is bitter.

❍ 6-9. ~씨 (Mr., Mrs., Miss)

Korean uses one handy word to cover Mr., Mrs., Miss., Ms. etc. 씨 is added after the person's full name. When translating 씨 it isn't always necessary to actually say "Mr" etc.

Example sentences

1. 김민준 씨는 대학생입니다.
   Mr. Min Jun Kim is a college student.

2. 최지우 씨는 미국 사람이 아니에요.
   Jiu Choi is not an American.

씨 does not require a translation, but you should have it after the name.

6 Question and Answer 질문과 대답

1. **이 영화는 재미있어요?**
   Is this movie interesting?

   네, 그 영화는 재미있어요.
   Yes, that movie is interesting.

   네, 좋아요.
   Yes, it's good.

2. **저 사람은 친구 입니까?**
   Is that person over there a friend?

   네, 친구예요.
   Yes, she's a friend.

   In the Korean sentence "he" or "she" isn't needed. It's assumed by the context.

   아니요, 친구가 아닙니다.
   No, he's not a friend.

3. **그 주스는 맛있어요?**
   Is that juice delicious?

   네, 이 주스는 맛있어요.
   Yes, this juice is delicious.

   아니요, 써요.
   No, it's bitter.

   네, 달아요.
   Yes, it's sweet.

6 Conversation 대화 K-E

1. Polite conversation between friends.

A: 이 신발은 커요?
B: 아니요, 작아요.
A: 비싸요?
B: 아니요, 싸요.

A: Are these shoes big?
B: No, they are small.
A: Are they expensive?
B: No, they are cheap.

2. Polite conversation between a Korean and someone in Korea for the first time.

A: 이것은 뭐예요?
B: 그것은 김밥이에요.
A: 맛있어요?
B: 아니요, 짜요.

A: What is this?
B: That is a seaweed roll.
A: Does it taste good?
B: No, it is salty.

6 Conversation 대화 E-K

1. Polite conversation between friends.

A: Is that person over there American?
B: No, he is Korean.
A: Is he a teacher?
B: No, he is a college student.

Remember, Korean verbs are "pronoun neutral" and you don't actually need to say "he", "she", "I", etc.

A: 저 사람은 미국 사람이에요?
B: 아니요, 한국 사람이에요.
A: 선생님이에요?
B: 아니요, 대학생이에요.

2. Polite conversation between people at a salad buffet.

A: Is that fruit?
B: No, this is a vegetable.
A: Is that a mushroom?
B: No, this is a cucumber.

A: 그것은 과일이에요?
B: 아니요, 이것은 야채예요.
A: 그것은 버섯이에요?
B: 아니요, 이것은 오이예요.

6 Sentence Building 문장 만들기

In each lesson we will build on a previous sentence. Watch it grow and transform each time new concepts are introduced.

이 피자는 맛있어요.
This pizza is delicious.

Compare how the sentence has changed from the prior lessons:

Lesson 4: 뭐예요?
What is it?

Lesson 5: 이것은 뭐예요?
What is this?

6 Workbook Area

❑ A6-1. Reading comprehension

At your current level, you should understand all of the grammar and words in the following sections. If you are struggling to understand them, review this and prior lessons.

① 바나나는 과일이에요.

② 과일은 맛있어요.

③ 주스는 달아요.

④ 멜론이 커요.

Dialogue

A: 바나나예요?

B: 아니요, 귤이에요.

A: 맛있어요?

B: 네, 달아요.

❑ A6-2. Reading comprehension questions

Answer the following questions about the reading comprehension in the prior section.

1. 주스는 달아요?

____

2. 귤은 짜요?

____

3. 멜론은 작아요?

____

❑ A6-3. Sentence Jumble

Using ONLY the words and particles provided, create Korean sentences that match the English translation. Conjugate verbs and reuse items as needed.

1. 사람, 고기, 이, 저, 그, 대학생, 맛있다, 선생님, 가, 은, 는, 이, 아닙니다, 입니다, 과일, 요

   ____

   This person is a college student.

   ____

   That fruit over there is delicious.

   ____

   That teacher isn't a college student.

2. 사람, 고기, 비싸다, 이, 그, 양말, 싸다, 맛있다, 가,달다, 은, 과일, 는, 쓰다, 요

   ____

   These socks are expensive.

   ____

   That meat is tasty.

   ____

   Fruit is bitter.

3. 달다, 이, 영화, 그, 여자, 좋다, 날씨, 나쁘다, 가, 은, 귤, 는, 이, 바나나, 과일, 재미있다

   ____

   This banana is sweet.

   ____

   The weather is nice.

   ____

   That movie is interesting.

❑ A6-4. Korean translation

Translate the following conversation into English.

1.
A: 이것은 뭐예요? B: 그것은 피자예요. A: 맛있어요? B: 아니요, 짜요.
A:
B:
A:
B:

❑ A6-5. English translation

Translate the following conversation into Korean.

1.
A: Is it a mushroom? B: No, it's a melon. A: Is it sweet? B: No, it's bitter.
A:
B:
A:
B:

❑ A6-6. BASIC form drill

Answer the questions about the verbs listed below. New words are used, but you should be able to create the necessary parts for each one based on what you learned in this lesson. Refer to section 6-4 for the BASIC rules.

1. 기쁘다 (to be happy)

A) What is the stem? ____________________

B) What is the last vowel in the stem? ____________________

C) What should 쁘 be changed to? ____________________

D) What is the BASIC form? ____________________

E) What rule applies? ____________________

2. 느리다 (to be slow)

A) What is the stem? ____________________

B) What is the last vowel in the stem? ____________________

C) Does the stem end with a 받침? ____________________

D) What is the BASIC form? ____________________

E) What rule applies? ____________________

3. 늦다 (to be late)

A) What is the stem? ____________________

B) What is the last vowel in the stem? ____________________

C) Is there a 받침? ____________________

D) What is the BASIC form? ____________________

E) What rule applies? ____________________

Lesson 7:

Pronouns and possession

7

Before This Lesson

1. Review the various vocabulary builder groups.
2. Know how to create the verb BASIC form.

Lesson Goals

1. Learn how to show possession, and how Korean pronouns work.
2. Learn the ㅂ irregular pattern.

From The Teachers

1. The concepts in this lesson are taught in specific order. They should be followed in that order.

Lesson Highlights

7-2.
ㅂ (비읍) irregular verbs

7-3.
Possession words and the particle 의

7-5.
The word "you" and pronoun usage

7 New Words 새로운 단어

누구	who?
저	I, me (polite)
나	I, me (casual)
당신	you (polite, formal)
너	you (casual)
케이크	cake
책상	desk
방	room
성적	grades
커피	coffee
차	tea

7 Word Usage 단어 사용법

❑ 7-1. 차 (car) and 차 (tea)

차 can mean "car" and "tea". They are pronounced the same. In modern Korean 한자 (Chinese characters) aren't used like in the past, however, it's fun to know that the 차 for "car" originated from the Chinese character 車 which means "wheel" and the 차 for "tea" comes from 茶.

7 New Descriptive Verbs 새로운 형용사

❑ 7-2. ㅂ (비읍) irregular verbs

In the prior lesson we learned how to conjugate verbs into the BASIC form. These following irregular verbs are the first in a series of irregular verbs that we will cover in this and following lessons. Let's look at four ㅂ irregular verbs.

다 form	BASIC form	English	Type
덥다	더워	hot (weather)	ㅂ irregular
춥다	추워	cold (weather)	ㅂ irregular
뜨겁다	뜨거워	hot to the touch	ㅂ irregular
차갑다	차가워	cold to the touch	ㅂ irregular

ㅂ irregular verbs BASIC form is made by removing the ㅂ from the stem then adding 워.

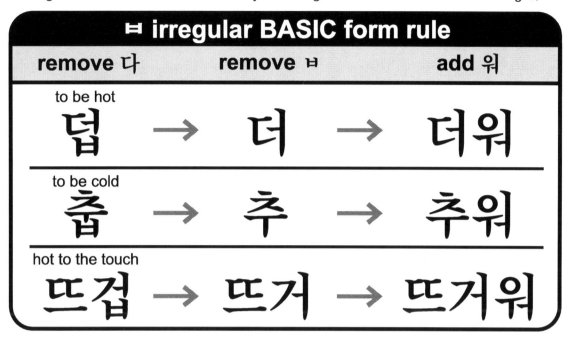

ㅂ irregular BASIC form rule

remove 다		remove ㅂ		add 워
to be hot 덥	→	더	→	더워
to be cold 춥	→	추	→	추워
hot to the touch 뜨겁	→	뜨거	→	뜨거워

In English we have one word for "hot" and "cold", however in Korean there are two words for hot and two for cold. 덥다 (hot) and 춥다 (cold) are used when talking about the weather or room temperature. When you are talking about things that you drink, eat, or touch then you must use 뜨겁다 (hot to the touch) and 차갑다 (cold to the touch).

Example sentences

1. 날씨가 더워요.	The temperature is hot.
2. 이 주스는 차가워요.	This juice is cold.
3. 이 국은 뜨거워요.	This soup is hot.
4. 그 방은 추워요.	That room is cold.

7 New Phrases 새로운 어구

1. 누구세요?
Who is it?

This is good for asking on the phone or to someone you don't know. If you are asking "Who is it?" in normal conversation say 누구예요?

2. 맞아요.
That's correct. / That's right.

7 Grammar 문법

❍ 7-3. Possession words and the particle 의

The possession marker 의 follows a word to make it possessive, or to make it a "modifier" of the following word. All you do is add 의 to the word to make it possessive.

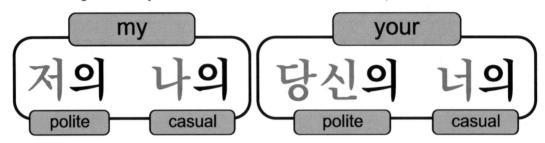

my		your	
저의	나의	당신의	너의
polite	casual	polite	casual

Example sentences

1. 저의 성적은 좋아요.
   My grades are good.
2. 저의 친구는 일본 사람입니다.
   My friend is Japanese.
3. 당신의 선생님은 지혜 선생님입니까?
   Is your teacher Mrs. Jihye?
4. 저의 남자친구가 서른 살이에요.
   My boyfriend is 30 years old.
5. 너의 차가 비싸?
   Is your car expensive?

   요 isn't used as it's too polite for 너.
6. 나의 차는 도요타예요.
   My car is a Toyota.

NOTE: The 의 hangul is pronounced like "we" with your bottom lip pulled back. HOWEVER, in the following cases you might hear it pronounced as 에.

1. When it's at the end of a word. (especially after 받침)
2. When it's spoken fast.

You can also use 의 after names and titles to show possession. After names it acts like ('s)

Example sentences

1. 조지의 차입니다.
   It is George's car.
2. 선생님의 사과입니다.
   It is teacher's apple.
3. 어머니의 바나나예요.
   It's my mother's banana.
4. 이것은 아버지의 펜입니까?
   Is this father's pen?
5. 이것은 친구의 책입니다.
   This is my friend's book.
6. 그것은 동생의 요거트예요.
   That's my younger sibling's yogurt.

You can combine 누구 with 의 to say "whose".

Example Q&A

1. **이것은 누구의 책이에요?**	**Whose book is this?**
친구의 책이에요.	It's my friend's book.
김민수 씨의 책입니다.	It's Minsu Kim's book.
2. **그것은 누구의 음식이에요?**	**Whose food is that?**
저의 음식이에요.	It's my food.
너의 음식이야.	It's your food.

너의 is very informal. 이야, the informal of 이다 is also used.

❍ 7-4. Short versions of "my" and "your"

나의 is often shortened to 내 and 저의 shortened to 제 to mean "my" or even "me / I". If it's in front of another noun then it's "my" and if not then it is "me / I".

저의 (my)	shortens to	제 (my, I)	used in polite speech
나의 (my)	shortens to	내 (my, I)	used in casual speech
너의 (your)	shortens to	네 (your, you)	used in casual speech

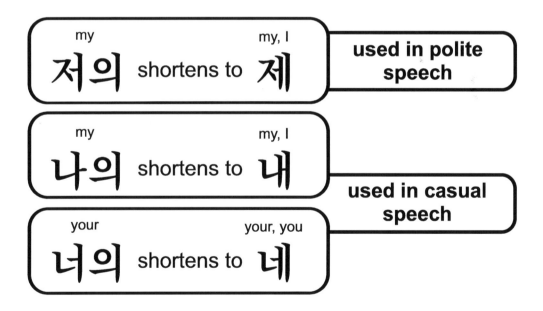

Korean unfortunately does not have different sounds for 네 and 내.
So the same sound can mean "you" and "me". To avoid this Koreans pronounce 네 as 니 when speaking. You usually won't see 니 in writing, but in speaking 니 is very common.

On a funny note, if you listen to KPOP music you might have wondered why they keep saying "NIGA". Well they aren't trying to be hip hop. They are actually saying "you are…".

Example sentences

1. 제 어머니는 마흔 살입니다.
   My mother is 40 years old.
2. 제 친구는 선생님이에요.
   My friend is a teacher.
3. 네 (니) 차가 도요타야?
   Is your car a Toyota?

   (네 = your; 내 = my; 야 = informal of 이다.)
4. 너는 내 친구가 아니야!
   You are not my friend!

   (아니야 is informal of 아닙니다.)
5. 제 누나는 대학생이에요.
   My older sister is a college student.
6. 제가 미국 사람이에요.
   I'm American.

   (Here 제 means "I" and not "my".)

It's important to know that words such as 제 (my), and 네 (your) will ALWAYS be followed by a noun. These words are modifying the noun they come before.

제 noun = my noun
네 noun = your noun

네, = yes　　네가 = you
네. = yes　　제가 = I

7-5. The word "you" and pronoun usage

Even though we just taught you how to say "you" and "your", it's REALLY important to understand that Korean doesn't use "you" and "your" as frequently as English does. It's almost as if they purposely avoid it. Sentences automatically determine pronouns such as, "you", "I", "he" and, "she" based on the context.

For example, "you" or "your" isn't part of "What is your name?"

~~당신의~~ 이름이 뭐예요?

This is because of the context. If this is said to you, you know it's YOUR name.

However, if you are talking to a friend about his new girlfriend, the same phrase could mean "What is HER name?"

So when do you actually say "you" in Korean?
You will hear 당신 in Korean pop music, dramas, and translated materials. Whenever the generic "you" is required, then 당신 is used. Because English often uses "you", it's very common to see 당신 in Korean translations, however avoiding it is best.

당신 is also used by couples when addressing each other.

EXECUTIVE SUMMARY
You should avoid using 당신 when talking to people as it's a bit weird and might even be considered rude. It's much more common to refer to people by their names or using 너 in casual speech.

❍ 7-6. Using 것 to say "thing"

In section 6-7 we took the first part of 이것 (this one) to make 이 which can go in front of any noun to say "this (noun)". This is very powerful, but so is the remaining 것 which just means "thing". 것 is a common part of many Korean grammar patterns. It can be used to refer to physical things, and ideas. In this lesson we use it to say "It's mine" and "whose is it" etc.

것 = physical and abstract "thing"

Although 것 can be translated as "thing", it is often not said in the English translation, despite it being a very important part of the grammar.

Example sentences

1. 누구의 것이에요?
   Whose thing is this? / Whose is it?

In spoken Korean 의 is often removed.

2. 그것이 제 것이에요?
   Is that my thing? / Is that mine?
3. 이 바나나는 선생님의 것입니까?
   Is this banana teacher's?
4. 이 음식은 누구의 것이에요?
   Whose is this food?
5. 그 개는 제 것이 아니에요.
   That dog isn't mine.

특별 정보 Special Information

In English we can say "Is this yours?" to a complete stranger. In Korea there is a layer of politeness with complete strangers. Directly referring to a person you don't know as YOU either using 당신 or 너 is not normal. For this reason you wouldn't ask "Is this yours" to someone UNLESS you know them. Also, since you know them, and since 너 is casual, you would use casual speech (which is covered in section 13-10)

You shouldn't say these sentences:

1. 이 잡지는 **너**의 것이에요? Is this magazine yours?
2. 이 잡지는 **당신**의 것이에요? Is this magazine yours?

If you are talking to your friend you can say these casual phrase:

1. 이 잡지는 **너**의 것이야? Is this magazine yours?
2. 이 잡지는 **네** 것이야? Is this magazine yours?

When talking to a stranger it's better to ask:

1. 이 잡지는 누구의 것이에요? Whose magazine is this?

7-7. "He" and "She" pronouns

In English we use "he" and "she" when talking about a person whom might be with us. However, in Korean you never say "he" or "she" about a person whom is with you.

"He" in Korean can be simply, 그 or 그 사람. 그 사람 can also mean "that person", so the context of the sentence will determine if it means "he" or not. 그녀 means "her" but it is never said in spoken Korean. It is only used in written Korean.

Although this has been said before, it's VERY important to understand that Korean does NOT continually use pronouns like English. Once a topic is introduced, it is typically NOT restated again in any form. For English speakers who are used to continually saying "he", "she", "I", "you" this might be a challenge.

Some books, including this one, will sometimes restate a topic, or use pronouns more than necessary in order to teach certain concepts. As this book progresses we will wean you off of overusing pronouns.

If you DO use pronouns when they don't have to be used, don't worry, it's a common mistake of new speakers of Korean. You may not sound natural, but will be understood.

7 Question and Answer 질문과 대답

1. **저 사과는 누구의 것이에요?**
   Whose apple is that?

   제 것이에요.
   It's mine.

   내 것이야.
   It's mine.

   > Remember 내 is only used in casual speech. For polite speech 제 would be used.

   제 누나의 것이에요.
   It's my older sister's.

2. **캐나다 사람이에요?**
   Are you Canadian?

   네, 맞아요.
   Yes, that's right.

   네. 나는 캐나다 사람이에요.
   Yes. I am Canadian.

   아니에요. 저는 한국 사람이에요.
   I'm not. I am Korean.

   아니요. 캐나다사람이 아니에요.
   No. I am not Canadian.

3. **저 여자는 미국 사람이에요?**
   Is that girl American?

   네, 맞아요.
   Yes, that's right.

   아니요, 영국 사람이에요.
   No, she is English.

   아니에요, 호주 사람이에요.
   She isn't. She is Australian.

4. **이 책상은 누구의 것이에요?**
Whose is this desk?

"Whose desk is this?" sounds more natural than "Whose is this desk?" in English but this sentence is not weird in Korean syntax.

조지의 것입니다.
It's George's.

저 여자의 것입니다.
It's that girl's.

선생님의 것입니다.
It's the teacher's.

5. **대학생이에요?**
Are you a college student?

네, 저는 대학생이에요.
Yes, I am a college student.

Here 네 means "yes". The 네 that means "your" will ALWAYS be followed by another noun.

아니요, 저는 대학생이 아니에요.
No, I am not a college student.

7 Conversation 대화 K-E

1. Polite conversation at a restaurant.

A: 이 국은 누구의 것이에요?
B: 제 것이에요.
A: 뜨거워요?
B: 네, 뜨거워요.

A: Whose soup is this?
B: It is mine.
A: Is it hot?
B: Yes, it is.

2. Polite conversation between friends.

A: 저 여자는 누구예요?
B: 제 누나예요.
A: 당신의 누나는 대학생이에요?
B: 아니요, 선생님이에요.

A: Who is that girl?
B: She is my older sister.
A: Is your older sister a college student?
B: No, she is a teacher.

3. Polite conversation when a friend visits for the first time.

A: 이 방은 당신의 방이에요?
B: 아니요, 제 남동생의 방이에요.
A: 이 방은 더워요.
B: 네, 더워요.

A: Is this room your room?
B: No, this room is my younger brother's room.
A: This room is hot.
B: Yes, it is.

7 Conversation 대화 E-K

1. Polite conversation in a parking lot.

A: Whose is this Hyundai car? (Whose Hyundai is this?)
B: This is my father's car.
A: Is it expensive?
B: Yes, it is.

A: 이 현대 차는 누구의 것이에요?
B: 이것은 제 아버지의 차예요.
A: 비싸요?
B: 네, 비싸요.

현대 is a major Korean car company. They also own KIA.

2. Polite conversation at a park.

A: Whose cat is that over there?
B: It's mine.
A: How old is that cat?
B: He is 2 years old.

A: 저 고양이는 누구 것이에요?

B: 제 것이에요.

A: 몇 살이에요?

B: 두 살이에요.

3. Polite conversation at school.

A: My grades are very good.

B: My grades are bad…

A: Who is the teacher?

B: It's Ms. Sunhee (teacher).

Many Koreans spell their name differently than the official Korean Romanization to make it easier to read. Sunhee is actually "Seonheui"

A: 제 성적은 너무 좋아요.

B: 제 성적은 나빠요…

A: 선생님은 누구예요?

B: 선희 선생님이에요.

7 Sentence Building 문장 만들기

In each lesson we will build on a previous sentence. Watch it grow and transform each time new concepts are introduced.

제 어머니의 피자는 차가워요.
My mother's pizza is cold.

Compare how the sentence has changed from the prior lessons:

Lesson 4: 뭐예요?
What is it?

Lesson 5: 이것은 뭐예요?
What is this?

Lesson 6: 이 피자는 맛있어요.
This pizza is delicious.

7 Workbook Area

❑ A7-1. Reading comprehension

At your current level, you should understand all of the grammar and words in the following sections. If you are struggling to understand them, review this and prior lessons.

New words for this comprehension: 제니 (Jenny), 외국인 (Foreigner)

① 제 동생의 여자친구의 이름은 제니예요.
② 제니는 대학생이에요.
③ 영국사람이에요.
④ 스무 살이에요.

Dialogue

A: 이 여자는 누구예요?
B: 제 남동생의 여자친구 제니예요
A: 외국인이에요? 어느 나라 사람이에요?
B: 영국사람이에요.

❑ A7-2. Reading comprehension questions

Answer the following questions about the reading comprehension in the prior section.

1. 제니는 어느 나라 사람이에요?

____

2. 제 동생의 여자친구의 이름은 선아예요?

____

3. 제니는 서른 살이에요?

____

❑ A7-3. Sentence Jumble

Using ONLY the words and particles provided, create Korean sentences that match the English translation. Conjugate verbs and reuse items as needed.

1. 은, 나쁘다, 주스, 성적, 이름, 뭐예요, 는, 의, 오빠, 차갑다, 당신, 커피, 그, 이, 가,

   ____
   My grades are bad.

   ____
   This coffee is cold.

   ____
   What is your name?

2. 날씨, 이름, 그녀, 은, 는, 선생님, 이, 가, 의, 제, 이다, 남동생, 뜨겁다, 신발, 그, 저, 덥다,

   ____
   She is my teacher.

   ____
   My younger brother's name is 선호.

   ____
   The weather is hot.

3. 어머니, 은, 는, 그녀, 이다, 차, 작다, 저, 이, 가, 국, 김밥, 의, 맛있다, 방, 도요타

   ____
   Her room is small.

   ____
   My mother's car is a Toyota.

   ____
   That soup over there is tasty.

❑ A7-4. Korean translation

Translate the following conversation into English.

1.
A: 이 커피는 뜨거워요? B: 아니요, 차가워요. A: 날씨는 더워요? B: 아니요, 추워요.
A:
B:
A:
B:

❑ A7-5. English translation

Translate the following conversation into Korean.

1.
A: Whose magazine is this? B: It's mine. A: Whose Toyota is this? B: It's my friend's car
A:
B:
A:
B:

❑ A7-6. Basic Form Drill

Answer the questions about the verbs listed below. New words are used, but you should be able to create the necessary parts for each one based on what you learned in this lesson. Refer to section 6-4 and 7-2 (ㅂ irregular) for the BASIC form rules.

1. 더럽다 (to be dirty) (ㅂ irregular)

A) What is the stem? ____________________

B) What is removed from the stem? ____________________

C) What is added to the stem? ____________________

D) What is the BASIC form? ____________________

2. 슬프다 (to be sad)

A) What is the stem? ____________________

B) What is the last vowel in the stem? ____________________

C) What should 프 be changed to? ____________________

D) What is the BASIC form? ____________________

E) What rule applies? ____________________

3. 흐리다 (to be cloudy)

A) What is the stem? ____________________

B) What is the last vowel in the stem? ____________________

C) Does the stem end with a 받침? ____________________

D) What is the BASIC form? ____________________

E) What rule applies? ____________________

4. 넓다 (to be wide)

A) What is the stem? ______________________________

B) What is the last vowel in the stem? ______________________________

C) Does the stem end with a 받침? ______________________________

D) What is the BASIC form? ______________________________

E) What rule applies? ______________________________

5. 바쁘다 (to be busy)

A) What is the stem? ______________________________

B) What is the last vowel in the stem? ______________________________

C) What should 쁘 be changed to? ______________________________

D) What is the BASIC form? ______________________________

E) What rule applies? ______________________________

7 Vocabulary Builder

Some of these words will be used in the following lessons. Even if they aren't used in the lessons you should learn them.

■ Group E: places 장소

집	house, home
학교	school
직장	workplace
병원	hospital
공항	airport
교실	classroom
아파트	apartment
교회	church
절	Buddhist temple
화장실	restroom
목욕탕	bathhouse
식당	restaurant
회사	company (work)

■ Group F: animals 동물

개	dog
고양이	cat
쥐	mouse
펭귄	penguin
곰	bear
하마	hippo
기린	giraffe
코끼리	elephant
물고기	fish

Lesson 8:

Having, not having, and locations

8

Before This Lesson

1. Know vocabulary groups: E (places) and F (animals).
2. Understand how to make the verb BASIC form.

Lesson Goals

1. Learn how to use the location marker 에.
2. Learn how to use location words.

From The Teachers

1. Keep reviewing the BASIC rules taught in section 6-4. They are important to upcoming verb patterns.

Lesson Highlights

8-4.
있다 (to exist, to have)

8-7.
Using location words

8-8.
안 vs 속

8 New Words 새로운 단어

어디	where?
여기	here
거기	there
저기	over there
의자	chair
비행기	airplane
가방	purse, bag
침대	bed
숙제	homework
물	water
마음	heart, mind
꿈	dream
악몽	nightmare

8 New Descriptive Verbs 새로운 형용사

In this lesson we add the first 하다 verb. We will learn some descriptive verbs that will help you reinforce the rules learned in prior lessons. If you need to, review the section on ㅂ irregulars in lesson 7 and "BASIC form" in lesson 6.

다 form	BASIC form	English	Type
많다	많아	a lot, many	regular
어렵다	어려워	difficult	ㅂ irregular
쉽다	쉬워	easy	ㅂ irregular
맵다	매워	spicy	ㅂ irregular
예쁘다	예뻐	pretty, beautiful	regular
착하다	착해	kind, nice	하다

❑ 8-1. 많다 (a lot, many)

많다 is a very common descriptive verb used in daily Korean. This is one of the first words in this book that has a 겹받침 (double final consonant). The final consonant in 많 is the "h" sound ㅎ (히읗). It's silent and the entire character should be pronounced as 만.

Example sentences

1. 많아요. (sounds like 마나요)
   There is a lot.
2. 숙제가 많아요.
   (I have) a lot of homework.
3. 친구는 숙제가 많아요.
   My friend has a lot of homework.
4. 선생님은 친구가 많아요.
   Teacher has many friends.

The "I have" isn't actually said in Korean, but it is implied based on context.

If you say "My sister is stressed" first, then it translates as "She has lots of homework."

Using the topic marker you can directly specify who you are talking about instead of relying on context or prior sentences.

❑ 8-2. 어렵다 (hard), 쉽다 (easy), and 맵다 (spicy)

These three descriptive verbs don't follow the standard BASIC pattern. You might eventually wonder why they are "irregular" when it seems most ㅂ descriptive verbs don't follow the regular pattern.

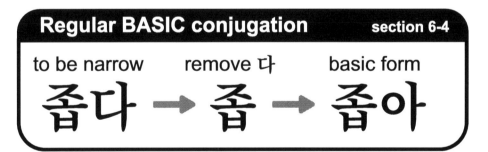

Regular BASIC conjugation section 6-4

to be narrow	remove 다	basic form
좁다 →	좁 →	좁아

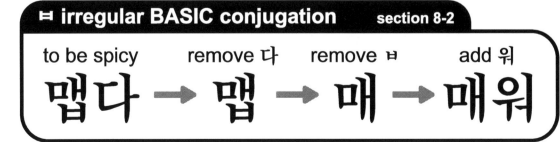

ㅂ irregular BASIC conjugation section 8-2

to be spicy	remove 다	remove ㅂ	add 워
맵다 →	맵 →	매 →	매워

Example sentences

1. 이 음식이 매워요?
   Is this food spicy?
2. 제 숙제가 어려워요.
   My homework is difficult.
3. 한국어는 쉬워요.
   Korean is easy.
4. 이 주스는 써요.
   This juice is bitter.

❑ 8-3. 예쁘다 (pretty, beautiful), 착하다 (kind, nice)

예쁘다 and 착하다 are both used to describe people. Scenery can also be 예쁘다.
If necessary, review section 6-4 to know how to make the BASIC form for each of these.

Example sentences

1. 제 여자친구가 예뻐요.
   My girlfriend is pretty.
2. 제 아버지는 착해요.
   My father is kind.

8 New Action Verbs 새로운 동사

Verb	Basic	English	Type
있다	있어	to exist, to have	regular
없다	없어	to not exist, to not have	regular

8 Verb Usage 동사 사용법

❑ 8-4. 있다 (to exist, to have)

You will use this verb everyday when speaking Korean. Even though 있다 has an "S" sound ㅅ (시옷), remember that when a ㅅ comes at the end of a character it sounds like a "T" unless followed by ㅇ in the next character. This is covered in more detail in section 5-4.

있다 is used to say things like, "there is a ~", and "I have a ~". When using 있다, the item that you "have" or "exists" is marked with the subject marker 이 / 가.

(thing) 이 / 가 있다
there is a (thing)
to have a (thing)

있다 isn't a descriptive verb but it still uses the rules from the prior lessons. The BASIC form is needed to fully use the verb. 요 after the BASIC form makes the sentence polite.

Example sentences

1. 고양이가 있어요.
   There is a cat. / I have a cat.

   Don't let the final 이 in 고양이 confuse you. This is just a part of the word and not the subject marker.

2. 야채가 있어요.
   There are / I have vegetables.
3. 펜이 있어요?
   Do you have a pen?
4. 김밥이 있어요.
   There is / I have gimbap.
5. 뭐가 있어요?
   What is there? / What do you have?

❑ 8-5. 없다 (to not exist, to not have)

없다 has the opposite meaning of 있다. It also has 겹받침 (double final consonant). When saying 없다 the ㅅ (시옷) is silent unless it's followed by a vowel. When it's in the BASIC form 없어 then both the ㅂ (비읍) and ㅅ (시옷) are sounded out much like the "obs" in the word "obscure". However, by no means is 없다 obscure in the Korean language. You will certainly use it every day you speak Korean.

Example sentences

1. 고양이가 없어요.
   There isn't a cat. / I don't have a cat.
2. 야채가 없어요.
   There aren't any / I don't have vegetables.
3. 저는 여동생이 없어요.
   I don't have a younger sister.
4. 김밥이 없어요.
   There isn't / I don't have gimbap.
5. 펜이 없어요?
   You don't have a pen?
6. 제 가방이 없어요.
   My bag isn't there.

8 Grammar 문법

❍ 8-6. Location marker 에

The location marker 에 is the Korean version of "in, on, at". You put it after a location to mark it as the location where something is or isn't. We will use the new words 여기 (here) etc. that were introduced in this lesson.

Example sentences

1. 여기에 있어요.
   It's here.
2. 거기에 없어요.
   It isn't there.
3. 어디에 있어요?
   Where is it?
4. 저기에 있어요.
   It's over there.

Now let's make bigger sentences that have subjects and locations.

Example sentences

1. 차가 여기에 있어요.
   A car is here.
2. 개가 거기에 없어요.
   Dogs aren't there.
3. 고양이가 어디에 있어요?
   Where is the cat?
4. 제 친구가 저기에 있어요.
   My friend is over there.

❍ 8-7. Using location words

Location words are used with objects to say things like "in front of the car" and "on top of the table". Simply add the location word after the item followed by the location marker 에.

위
above, on top, up

밑
below, under, down

속 / 안
inside, in

옆
side, next to

앞
in front

뒤
behind

Example sentences

See if you can cover the English of the following sentences and guess the English based on the pictures in the prior section.

1. 책상 위에 고양이가 있어요.
   There is a cat on top of the desk.
2. 책상 밑에 쥐가 있어요.
   There is a mouse under the desk.
3. 책상 속에 펭귄이 있어요.
   There is a penguin in the desk.
4. 책상 옆에 곰이 있어요.
   There is a bear next to the desk.
5. 책상 앞에 하마가 있어요.
   There is a hippo in front of the desk.
6. 책상 뒤에 기린이 있어요.
   There is a giraffe behind my desk.

All of the prior sentences had a pattern of "There is an animal on top of the desk." with the topic of the sentence being the location. However, if we want to make the animal the primary topic, we would change the sentences to the ones below.

Example sentences

1. 고양이는 책상 위에 있어요.
   The cat is on top of the desk.
2. 쥐는 책상 밑에 있어요.
   The mouse is under the desk.
3. 펭귄은 책상 속에 있어요.
   The penguin is in the desk.
4. 곰은 책상 옆에 있어요.
   The bear is next to the desk.
5. 하마는 책상 앞에 있어요.
   The hippo is in front of the desk.
6. 기린은 책상 뒤에 있어요.
   The giraffe is behind my desk.

What just happened?

What is different between the first and second set of sentences? 이 / 가 subject markers have changed to 은 / 는 topic markers. Furthermore, the order of the sentences are different since a topic should start the sentence. The English also completely changes.

Further down the rabbit hole…

So why isn't a 은 / 는 topic marker used after the location in the first set of sentences? You actually CAN say 에는. The 는 isn't needed unless you wish to stress the specific location.

책상 위에**는** 고양이가 있어요.

There is a cat on TOP of the desk. (as opposed to other places)

❍ 8-8. 안 vs 속

속 and 안 both mean "inside, in". Let's look at when to use each one.

안 is used when you can OPEN and look inside.
Bags and refrigerators can be opened. Buildings, and other structures have doors.

1. 비행기 **안**에 있어요?	Are you **inside** an airplane?
2. 친구는 학교 **안**에 있어요.	My friend is **inside** the school.
3. 집 **안**에 있어요.	It's inside the house. / I'm in my house.
4. 어머니는 병원 **안**에 없어요.	My mother is not inside the hospital.

속 is used in abstract spaces that you cannot OPEN, or SEE inside.
Liquids and non-physical locations such as dreams, your head, and your heart use 속.

1. 머리 **속**에 있어요.	It's **in** my head.
2. 제 악몽 **속**에 하마가 있어요.	There is a hippo **in** my nightmare.
3. 제 마음 **속**에 당신이 있어요.	You are **in** my heart.
4. 꿈 **속**에는 친구가 많아요.	**In** my dreams there are many friends.

속 and 안 are sometimes interchangeable with smaller physical locations.

1. 가방 **안**에 김밥이 있어요.	There is gimbap **in** my bag.
2. 가방 **속**에 김밥이 있어요.	There is gimbap **in** my bag.
3. 책상 **안**에 펜이 없어요.	There isn't a pen **in** the desk.
4. 책상 **속**에 펜이 없어요.	There isn't a pen **in** the desk.

❍ 8-9. 누구 vs 누가

누구 and 누가 both mean "Who". 누구 is used when "who" is the object (such as "Who do you love?". 누가 is used when "who" is the subject (such as, "Who is coming?").
If you ever want to say 누구가 just shorten it to 누가.

누구가 shortens to **누가**

1. **누가** 있어요?	Who is there?
2. 방 안에 **누가** 있어요?	Who is in the room?

8 Question and Answer 질문과 대답

1. **여동생이 있어요?**
   Do you have a younger sister?

   네, 있어요.
   Yes, I have.

   아니요, 없어요.
   No, I don't have

   아니요, 없어요. 저는 남동생이 있어요.
   No, I don't have. I have a younger brother.

2. **지혜 선생님은 어디에 있어요?**
   Where is teacher Jihye?

   저기에 있어요.
   She is over there.

   병원에 있어요.
   She is at a hospital.

   식당에 있어요.
   She is at a restaurant.

3. **귤은 어디에 있어요?**
   Where is the tangerine?

   가방 안에 있어요.
   가방에 있어요.
   It's in the bag.

   Both of these sentences are correct.

   책상 뒤에 있어요.
   It's behind the desk.

   귤이 없어요.
   I don't have a tangerine.

8 Conversation 대화 K-E

1. Polite conversation between co-workers.

A: 누나가 있어요?
B: 네, 있어요.
A: 어디에 있어요?
B: 프랑스에 있어요.

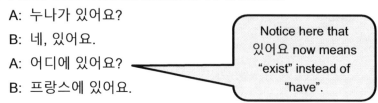

> Notice here that 있어요 now means "exist" instead of "have".

A: Do you have an older sister?
B: Yes, I do.
A: Where is she?
B: She is in France.

2. Polite conversation between friends on the phone.

A: 어디예요?
B: 저는 집에 있어요.
A: 엄마는 어디에 있어요?
B: 병원에 있어요.

A: Where are you?
B: I am in my house.
A: Where is your mother?
B: She is in the hospital.

3. Casual conversation between friends after school.

A: 숙제가 많아?
B: 응, 많아.
A: 숙제가 어려워?
B: 아니, 쉬워.

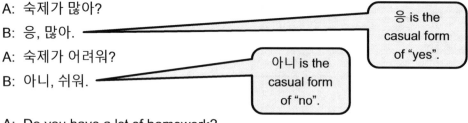

> 응 is the casual form of "yes".

> 아니 is the casual form of "no".

A: Do you have a lot of homework?
B: Yeah, lots.
A: Is the homework hard?
B: No, it's easy.

4. Polite conversation on the phone.

A: 누구세요?

B: 저는 선아의 친구 조지예요. 선아는 집에 있어요?

A: 아니요, 선아는 공항에 있어요.

B: 알겠습니다. 감사합니다.

> 선아 is a Korean girl's name.

> 알겠습니다 is a polite way to say "Okay".

A: Who is it?

B: This is Seona's friend George. Is Seona at home?

A: No, she's at the airport.

B: Okay. Thank you.

8 Conversation 대화 E-K

1. Polite conversation between friends.

A: Do you have a car?

B: No, I don't have a car.

A: Does your older brother have one?

B: Yes, he has a Hyundai.

A: 차가 있어요?

B: 아니요, 차가 없어요.

A: 오빠는 차가 있어요?

B: 네, 현대 있어요.

> "Your" is not needed because we know WHOSE brother we are talking about based on the context.

> It's common in Korean to drop particles when speaking. 가 is dropped here.

> 현대 (Hyundai) is a large Korean car manufacturer.

2. Polite conversation between friends.

A: Who is at school?

B: My older brother is at school.

A: Is your younger sister there also (도)?

B: No, she isn't. She is at home.

A: 학교에 누가 있어요?

B: 제 오빠가 있어요.

A: 여동생도 학교에 있어요?

B: 아니요, 없어요. 집에 있어요.

> 누가 학교에 있어요 is also a good sentence. As long as you keep the particles with the proper word you can move them without affecting the meaning.

> 도 is taught later in the book. It means "also".

3. Polite conversation at a restaurant.

A: Is that meat spicy?
B: Yes. It is spicy. Do you have orange juice?
A: I don't have orange juice. I have water.

A: 그 고기는 매워요?
B: 네, 매워요. 오렌지 주스가 있어요?
A: 오렌지 주스가 없어요. 물이 있어요.

8 Sentence Building 문장 만들기

In each lesson we will build on a previous sentence. Watch it grow and transform each time new concepts are introduced.

제 어머니는 가방이 없어요.
My mother doesn't have a bag.

Compare how the sentence has changed from the prior lessons:

Lesson 5: 이것은 뭐예요?
What is this?

Lesson 6: 이 피자는 맛있어요.
This pizza is delicious.

Lesson 7: 제 어머니의 피자는 차가워요.
My mother's pizza is cold.

8 Workbook Area

❑ A8-1. Reading comprehension

At your current level, you should understand all of the grammar and words in the following sections. If you are struggling to understand them, review this and prior lessons.

① 바나나 옆에 책이 있어요.
② 그 책은 민수 씨의 책이에요.
③ 민수 씨의 잡지는 어디에 있어요?
④ 가방 안에 없어요.

Dialogue

A: 의자 위에 책이 있어요?
B: 아니요. 없어요.
A: 잡지는 어디에 있어요?
B: 사과 옆에 있어요.

❑ A8-2. Reading comprehension questions

Answer the following questions about the reading comprehension in the prior section.

1. 잡지는 바나나 옆에 있어요?

____

2. 잡지는 가방 안에 있어요?

____

3. 그 책은 누구의 책이에요?

____

❑ A8-3. Sentence Jumble

Using ONLY the words and particles provided, create Korean sentences that match the English translation. Conjugate verbs and reuse items as needed.

1. 에, 그, 은, 네, 위에, 숙제, 오빠, 의, 양말, 는, 이, 있다, 가, 여기, 책상, 쉽다, 제, 안에, 요

   ____

   My socks are on the desk.

   ____

   His homework is easy.

   ____

   Your older brother is here.

2. 에, 의자, 귤, 그, 안, 침대, 이다, 학교, 선생님, 그녀, 은, 는, 교실, 뒤. 이, 가, 병원, 요

   ____

   She is at the hospital.

   ____

   There is a tangerine behind the chair.

   ____

   Is the teacher in the classroom?

3. 있다, 숙제, 그녀, 누나, 너, 앞, 에, 고양이, 은, 없다, 는, 이, 가, 그, 의, 학교, 개, 어디, 요

   ____

   Where is his older sister?

   ____

   Do you have a dog?

   ____

   She has no homework.

❑ A8-4. Korean translation

Translate the following conversation into English.

1.
A: 선희의 가방은 어디에 있어요? B: 책상 옆에 있어요. A: 이 숙제는 쉬워요? B: 아니요, 어려워요.
A:
B:
A:
B:

❑ A8-5. English translation

Translate the following conversation into Korean.

1.
A: Do you have a chair? B: No, I don't. A: Is mom in her room? B: Yes, she is.
A:
B:
A:
B:

8 Vocabulary Builder

The more words you know, the less you will get stuck when speaking Korean. Keep reviewing the prior words until you know them well. These new words will pop up in following lessons.

Group G: more places 더 많은 장소

은행	bank
가게	store
백화점	department store
서점	book store
약국	pharmacy
편의점	convenience store
영화관	movie theater
도서관	library

Group H: food and drink 음식과 마실것

빵	bread
계란	egg
우유	milk
사탕	candy
떡	rice cakes
음료수	beverage (non-alcoholic)
라면	ramen noodles
감자	potato
감자튀김	french fries

Lesson 9:

Asking for things and counters

9

Before This Lesson

1. Know the vocabulary groups: G (more places) and H (food and drink).
2. Take a quick look at Lesson 2 to refresh your grasp of numbers. This lesson uses them heavily.
3. Take a 15 minute break. When was the last time you relaxed?

Lesson Goals

1. Continue learning new descriptive verbs.
2. Learn a variety of counter types.

From The Teachers

1. This lesson heavily uses Korean numbers and even teaches you higher numbers. Make sure you review lesson 2 if you need to study up.

Lesson Highlights

9-1.
Ways to say "very" in Korean

9-5.
Asking for something with 주세요

9-7.
Korean Counters

9-10.
Sounding more natural with 그럼

9 New Words 새로운 단어

얼마	how much?
원	won (Korean money)
달러	dollar
엔	yen (Japanese money)
유로	euro (EU money)
강아지	puppy
콜라	cola (Coke ®)
콜라 라이트	cola light (Diet Coke ®)
맥주	beer
물	water
밥	dinner, lunch etc., cooked rice

9 New Phrases 새로운 어구

1. 알겠습니다. (polite)

Got it. / I understand. / Okay.

This is very commonly said after you have given instructions or information to someone. The person who heard the information says this to mean "understood".

2. 여기요. / 저기요.

Come here please. (in a restaurant etc.)

This means "here" / "over there". 여기요 is most common to say "I'm here", but many Koreans say 저기요 to mean "hey over there". Both will get a waiter to come.

9 New Descriptive Verbs 새로운 형용사

We introduce a new verb type, 르 irregulars in this lesson and some new words for types already know. Review the section on ㅂ irregulars in lesson 7 and BASIC form in lesson 6.

다 form	BASIC form	English	Type
빠르다	빨라	to be fast	르 irregular
귀엽다	귀여워	to be cute	ㅂ irregular
맛없다	맛없어	to be tasteless	regular
재미없다	재미없어	to be uninteresting	regular

❑ 9-1. Ways to say "very" in Korean

There are multiple ways to say "very" in Korean. Here are some of the most common ways. No matter what anyone tells you… all of these words are used to mean "very". It's pure semantics to say one is a "different" version of "very".

너무	very
매우	very (mostly written only)
아주	very (quite~)
정말	very (really~)
진짜	very (really~)

When 너무 is used in a sentence where the verb is perceived as "negative" then, in most cases, it means "too". When used in a positive sentence it means "very".

너무 + negative meaning = too~
너무 + positive meaning = very~

Example sentences

1. 이 책은 **너무** 좋아요!	This book is **very** good!
2. 이 책은 **너무** 비싸요!	This book is **too** expensive!
3. 이 라면은 **너무** 맛있어요!	This ramen is **very** delicious!
4. 이것은 **너무** 매워요!	This is **too** spicy!
5. 이것은 **너무** 싸요!	This is **very** cheap!
6. 이것은 **너무** 작아요!	This is **too** small!

매우 and 아주 are placed in front of verbs like just like 너무 but they only mean "very".

Example sentences

1. 이 책은 **아주** 좋아요!	This book is **very** good!
2. 이 책은 **매우** 비싸요!	This book is **very** expensive.
3. 이 라면은 **아주** 맛있어요!	This ramen is **very** delicious!
4. 이 라면은 **매우** 매워요!	This ramen is **very** spicy.
5. 이것은 **아주** 싸요!	This is **very** cheap!
6. 이것은 **매우** 작아요!	This is **very** small!

정말 and 진짜 both mean "really" or "very" when placed in front of descriptive verbs.

Example sentences

1. 이 책은 **정말** 좋아요! — This book is **really** good!
2. 이 라면은 **진짜** 매워요! — This ramen is **really** spicy.

특별 정보 Special Information

정말 and 진짜 both can mean "are you serious?", or "really?". 진짜 can even mean "real, genuine" as opposed to "fake".

Example sentences

1. 피노키오는 **진짜** 사람입니까? — Is Pinocchio a **real** person?
2. **정말**요? — Are you **serious**?

❑ 9-2. 빠르다 (fast), 르 irregular verb types

르 irregulars still follow the BASIC form rules taught in section 6-4. They are irregular because the ㄹ (리을) sound is doubled by adding a ㄹ to the bottom of the first character. Most verbs that have 르 in them are this type.

The 르 changes based on the BASIC form rules (section 6-4) rule #5. Then a ㄹ is added to the first character of the stem. The bottom 2 examples are verbs you don't know yet.

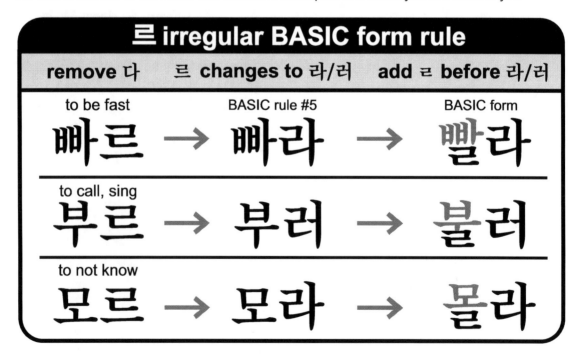

르 irregular BASIC form rule

remove 다	르 changes to 라/러	add ㄹ before 라/러
to be fast 빠르 →	BASIC rule #5 빠라 →	BASIC form 빨라
to call, sing 부르 →	부러 →	불러
to not know 모르 →	모라 →	몰라

Example sentences

1. 김민수 씨는 너무 빨라요! — Minsu Kim is very fast!
2. 선생님의 차는 빨라요. — Teacher's car is fast.

특별 정보 Special Information

SUMMARY: Always use the PRIOR to LAST character of the stem with BASIC rule #5. When the LAST character in the stem has ㅡ, BASIC rule #5 is used, and it's changed to ㅏ or ㅓ based on the PRIOR character's vowel. It's easy to mistakenly use the FIRST character for the vowel change with longer words. For example:

떠오르다 (to rise up; to occur) type: 르 irregular

If you mistakenly use the FIRST character, the stem would be 떠올러. Since the character just before the FINAL in the stem is used, the BASIC is actually 떠올라.

❑ 9-3. 귀엽다 (cute)

Nothing really much to say about this, except that Korean girls and boys are pretty cute… so you will need this word. It is a ㅂ irregular verb, so the ㅂ changes to 워.

Example sentences

1. 제 여자친구는 정말 귀여워요. — My girlfriend is really cute.
2. 제 친구의 여동생이 귀여워요. — My friend's younger sister is cute.
3. 그 강아지는 귀여워요. — That puppy is cute.
4. 학교에서 누가 귀여워요? — Who is cute in school?

누구가 changes to 누가

❑ 9-4. 맛없다 (tasteless), 재미없다 (uninteresting)

맛 means "flavor" and 재미 means "fun" or "interest". When you say 맛있다 or 맛없다 you are actually saying "there is flavor" or "there is no flavor". You learned the opposites of 맛없다 and 재미없다 in lesson 6.

Example sentences

1. 그 책이 재미없어요. — That book isn't interesting.
2. 그 책이 재미있어요. — That book is interesting.
3. 이 요거트가 맛없어요! — This yogurt is tasteless.
4. 이 요거트가 아주 맛있어요! — This yogurt is very tasty.

The pronunciation difference between 맛없다 (tasteless) and 맛있다 (tasty) is significant. 맛없다 has a “D” sound at the end of 맛 and 맛있다 has an “SH” sound at the end of 맛.

mash itt da — 맛있다

mad eob da — 맛없다

9 Grammar 문법

9-5. Asking for something with 주세요

주세요 means “please give” or just “please”. It comes from the verb 주다 (to give). The item that is being asked for is marked with the object marker 을 / 를.

(object) 을/를 주세요
Please give me (object)

Use 을 if the object has a 받침 and 를 if it doesn’t.

with 받침 use 을 계란을 주세요.

no 받침 use 를 우유를 주세요.

Example sentences

1. 책을 주세요.
   Give me a book please.
2. 차를 주세요.
   Some tea please.
3. 커피 주세요.
   Coffee please.
4. 귤을 주세요.
   A tangerine please.
5. 숙제를 주세요.
   Give me some homework please.

In spoken Korean, the object marker 을/를 is often dropped.

❍ 9-6. Saying "and" in lists

와 and 과 are used to connect nouns in a list. If the item just before "and" has a 받침, then 과 is used, and if there isn't a 받침 then 와 is used. This "and" is only ever used to connect nouns and NEVER sentences. The 와 or 과 has no space before, and always one after.

Example sentences

1. 김밥과 국을 주세요.
   Give me gimbap and soup.
2. 바나나와 귤이 맛있어요.
   Bananas and tangerines are tasty.
3. 한국어와 일본어가 진짜 어려워요.
   Korean and Japanese are really hard.
4. 차와 커피를 주세요.
   A tea and a coffee please.
5. 고양이와 강아지가 귀여워요.
   Cats and puppies are cute.
6. 제 어머니와 아버지는 너무 착해요.
   My mother and father are really kind.

In English, a comma is used for word lists, then "and" is used on the last word: (cats, dogs, and pigs). For Korean, 와 or 과 is required between every word in the list.

Example sentences

1. 김밥과 국과 바나나를 주세요.
   Give me gimbap, soup, and a banana.
2. 누나의 머리와 얼굴이 아주 예뻐요.
   Your older sister's hair and face are very pretty.
3. 바나나와 귤과 멜론이 맛있어요.
   Bananas, tangerines, and melons are tasty.

머리 means "head", but is also used to say "hair".

Each item in the "and" changes whether 와 or 과 is used.

❍ 9-7. Korean Counters

In English we have "slices of pizza", "cups of coffee", "reams of paper", "schools of fish", "packs of wolves", and "wads of cash". Just like English, Korean will count things in unique ways based on what is being counted.

The first counter is the 개 counter. 개 is the generic counter used for everyday items. 개 counter is sometimes used even when a more appropriate counter exists. It is never used for people, animals, machines, cars etc. as these types of items already have well defined counters.

If you are ever at a loss as to which counter to use, use this one. You might be wrong, but at least you will have said a counter in the spot where one is needed.

generic counter 개			
Number	Korean Number	Number with Counter	Never
one	하나	한 개	~~하나개~~
two	둘	두 개	~~둘개~~
three	셋	세 개	~~셋개~~
four	넷	네 개	~~넷개~~
five	다섯	다섯 개	
six	여섯	여섯 개	
seven	일곱	일곱 개	
eight	여덟	여덟 개	
nine	아홉	아홉 개	
ten	열	열 개	
eleven	열하나	열한 개	~~열하나 개~~
twenty	스물	스무 개	~~스물 개~~
how many?	몇 개?		

You will notice that there are slight changes to the numbers 1,2,3,4 and 20 when adding the counter. These changes occur in ALL counters using native Korean numbers. From 1-99, Korean numbers are used, but for 100 and up Chinese numbers are used.

Examples

스무 개 (20)
아흔 개 (90)
서른 개 (30)
쉰 개 (50)
스물두 개 (22)
열일곱 개 (17)
마흔다섯 개 (45)
예순한 개 (61)

❍ 9-8. How to say a certain number of something

To say things like “4 apples” and “2 pens” you simply put the number + counter word directly after the item.

item	+ number	+ counter	= English
사과	한	개	1 apple
오이	두	개	2 cucumbers
버섯	열	개	10 mushrooms
귤	여덟	개	8 tangerines

Example sentences

Notice how "and" is used.

1. 사과 네 개를 주세요.
   4 apples please.
2. 저는 귤이 한 개 있어요.
   I have 1 tangerine.
3. 계란 세 개 주세요.
   3 eggs please.
4. 멜론 두 개와 바나나 한 개를 주세요.
   2 melons and 1 banana please.

Now let's learn some more specific Korean counters.

How Many?	animals / fish	glasses / cups	bottles
	몇 마리?	몇 잔?	몇 병?
1	한 마리	한 잔	한 병
2	두 마리	두 잔	두 병
3	세 마리	세 잔	세 병
4	네 마리	네 잔	네 병
5	다섯 마리	다섯 잔	다섯 병
6	여섯 마리	여섯 잔	여섯 병
7	일곱 마리	일곱 잔	일곱 병
8	여덟 마리	여덟 잔	여덟 병
9	아홉 마리	아홉 잔	아홉 병
10	열 마리	열 잔	열 병
11	열한 마리	열한 잔	열한 병
20	스무 마리	스무 잔	스무 병
The remaining numbers follow the same pattern until 99.			

The counters follow the same rules as the 개 counter.

Notice (잔) from sentence 3 is changed to (병).

Example sentences

1. 고양이가 두 마리 있어요.
   There are 2 cats. / I have 2 cats.
2. 콜라 세 잔 주세요.
   3 glasses of cola please.
3. 물 여섯 잔 주세요.
   6 glasses of water please.
4. 물 여섯 병 주세요.
   6 bottles of water please.
5. 커피 두 잔과 차 한 잔을 주세요.
   2 coffees and 1 tea please.
6. 학교에 쥐가 몇 마리 있어요?
   How many rats are in the school?

❍ 9-9. Human Counters

명 is used to count people. 분 is also used to count people but it is more formal and isn't used when referring to people in your own group. 인분 is commonly used in restaurants to count servings.

NOTE: In this book we are actually spelling out the numbers to help you remember which version (Chinese or Korean) are being used. In actual usage numbers are normally not spelled out and you will have to remember which number version is used.

	people	people (formal)	servings
How Many?	몇 명?	몇 분?	몇 인분?
1	한 명	한 분	일 인분
2	두 명	두 분	이 인분
3	세 명	세 분	삼 인분
4	네 명	네 분	사 인분
5	다섯 명	다섯 분	오 인분
6	여섯 명	여섯 분	육 인분
7	일곱 명	일곱 분	칠 인분
8	여덟 명	여덟 분	팔 인분
9	아홉 명	아홉 분	구 인분
10	열 명	열 분	십 인분
11	열한 명	열한 분	십일 인분
20	스무 명	스무 분	이십 인분
The remaining numbers follow the same pattern until 99.			

인분 uses the Chinese numbers. Other than that, the rules are the same.

Example sentences

1. 친구가 몇 명 있어요? — How many friends do you have?
2. 학교에 선생님이 열 분 있어요. — There are 10 teachers in the school.
3. 김밥은 몇 인분 있어요? — How many servings of gimbap are there?
4. 김밥은 이십 인분 있어요. — There are 20 servings of gimbap.

❍ 9-10. Sounding more natural with 그럼

그럼 means "well, then~" or "if that's the case~". It can be added to the front of any sentence. For example, if someone tells you they don't have any apples, you can respond with 그럼, 바나나 주세요. (Well then, give me a banana.)

Example conversations

1. A: 사탕 열두 개 주세요.
   B: 사탕은 없어요.
   A: **그럼**, 사과 세 개 주세요.

   A: Give me 12 pieces of candy please.
   B: We don't have any candy.
   A: **Well then**, give me 3 apples.

2. A: 여동생이 있어요?
   B: 아니요, 없어요.
   A: **그럼**, 남동생이 있어요?
   B: 네, 있어요.

   A: Do you have a younger sister?
   B: No, I don't.
   A: **Well then**, do you have a younger brother?
   B: Yes, I do.

3. A: 이 김밥은 매워요?
   B: 네, 진짜 매워요!
   A: **그럼**, 그 김밥은요?
   B: 몰라요.

   A: Is this gimbap spicy?
   B: Yes, it's really spicy.
   A: **Well then**, what about that gimbap?
   B: I don't know.

> You can end a sentence with topic marker 은/는 + 요? to say "what about~?"

❍ 9-11. 100, 1000, and 10000 (Numbers Part II)

백 100

천 1,000

만 10,000

By learning just three more words you can count up to 99,999,999.

In lesson 2 you learned how to count number 1-99. For the higher numbers the pattern continues.

The hundreds (100-900) are very easy. Just add 백 (100) in front of the single numbers 1-9.

the hundreds (100-900)		
Number	Korean Number	Never
100	백	~~일백~~
200	이백	
300	삼백	
400	사백	
500	오백	
600	육백	
700	칠백	
800	팔백	
900	구백	

Example numbers

1. 오백오십
   550
2. 구백삼십일
   931
3. 사백이십
   420
4. 삼백팔십삼
   383
5. 백칠십육
   176
6. 이백사십사
   244
7. 팔백구십구
   899
8. 칠백십일
   711

The thousands (1000-9000) are just as easy. Just add 천 (1000) after the single numbers .

the thousands (1000-9000)		
Number	Korean Number	Never
1000	천	~~일천~~
2000	이천	
3000	삼천	
4000	사천	
5000	오천	
6000	육천	
7000	칠천	
8000	팔천	
9000	구천	

The 1,000 unit in Korean ends at 9,000. After 9,000, Korean begins counting in units of 10,000. Each unit of 10,000 is called 만. So, 20,000 is 이만 because it is 2 (이) units of 10,000 (만). And 50,000 is 오만 because it is 5 (오) units of 10,000 (만).

the ten thousands (10,000-90,000)		
Number	Korean Number	Never
10,000	만	~~일만~~
20,000	이만	
30,000	삼만	
40,000	사만	
50,000	오만	
60,000	육만	
70,000	칠만	
80,000	팔만	
90,000	구만	

You can have up to 9999 units of 10,000 which is 99,990,000. Knowing this, and with practice you can now count up just under 100 million.

Example numbers (thousands)

1. 사천육백이십
   4,620
2. 구천오백십일
   9,511
3. 오천삼백사십팔
   5,348
4. 칠천이백구십칠
   7,297
5. 천이
   1,002
6. 팔천팔백팔십팔
   8,888
7. 이천십사
   2,014
8. 삼천칠백
   3,700

Example numbers (ten thousands)

1. 만 오천
   15,000
2. 오만 이천이백칠십삼
   52,273
3. 육만 육백
   60,600
4. 만 천백십
   11,110
5. 구만 사천오백
   94,500
6. 삼만 팔천이백오십이
   38,252
7. 이만 칠천삼백삼
   27,303
8. 사만 사천
   44,000

Example numbers (bigger number)

1. 백만
   1,000,000
2. 오백만
   5,000,000
3. 천만
   10,000,000
4. 삼백만
   3,000,000
5. 팔천오만
   80,050,000
6. 구천구백구십구만 구천구백구십구
   99,999,999

❍ 9-12. Using money counters

Money is always counted using Chinese numbers. To use the money counters such as 원 (Won), 엔 (Yen), and 달러 (Dollars) you just add the counter word for the money after the number. There is always a space before the money counter.

Example sentences

1. 만 원 있어요.
   I have 10,000 won.
2. 이백 달러 주세요.
   Give me 200 dollars please.
3. 이 펜은 오만 엔이에요.
   This pen is 50,000 yen.
4. 만 원은 십 달러예요.
   10,000 won is 10 dollars.
5. 이만 오백육십 유로는 너무 비싸요.
   20,560 Euro is too expensive.
6. 제 집은 이십만 달러입니다.
   My house is 200,000 dollars.

❍ 9-13. My school, my bank, my company

In Korean language when referring to places that you don't actually own, such as the school you attend, the bank that you have an account with, the company you work at, and even your own house, it's common to use 우리 (we, our) instead of 제 or 내 (my). If 제 or 내 are used then ownership is implied.

Examples

1. 우리 학교	My school / our school
2. 우리 대학교	My college / our college
3. 우리 은행	My bank / our bank
4. 우리 집	My house / our house

9 Question and Answer 질문과 대답

1. **사탕 두 개 있어요?**
   Do you have two pieces of candy?

   네, 사탕 두 개 있어요.
   Yes, I have two pieces of candy.

   아니요, 저는 사탕이 없어요.
   No, I don't have any candy.

2. **서울에 가게가 몇 개 있어요?**
How many stores are in Seoul?

서울에는 가게가 만 개 있어요.
There are 10,000 stores in Seoul.

> The double particle 에는 is stressing that "in" Seoul, as opposed to other cities there are 10,000 stores

천 개가 있어요.
There are 1,000.

가게는 팔십칠 개가 있어요.
There are 87 stores.

> Even though the 개 counter SHOULD use Korean numbers, once the numbers go above 20 some Koreans use the Chinese numbers.

3. **이 요거트는 차가워요?**
Is this yogurt cold?

네, 차가워요.
Yes, it's cold.

아니요, 뜨거워요.
No, it's hot.

몰라요.
I don't know.

9 Conversation 대화 K-E

1. **Polite conversation at a coffee shop.**

A: 커피는 얼마예요?
B: 오천 원이에요.
A: 그럼... 두 잔 주세요.
B: 만 원입니다.

A: How much is coffee?
B: It's 5000 Won.
A: Well then, give me two cups.
B: It's 10000 Won.

2. Polite conversation at a restaurant.

A: 몇 명이에요?

B: 다섯 명이에요. 피자와 콜라를 주세요.

A: 알겠습니다.

A: How many people?

B: Five people. Give us pizza and coke please.

A: Understood.

3. Polite conversation at a park.

A: 저 고양이는 당신의 고양이에요?

B: 네, 제 고양이에요.

A: 너무 귀여워요.

B: 고마워요.

> 당신 is really the only option to use when you don't know a person and need to say "your".

A: Is that cat over there your cat?

B: Yes, it's my cat.

A: It's really cute.

B: Thanks.

9 Conversation 대화 E-K

1. Polite conversation at a Mexican restaurant.

A: Does this food taste good?

B: No, it's spicy. Do you have water?

A: Yes, I have some.

B: Give me some water please.

A: 이 음식은 맛있어요?

B: 아니요, 매워요. 물 있어요?

A: 네, 있어요.

B: 물 주세요.

2. Polite conversation between friends.

A: How many teachers are there in the school?
B: There are ten.
A: Well then, how many students are there?
B: There are 500.

A: 학교에 선생님이 몇 분 있어요?
B: 열 분이 있어요.
A: 그럼, 학생은 몇 명 있어요?
B: 오백 명이 있어요.

3. Informal conversation about… a drug deal?? No idea.

> You can't tell us this isn't funny. Lighten up… it's a joke.

A: How many you got?
B: I got ten.
A: Give me one.
B: A'ight.

A: 몇 개 있어?
B: 열 개 있어.
A: 한 개 줘.
B: 응.

> 줘 is casual for 주세요. You really can't expect drug deals to be polite can you? 응 is casual for "yes" or in this case "a'ight"

9 Sentence Building 문장 만들기

In each lesson we will build on a previous sentence. Watch it grow and transform each time new concepts are introduced.

콜라 두 병과 물 세 잔을 주세요.
2 bottles of cola and 3 cups of water please.

Compare how the sentence has changed from the prior lessons:

Lesson 6: 이 피자는 맛있어요.
This pizza is delicious.

Lesson 7: 제 어머니의 피자는 차가워요.
My mother's pizza is cold.

Lesson 8: 제 어머니는 가방이 없어요.
My mother doesn't have a bag.

9 Workbook Area

☐ A9-1. Reading comprehension

At your current level, you should understand all of the grammar and words in the following sections. If you are struggling to understand them, review this and prior lessons.

New words for this comprehension: 켈리 (Kelly), 영화표 (movie ticket), 장 (paper / ticket counter), 팝콘 (popcorn)

① 우리 학교 옆에 영화관이 있어요.

② 켈리는 영화표 두 장이있어요.

③ 영화표 두 장은 만 칠천 원이에요.

④ 팝콘은 오천 원이에요.

Don't confuse 잔 (glasses / cups counter) and 장 (paper / ticket counter) since they sound alike.

Dialogue

A: 안녕하세요.

B: 영화표 세 장 주세요. 얼마예요?

A: 이만 오천오백 원이에요.

B: 팝콘 두 개 주세요.

A: 알겠습니다.

☐ A9-2. Reading comprehension questions

Answer the following questions about the reading comprehension in the prior section.

1. 켈리는 영화표 몇 장이 있어요?

____

2. 팝콘은 얼마예요?

____

3. 공항 옆에 영화관이 있어요?

____

❑ A9-3. Sentence Jumble

Using ONLY the words and particles provided, create Korean sentences that match the English translation. Conjugate verbs and reuse items as needed.

1. 를, 을, 빠르다, 의, 주세요, 콜라, 맛없다, 물, 나, 맥주, 은, 는, 이, 가, 맛있다, 제, 그, 차

____

This beer is tasteless.

____

My car is fast.

____

Give me some water.

2. 가, 인분, 열, 제, 마리, 주세요, 아버지, 있다, 재미없다, 을, 에, 은, 음식, 명, 는 를, 오, 이, 개, 요.

____

Please give me five portions of food.

____

My father is not interesting.

____

There are 10 dogs.

3. 백,은, 맥주, 에, 너무, 있다, 당신, 명, 의, 귀엽다, 학교, 는, 이, 가, 네, 남동생, 를, 춥다

____

Do you have some beer?

____

There are 100 people at this school.

____

Your younger brother is very cute.

❑ A9-4. Korean translation

Translate the following conversation into English.

1.
A: 사탕 한 개는 얼마예요? B: 천 원이에요. A: 다섯 개 주세요. B: 오천 원이에요.
A:
B:
A:
B:

❑ A9-5. English translation

Translate the following conversation into Korean.

1.
A: Is this gimbap delicious? B: No, it's too salty. A: Well then, please give me 3 eggs. B: I don't have 3. I have 2 eggs.
A:
B:
A:
B:

❑ A9-6. Basic form drill

Answer the questions about the verbs listed below. New words are used, but you should be able to create the necessary parts for each one based on what you learned in this lesson. Refer to section 6-4 for the rules.

1. 어렵다 (to be difficult) ㅂ irregular (section 7-2)

A) What is the stem? ______________________

B) What is removed from the stem? ______________________

C) What is added to the stem? ______________________

D) What is the BASIC form? ______________________

2. 빠르다 (to be fast) 르 irregular (section 9-2)

A) What is the stem? ______________________

B) What is the last vowel in the stem? ______________________

C) What should 르 be changed to? ______________________

D) What gets added to 빠? ______________________

E) What is the BASIC form? ______________________

3. 머무르다 (to stay, remain) 르 irregular (section 9-2)

A) What is the stem? ______________________

B) What is the last vowel in the stem? ______________________

C) What should 르 be changed to? ______________________

D) What gets added to 무? ______________________

E) What is the BASIC form? ______________________

4. 입다 (to wear) regular

A) What is the stem? ______________________________

B) What is the last vowel in the stem? ______________________________

C) Does the stem end with a 받침? ______________________________

D) What is the BASIC form? ______________________________

E) What rule applies? ______________________________

5. 가르치다 (to teach) type: regular

A) What is the stem? ______________________________

B) What is the last vowel in the stem? ______________________________

C) Does the stem end with a 받침? ______________________________

D) What is the BASIC form? ______________________________

E) What rule applies? ______________________________

9 Vocabulary Builder

Days of the week will be used a lot in the next lesson.

■ Group I: days of the week 요일

일요일	Sunday
월요일	Monday
화요일	Tuesday
수요일	Wednesday
목요일	Thursday
금요일	Friday
토요일	Saturday

Lesson 10:

Future, Past, and Present Tenses

10

Before This Lesson

1. Understand how to convert verbs into the BASIC form.
2. Understand what it means to be a ㅂ (비읍) irregular verb.

Lesson Goals

1. Learn how to make any verb into the future and past tense.

From The Teachers

1. Don't worry if you haven't learned everything perfectly from past lessons. A lot of sentences are designed to review prior concepts. If you have some extra time you can always go back and scan prior lessons.

Lesson Highlights

10-1.
Past tense

10-3.
BASIC future tense and present tense

10-5.
Future tense for ㅂ irregular verbs

10-8.
The months

10 New Words 새로운 단어

무슨 요일	what day of the week?
언제	when?
지금	now, right now
어제	yesterday
오늘	today
내일	tomorrow
매일	every day
매주	every week
매달	every month
매년	every year
시험	test, exam

10 New Action Verbs 새로운 동사

Verb	Basic	English	Type
가다	가	to go	regular
오다	와	to come	regular

10 Grammar 문법

In this lesson we introduce "action" verbs. Up until now we have learned mostly "descriptive" verbs. The good news is that the conjugation methods, such as BASIC form, taught in section 6-4 work for both types.

❍ 10-1. Past tense

Up until this point, we have only used the present tense of verbs to say things like "There are 2 cats" and "It is cold". If we want to say "There WERE 2 cats" and "It WAS cold" we need to create the past tense form of the verbs.

To make verbs past tense you add ㅆ to the bottom of the BASIC form then add 어.

it IS cold	add ㅆ then add 어	it WAS cold
추워 →	추웠 →	추웠어

it IS small	add ㅆ then add 어	it WAS small
작아 →	작았 →	작았어

Example sentences

1. 어제는 추웠어요.
   It was cold yesterday.
2. 금요일은 더웠어요.
   Friday was hot.
3. 그 김밥은 매웠어요.
   That gimbap was spicy.
4. 이 책이 어려웠어요.
   This book was difficult.
5. 집에 있었어요.
   I was at home.
6. 고양이가 없었어요.
   There wasn't a cat.
7. 그 주스는 달았어!
   That juice was sweet!
8. 영화는 재미있었어요.
   The movie was interesting.

Without 요 this is a casual sentence. Use with friends only!

NOTE: Sentence #5, #6, and #8 can be tricky. The present tense of verbs like 있다 and 없다 sound similar to the past tense of other verbs. These verbs need a DOUBLE ㅆ어 sound for past tense.

isseo-sseo yo	oebseo-sseo yo
있었어요	없었어요
(there was~, I had~)	(there wasn't~, I didn't have~)

❍ 10-2. 가다 (to go), 오다 (to come)

The location is marked with the location marker 에.

(place) 에 가다 / (place) 에 오다
go to (place) / come to a (place)

The past tense for 가다 and 오다 follows the pattern taught in the prior grammar point.

Example sentences (using locations)

1. 저는 학교에 갔어요.
   I went to school.
2. 아버지는 서울에 갔어요.
   My father went to Seoul.
3. 제가 친구의 집에 갔어요.
   I went to a friend's house.
4. 개가 여기에 왔어요.
   The dog came here.

Time is marked with the time marker 에. The time marker is exactly the same as the location marker in sound.

(time) 에 가다 / (time) 에 오다
go at (time) / come at (time)

Example sentences (using times)

1. 저는 화요일에 갔어요.
   I went on Tuesday.
2. 친구가 금요일에 왔어요.
   My friend came on Friday.
3. 어머니가 목요일에 갔어요.
   My mother went on Thursday.
4. 토요일에 왔어요.
   I came on Saturday.

You can use the time and location markers in the same sentence.

Example sentences (using times and locations)

1. 남동생이 화요일에 서울에 왔어요.
   My younger brother came to Seoul on Tuesday.
2. 목요일에 여동생의 집에 갔어요.
   I went to my younger sister's house on Thursday.
3. 제 여자친구가 토요일에 편의점에 갔어요.
   My girlfriend went to the convenience store on Saturday.
4. 저는 금요일에 태국에 왔어요.
   I came to Thailand on Friday.

❍ 10-3. BASIC future tense and present tense

Depending on the context of the sentence BASIC form can be future and present tense. You can force context by adding appropriate time words such as 내일 (tomorrow), 매일 (every day), and 지금 (now). Pay attention to how by changing just ONE word the tense of the sentence changes.

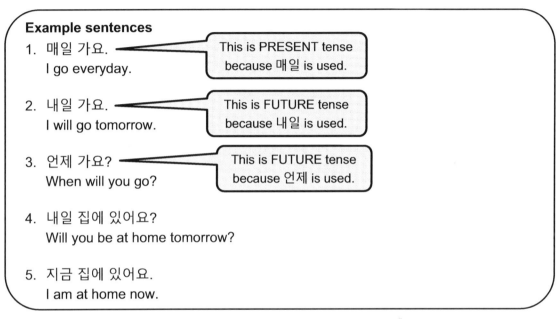

Example sentences

1. 매일 가요.
   I go everyday.
   (This is PRESENT tense because 매일 is used.)

2. 내일 가요.
   I will go tomorrow.
   (This is FUTURE tense because 내일 is used.)

3. 언제 가요?
   When will you go?
   (This is FUTURE tense because 언제 is used.)

4. 내일 집에 있어요?
   Will you be at home tomorrow?

5. 지금 집에 있어요.
   I am at home now.

In spoken Korean using the BASIC form is very common.

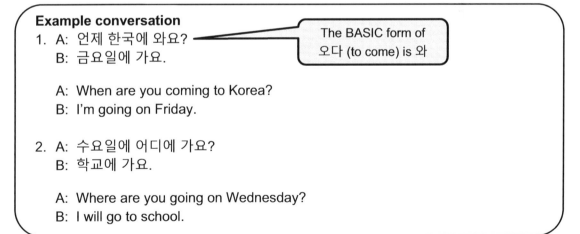

Example conversation

1. A: 언제 한국에 와요?
   B: 금요일에 가요.
   (The BASIC form of 오다 (to come) is 와)

   A: When are you coming to Korea?
   B: I'm going on Friday.

2. A: 수요일에 어디에 가요?
   B: 학교에 가요.

   A: Where are you going on Wednesday?
   B: I will go to school.

특별 정보 Special Information

BASIC form can only be future and present tense. The BASIC form is NEVER past tense. To make past tense you must use the pattern taught in section 10-1. Also, without the proper context BASIC form defaults to present tense.

❍ 10-4. Future tense (will do, going to do)

Another way to make future tense verbs is ㄹ/을 거예요 form. This form has benefits over the BASIC future tense since it doesn't require context to make it future tense. ㄹ/을 거예요 for regular, and also 르 irregular verbs, is made using the pattern below.

Future Tense (NO 받침) (add ㄹ)

remove 다		add ㄹ to stem		add 거예요
to go 가	→	갈	→	Will go. 갈 거예요
to come 오	→	올	→	Will come. 올 거예요
to be fast 빠르	→	빠를	→	Will be fast. 빠를 거예요

Future Tense (WITH 받침) (add 을)

remove 다		add 을 after stem		add 거예요
to be, to have 있	→	있을	→	Will be. / Will have. 있을 거예요
a lot, many 많	→	많을	→	Will be many. 많을 거예요
to be good 좋	→	좋을	→	Will be good. 좋을 거예요

Example sentences

1. 서울에 갈 거예요. — I will go to Seoul.
2. 수요일에 친구가 올 거예요. — My friend is coming on Wednesday.
3. 내일 사람이 많을 거예요. — There will be many people tomorrow.
4. 오늘은 집에 있을 거예요. — I will be at home today.

10-5. Future tense for ㅂ (비읍) irregular verbs

ㅂ irregular verbs conjugate into the future tense by removing ㅂ from the stem and then adding 울 거예요. NOTE!!! This is 울 not 을.

Future Tense (ㅂ irregular) (add 울 거예요)

remove 다 then ㅂ		add 울 (not 을!)	add 거예요
to be cold			Will be cold.
춥 →	추 →	추울 →	추울 거예요
to be hot			Will be hot.
덥 →	더 →	더울 →	더울 거예요
to be spicy			Will be spicy.
맵 →	매 →	매울 →	매울 거예요

Example sentences

1. 내일은 추울 거예요? — Will it be cold tomorrow?
2. 금요일은 더울 거예요. — Friday will be hot.
3. 시험이 어려울 거예요. — The test will be hard.
4. 시험이 쉬울 거예요. — The test will be easy.

10-6. ㄹ/을 거예요 for probable future outcomes

While it's true that ㄹ/을 거예요 means, "I will~", or "I am going to~", it is also used to assume probable future outcomes. For example with any descriptive verb, it is more natural to translate ㄹ/을 거예요 to "It will probably be~" or "It might be~", instead of, "It will be~".

Example sentences

1. 내일은 추울 거예요. — Tomorrow will probably be cold.
2. 이 김밥은 매울 거예요. — This gimbap might be hot.
3. 시험이 어려울 거예요. — The test might be hard.
4. 시험이 쉬울 거예요. — The test will probably be easy.

⚠ 특별 정보 Special Information ⚠

SUMMARY: To verb "to rain" or "to snow" uses the verb 오다 (to come).
When 비 (rain) and 눈 (snow) fall, Koreans say "it's coming" using 오다 (to come).

Example sentences

1. 내일 비가 올 거예요.	It will rain tomorrow.
2. 지금 눈이 와요.	It's snowing now.
3. 화요일에 비가 왔어요.	It rained on Tuesday.
4. 어제 눈이 왔어요.	It snowed yesterday.

❍ 10-7. A note about the time marker 에

The time marker 에 translates to "in", "on", or "at" in relation to times.
You should not use time marker 에 with 오늘 (today), 어제 (yesterday), and 내일 (tomorrow). You should use 에 after named times like "Sunday", "March", or "3pm".
NOTE: 에 is often dropped in spoken Korean.

Example sentences

1. 내일 한국에 가요.	I will go to Korea tomorrow.
2. 일요일에 친구가 와요.	On Sunday a friend will come.
3. 어제 선생님은 여기에 있었어요.	The teacher was here yesterday.
4. 월요일에 시험이 없을 거예요.	There won't be a test on Monday.

❍ 10-8. The months

Korean months are just Chinese number + 월. For practice, the number part will be hangul.

the months (Jan – Dec)					
What month? 몇월					
January	일월	1 월	July	칠월	7 월
February	이월	2 월	August	팔월	8 월
March	삼월	3 월	September	구월	9 월
April	사월	4 월	October	시월 (not 십)	10 월
May	오월	5 월	November	십일월	11 월
June	유월 (not 육)	6 월	December	십이월	12 월

Example sentences

1. 이월에 중국에 갔어요.
   I went to China in February.
2. 유월에 여기에 없을 거예요.
   I won't be here in June.
3. 팔월에 비가 많이 왔어요.
   It rained a lot in August.
4. 십이월에 눈이 왔어요.
   It snowed in December.

❍ 10-9. Every Monday, every January etc.

You can add 매주 (every week) in front of any week day, or 매년 (every year) in front of any month, to say things like "every Monday", and "every January".

Example sentences

1. 매주 금요일에 서울에 가요. I go to Seoul every Friday.
2. 매주 일요일에 교회에 가요. I go to church every Sunday.
3. 매년 삼월에 병원에 가요. I go to the hospital every March.
4. 매년 오월이 더워요. It's hot every May.

❍ 10-10. Past tense for 이다 and 아니다

In section 10-1 we introduce past tense. 이다 (it is, I am, he is, she is etc) and 아니다 (it isn't, I am not, he isn't, she isn't etc) can be conjugated into the past tense as shown:

Verb	Past tense (with 받침)	Past tense (without 받침)
이다	이었어요	였어요
아니다	아니었어요	아니었어요

Example Q&A

1. **얼마였어요.** **How much was it?**
   천 원이었어요. It was 1000 won.
   삼만 원이었어요. It was 30,000 won.
2. **언제 였어요?** **When was it?**
   토요일이었어요. It was Saturday.
   어제가 아니었어요. It wasn't yesterday.

10 Question and Answer 질문과 대답

1. **매일 학교에 가요?**
   Do you go to school everyday?

   네, 매일 학교에 가요.
   Yes, I go to school everyday.

   아니요, 매주 월요일에 가요.
   No, I go to school every Monday.

2. **언제 서울에 와요?**
   When do you come to Seoul?

   내일 가요.
   I'll go tomorrow.

   저는 매주 화요일에 서울에 가요.
   I go to Seoul every Tuesday.
   저는 매달 서울에 갈 거예요.
   I will go to Seoul every month.

3. **어제 날씨가 추웠어요?**
   Was the weather cold yesterday?

   네, 추웠어요.
   Yes, it was cold.

   아니요, 더웠어요.
   No, it was hot.

10 Conversation 대화 K-E

1. Polite conversation between schoolmates.

A: 내일 학교에 갈 거예요?

B: 아니요, 집에 있을 거예요.

A: 숙제 있어요?

B: 아니요, 없어요.

A: Will you go to school tomorrow?

B: No, I will be at home.

A: Do you have homework?

B: No, I don't.

2. Polite conversation between penpals.

A: 오늘 미국에 가요?

B: 아니요, 내일 갈 거예요.

A: 언제 한국에 올 거예요?

B: 삼월에 올 거예요.

A: Are you going to America today?

B: No, I will go tomorrow.

A: When will you come to Korea?

B: I will come in March.

3. Polite conversation between two people living in different parts of Korea.

A: 오늘 추워요?

B: 네, 진짜 추워요.

A: 목요일은 추워요?

B: 아니요, 금요일이 추울 거예요.

A: Is today cold?

B: Yes, it's really cold.

A: Will it be cold on Thursday?

B: No, it will be cold on Friday.

10 Conversation 대화 E-K

1. Polite conversation between friends.

A: What day of the week is it today?
B: It's Sunday.
A: Are you going to go to church? (Will you go to church?)
B: Yes, I go every Sunday.

A: 오늘은 무슨 요일이에요?
B: 일요일이에요.
A: 교회에 갈 거예요?
B: 네, 매주 일요일에 가요.

2. Polite conversation between friends.

A: Was there a rice cake on the desk?
B: No, there wasn't.
A: Well then, what was there?
B: There were books.

A: 책상 위에 떡이 있었어요?
B: 아니요, 없었어요.
A: 그럼, 뭐가 있었어요?
B: 책이 있었어요.

3. Polite conversation between a wife and her husband.

A: Did you go to the bank yesterday?
B: No, I went on Wednesday.
A: When will you go to bookstore?
B: I will go tomorrow.

A: 어제 은행에 갔어요?
B: 아니요, 수요일에 갔어요.
A: 언제 서점에 갈 거예요?
B: 내일 갈 거예요.

10 Sentence Building 문장 만들기

In each lesson we will build on a previous sentence. Watch it grow and transform each time new concepts are introduced.

내일 콜라 두 병을 살 거예요.
I will buy 2 bottles of cola tomorrow.

Compare how the sentence has changed from the prior lessons:

Lesson 7: 제 어머니의 피자는 차가워요.
My mother's pizza is cold.

Lesson 8: 제 어머니는 가방이 없어요.
My mother doesn't have a bag.

Lesson 9: 콜라 두 병과 물 세 잔을 주세요.
2 bottles of cola and 3 cups of water please.

10 Workbook Area

❑ A10-1. Reading comprehension

At your current level, you should understand all of the grammar and words in the following sections. If you are struggling to understand them, review this and prior lessons.

New words in this comprehension: 리키 (Ricky), 가족 (family)

① 리키는 매년 칠월에 멕시코에 가요.

② 멕시코에 친구와 가족이 많아요.

③ 리키의 아버지는 멕시코 사람이에요.

④ 멕시코는 아주 예뻐요.

Dialogue

A: 준호 씨 언제 멕시코에 가요?

B: 칠월에 갈 거예요.

A: 무슨 요일에 갈 거예요?

B: 월요일에 갈 거예요.

❑ A10-2. Reading comprehension questions

Answer the following questions about the reading comprehension in the prior section.

1. 준호는 언제 멕시코에 갈 거예요?

____

2. 리키의 아버지는 어느 나라 사람이에요?

____

3. 멕시코에 누가 많아요?

____

❑ A10-3. Sentence Jumble

Using ONLY the words and particles provided, create Korean sentences that match the English translation. Conjugate verbs and reuse items as needed.

1. 제, 이, 오늘, 오다, 서울, 어제, 절, 가다, 이다, 금요일, 는, 가, 친구, 에, 토요일, 저

____

My friend will come to Seoul on Friday.

____

I am going to go to a Buddhist temple tomorrow.

____

On Friday and Saturday I went to Seoul.

2. 덥다, 에, 집, 은, 는, 가다, 너무, 이, 가, 십이월, 십일월, 국, 저, 뜨겁다, 제, 의

____

Will November be hot? (casual)

____

This soup is too hot.

____

I went to my friend's house.

3. 매년, 어머니, 약국, 는, 이, 어렵다, 여기, 제, 가다, 어제, 가, 오다, 숙제, 에, 삼월, 정말

____

I went to a pharmacy yesterday.

____

My mother comes here every March.

____

This homework was really difficult.

❑ A10-4. Korean translation

Translate the following conversation into English.

1.
A: 시험은 언제예요? B: 수요일이에요. A: 지금 성적이 좋아요? B: 아니요... 나빠요.
A:
B:
A:
B:

❑ A10-5. English translation

Translate the following conversation into Korean.

1.
A: What month did your younger brother go to Australia? B: He went in December. A: Does he go every December? B: Yes, he goes every December and May.
A:
B:
A:
B:

10 Vocabulary Builder

Keep learning new words. As you learn more grammar you will realize that grammar isn't the hard part. You won't get stuck on grammar, but you will easily get stuck on a word you don't know.

■ Group J: things around the house 집안에 있는 것

침대	bed
거울	mirror
문	door
창문	windows
텔레비전	television
티브이	TV
약	medicine
가구	furniture
컴퓨터	computer
에어컨	air conditioning

■ Group K: events 이벤트

생일	day of birth
파티	party
생일 파티	birthday party
선물	present
여행	trip, travel
결혼식	wedding
크리스마스	Christmas
설날 (설랄)	New Year's Day

We hereby bequeath this blank page to you. Do ANYTHING you want with it, UNLESS this is a library book. DO NOT WRITE in the library book!

Lesson 11:

Dates and Time

11

Before This Lesson

1. Learn vocabulary groups: J (things around the house) and K (events).

2. Review the future and past tense verb conjugations.

Lesson Goals

1. Learn four new action verbs.
2. Learn how to tell time and make dates.

From The Teachers

1. This is a numbers heavy lesson since both Chinese and Korean numbers are used to tell time. Make sure you are strong with the numbers.

2. As you learn more action verbs you will BE ABLE to say more everyday actions. One great way to practice your Korean is to say as many things you can in Korean as you do them. For example, “I will go to the store.” etc. Sure… you will look crazy if anyone sees you, but your Korean will improve the more you ACTUALLY speak it.

Lesson Highlights

11-8.
Telling time in Korean

11-10.
Next Friday, Last Monday, Next January, This March

11-11.
The event location marker 에서

11-13.
How to say complete dates in Korean

11 New Words 새로운 단어

지난주	last week
이번 주	this week
다음 주	next week
지난달	last month
이번 달	this month
다음 달	next month
지난해	last year
이번 해	this year
다음 해	next year
비행기표	airline ticket
햄버거	hamburger
부모님	parents
많이	a lot
같이	together
오늘 밤	tonight
어젯밤	last night
싸이	PSY (Korean singer)

11 Word Usage 단어 사용법

❑ 11-1. Other versions of this, last, and next year

지난해 (last year), 이번 해 (this year), and 다음 해 (next year) can be used normally, and are nice because they have the same pattern as the weeks and months. The following versions are more used however, just not as easy to remember.

작년	last year
올해	this year
내년	next year

NOTE: Spaces are NOT needed for 지난해 (last year), 지난달 (last month), and 지난주 (last week).

❑ 11-2. 많이 (a lot, many)

많이 (pronounced 만이) is the adverb form of 많다 (many, a lot). An adverb modifies the following verb. Put 많이 in front of ANY verb to say "I did this a lot". It also shows amount.

많이 (verb)
to (verb) a lot
many (verbed)

Example sentences

1. 친구가 많이 있어요.	I have a lot of friends.
2. 한국에 많이 갔어요.	I went to Korea a lot.
3. 파티에 친구가 많이 왔어요.	Many friends came to the party.

❑ 11-3. Doing actions with someone and "with" words

You can add 같이 (together) (pronounced 가치) in front of a verb to say you did something "together" with someone.

같이 (verb)
to do a (verb) together

(somebody) 하고 같이 (verb)
to do a (verb) together with (someone)

There are three ways to say "with" someone.

1. 와 / 과

You can use the 와 / 과 that you already learned in section 9-4. If the person you are doing something with has a 받침, then use 과 and if not use 와.

친구와 갔어요.
I went with a friend.

2. 하고

You can also use 하고. 하고 never changes regardless of if there is or isn't a 받침.

친구**하고** 갔어요.
I went **with** a friend.

3. 랑 / 이랑

If the person you are doing something with has a 받침 use 이랑 and if not use 랑.

친구**랑** 갔어요.
I went **with** a friend.

Use the "with" words to say you did something with someone. Adding 같이 is not required, but it strengthens the sentence.

와 / 과 are typically used in written Korean, and in more formal situations like news reports or talking to your boss.

랑 / 이랑 and 하고 are used in more casual / spoken situations. You can always use 하고 if you don't want to worry about 받침 usage.

Example sentences

1. 여동생이**랑** 같이 갔어요.
   I went together with my younger sister.

2. 누나**하고** 영국에 갈 거예요.
   I will go to England with my older sister.

3. 부모님**하고** 식당에 갔어요.
   I went to a restaurant with my parents.

4. 유월에 친구**랑** 태국에 갈 거예요.
   I will go to Thailand with a friend in June.

5. 시월에 오빠**와** 캐나다에 갔어요.
   I went to Canada with my older brother in October.

특별 정보 Special Information

SUMMARY: 와/과, 하고, and 랑/이랑 also mean "and".
In Korean, the three ways to say "with" can all be used as "and".

Example sentences

1. 김밥하고 김치가 맜있어요.
   Gimbap and kimchi are delicious.
2. 개랑 고양이가 너무 귀여워요.
   Dogs and cats are very cute.
3. 조지 씨하고 김민수 씨하고 가게에 같이 갈 거예요.
   I will go to the store (together) with George and Minsu Kim.
4. 사탕하고 바나나가 달아요.
   Candy and bananas are sweet.
5. 그 사람이랑 그 사람은 착해요.
   That person and that person are kind.

Both "and" and "with" are used in this sentence.

11 New Action Verbs 새로운 동사

Verb	Basic	English	Type
사다	사	to buy	regular
보다	봐	to see, to watch	regular
먹다	먹어	to eat	regular
마시다	마셔	to drink	regular

11 Verb Usage 동사 사용법

The item being, bought, watched, eaten, or drank is marked with the object marker 을/를.
If the item has a 받침 then 을 will be used and 를 when there is not 받침.

❑ 11-4. 사다 (to buy)

The item being bought is marked with the object marker 을/를.

(item) 을/를 사다
to buy an (item)

Example sentences

1. 어제 사과를 샀어요.
   I bought an apple yesterday.
2. 내일 비행기표를 살 거예요.
   I will buy an airline ticket tomorrow.
3. 누가 책을 샀어요?
   Who bought the book?
4. 멜론 몇 개 살 거예요?
   How many melons will you buy?

Koreans often drop the object marker.

Example conversations

1. A: 이 차는 언제 샀어요?
   B: 지난주에 샀어요.
   A: 얼마였어요?
   B: 이백만 원이었어요.

   A: When did you buy this car?
   B: I bought it last week.
   A: How much was it?
   B: It was 2,000,000 won.

였어요 is past tense of 이다. It means "it was". With a 받침 it would be 이었어요.

2. A: 비행기표를 언제 살 거예요?
   B: 지난주에 샀어요.
   A: 비쌌어요?
   B: 네, 진짜 비쌌어요.

   A: When will you buy the airline ticket?
   B: I bought it last week.
   A: Was it expensive?
   B: Yes, it was really expensive.

Non-specific times such as "today" don't use time marker 에. However, words such as "next week", and "last month" can use 에.

❑ 11-5. 보다 (to see, to watch)

The item being watched, is marked with the object marker 을/를.

(item) 을/를 보다
to see an (item)

Example sentences

1. 일요일에 영화를 볼 거예요. I will watch a movie on Sunday.
2. 제 고양이를 봤어요? Did you see my cat?
3. 지난주에 한국 사람을 봤어요. I saw a Korean person last week.
4. 아버지하고 매일 텔레비전을 봐요. I watch TV everyday with my father.

특별 정보 Special Information

In Korea you don't "take" a test you "see" a test using 보다.

1. 시험을 봤어요. I took a test.
2. 언제 시험을 볼 거예요? When will you take the test?

❑ 11-6. 먹다 (to eat)

The item being eaten, is marked with the object marker 을/를.

(item) 을/를 먹다
to eat an (item)

Example sentences

1. 매일 김밥을 먹어요. I eat gimbap everyday.
2. 어제 사과 세 개 먹었어요. I ate 3 apples yesterday.
3. 제 오빠는 귤을 먹을 거예요. My older brother will eat a tangerine.
4. 월요일에 햄버거를 먹었어요. On Monday I ate a hamburger.

특별 정보 Special Information

In Korean you do not "take" medicine. You "eat" it.

1. 약을 먹을 거예요. I will take some medicine.
2. 언제 약을 먹었어요? When did you take your medicine?

Soup is also "eaten" even though it is a liquid.

1. 국을 먹었어요. I ate soup.

❑ 11-7. 마시다 (to drink)

The item being drunk, is marked with the object marker 을/를.

(item) 을/를 마시다
to drink an (item)

Example sentences

1. 매일 차와 커피를 마셔요.
   I drink tea and coffee everyday.
2. 지난주에 주스를 많이 마셨어요.
   I drank a lot of juice last week.
3. 지난달에 친구랑 맥주를 많이 마셨어요.
   I drank a lot of beer with my friend last month.
4. 오늘 밤에 물을 많이 마실 거예요.
   I will drink a lot of water tonight.

11 Grammar 문법

❍ 11-8. Telling time in Korean

Telling time in Korean is as easy as learning the "o'clock" and the "minutes" counter. The "o'clock" counter uses Korean numbers and the "minutes" counter uses Chinese numbers.

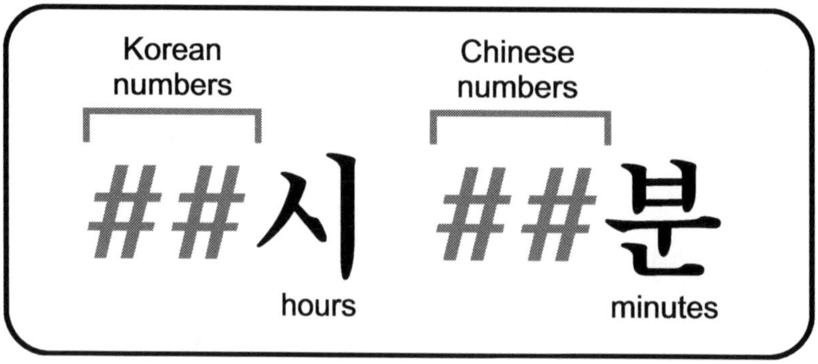

몇 시	what time?	몇 분	how many minutes?
한 시	1 o'clock	일 분	1 minute
두 시	2 o'clock	이 분	2 minutes

세 시	3 o'clock
네 시	4 o'clock
다섯 시	5 o'clock
여섯 시	6 o'clock
일곱 시	7 o'clock
여덟 시	8 o'clock
아홉 시	9 o'clock
열 시	10 o'clock
열한 시	11 o'clock
열두 시	12 o'clock

삼 분	3 minutes
사 분	4 minutes
오 분	5 minutes
육 분	6 minutes
칠 분	7 minutes
팔 분	8 minutes
구 분	9 minutes
십 분	10 minutes
십오 분	15 minutes
이십 분	20 minutes

Now you just put the two counters together to make a valid time.

여덟 시 오 분
8:05

열 시 삼십 분
10:30

다섯 시 오십 분
5:50

세 시
3:00

You can now use time with the grammar and verbs you already know.

Example Q&A

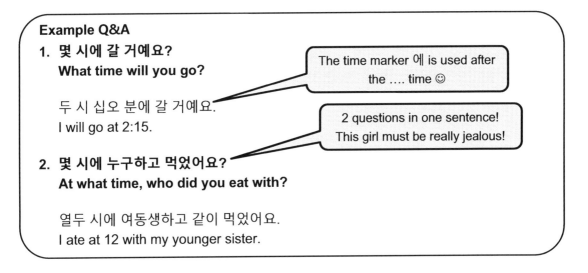

1. **몇 시에 갈 거예요?**
   What time will you go?

   두 시 십오 분에 갈 거예요.
   I will go at 2:15.

   The time marker 에 is used after the …. time ☺

2. **몇 시에 누구하고 먹었어요?**
   At what time, who did you eat with?

   2 questions in one sentence! This girl must be really jealous!

   열두 시에 여동생하고 같이 먹었어요.
   I ate at 12 with my younger sister.

❍ 11-9. Half past, a.m. / p.m.

반 means "half" and you can use it instead of 삼십분 (30 minutes). If you want to denote a.m. and p.m. you use 오전 (before noon) and 오후 (after noon) before the time.

오후 열두 시 사십 분
12:40 p.m

오전 여덟 시 오 분
8:05 a.m.

오전 여섯 시 이십 분
6:20 a.m.

오후 두 시 반
2:30 p.m.

❍ 11-10. Next Friday, Last Monday, Next January, This March

In order to say "next Friday", or "last Monday" you just say "next week Friday" or "last week Monday". Nothing needs to come in between the words, just line them up.

Examples

1. 다음 주 금요일	next Friday (Friday of next week)
2. 이번 주 화요일	this Tuesday (Tuesday of this week)
3. 지난주 월요일	last Monday (Monday of last week)
4. 다음 주 일요일	next Sunday (Sunday of next week)

Example sentences

1. 이번 주 토요일에 중국에 갈 거예요.	I am going to China this Saturday.
2. 지난주 화요일에 학교에 있었어요.	I was in school last Tuesday.
3. 다음 주 월요일에 미국에 갈 거예요.	I will go to America next Monday.
4. 다음 주 일요일에 어디에 있을 거예요?	Where will you be next Sunday?

You can put "last year", "this year", and "next year" in front of any month just like the days.

Examples

1. 작년 일월	last January (January of last year)
2. 올해 십이월	this December (December of this year)
3. 내년 유월	next June (June of next year)

NOTE: 내년 오월 means, "May of next year", not the coming May in the same year.

❍ 11-11. The event location marker 에서 (and from)

When you are saying that you DID something SOMEWHERE then you cannot use the location marker 에. Instead you must use the "event location" marker 에서 (in, at, on).

Example sentences

1. 미국에서 책상을 샀어요.
   I bought a desk in America.
2. 지난주 화요일에 학교에 있었어요.
   I was in school last Tuesday.
3. 다음 주 월요일에 미국에 갈 거예요.
   I will go to America next Monday.
4. 어디에서 먹었어요?
   Where did you eat at?

❍ 11-12. 이미, 벌써 (already)

이미 and 벌써 are added in front of past tense action verbs to say "I already ate." etc. 이미 is used to express that something was done ahead of time. 벌써 is a much stronger word, used when the speaker is surprised that the thing was done. Despite these slightly different nuances of the words, many people interchange them freely regardless of the situation.

Example sentences

1. 이미 샀어요.
   I already bought it.
2. 그는 벌써 갔어요.
   He already went.

   Here 그 means "he".
3. 벌써 먹었어요?
   You already ate?
4. 이 영화를 이미 봤어요.
   I already watched this movie.

❍ 11-13. How to say years and complete dates in Korean

To say years you will just say the full number, such as 2015 or 1998, then add the word 년 (year). Korean doesn't break up the year into two parts like we do in English. For example, they don't say 19-80 (nineteen – eighty).

Examples

1. 이천십오년	year 2015
2. 천구백팔십년	year 1980
3. 천구백구십사년	year 1994
4. 천구백칠십이년	year 1972
5. 천팔백십이년	year 1812

You already know months, so let's look at days of the month. You will just say the Chinese numbers plus the word for "day" which is 일.

the days of the month (월일)					
what day?		며칠?	16	16 일	십육일
1	1 일	일일	17	17 일	십칠일
2	2 일	이일	18	18 일	십팔일
3	3 일	삼일	19	19 일	십구일
4	4 일	사일	20	20 일	이십일
5	5 일	오일	21	21 일	이십일일
6	6 일	육일	22	22 일	이십이일
7	7 일	칠일	23	23 일	이십삼일
8	8 일	팔일	24	24 일	이십사일
9	9 일	구일	25	25 일	이십오일
10	10 일	십일	26	26 일	이십육일
11	11 일	십일일	27	27 일	이십칠일
12	12 일	십이일	28	28 일	이십팔일
13	13 일	십삼일	29	29 일	이십구일
14	14 일	십사일	30	30 일	삼십일
15	15 일	십오일	31	31 일	삼십일일

Complete dates in Korean always in the order of year, month, day of the month. Remember that the order is always from the largest time span to the smallest.

Example sentences

1. 이천십사년 이월 십사일 — 2014, February 14
   2014 년 2 월 14 일
2. 이천이십년 오월 오일 — 2020, May 5
   2020 년 5 월 5 일
3. 천구백칠십이년 시월 이십구일 — 1972, October 29
   1972 년 10 월 29 일
4. 이천이년 칠월 십오일 — 2002, July 15
   2002 년 7 월 15 일

From this point, we will write numbers as they are normally written in Korea, which is, 1,2,3,4 etc. We assume that by now you know the number system. Also it's REALLY tedious to keep typing out the numbers!

It's handy to know 태어나다 (to be born) in Korean for the next set of examples. Since you know how to conjugate verbs, you already know how to ask when someone was born.

언제 태어났어요?
When were you born?

Example sentences

1. 제 생일은 1999 년 3 월 10 일입니다.
   My birthday is March 10, 1999.

2. 저는 1986 년 1 월 8 일에 태어났어요.
   I was born on January 8, 1986.

3. 제 여동생은 1991 년 9 월 14 일에 태어났어요.
   My younger sister was born on September 14, 1991.

4. 싸이 씨의 생일은 1977 년 12 월 31 일입니다.
   Psy's birthday is December 31, 1977.

11 Question and Answer 질문과 대답

1. **다음 주에 저와 영국에 갈 거예요?**
   Are you going to England with me next week?

   네, 갈 거예요.
   Yes, I will go.

   아니요, 저는 다음 주에 일본에 가요.
   No, I will go to Japan next week.

2. **비행기표를 벌써 샀어요?**
   Did you already buy an airline ticket?

   네, 지난주 월요일에 샀어요.
   Yes, I bought it last Monday.

   아니요, 오늘 살 거예요.
   No, I will buy it today.

3. **몇 시에 약 먹을 거예요?**
   What time will you take your medicine?

   오후 다섯 시 반에 먹을 거예요.
   I'll take it at 5:30 pm.

   이미 먹었어요.
   I already took it.

11 Conversation 대화 K-E

1. **Polite conversation between co-workers.**

   A: 몇 시에 부산에 갈 거예요?
   B: 다섯 시 오십 분에 갈 거예요.
   A: 누구하고 갈 거예요?
   B: 부모님하고 갈 거예요.

   부산 is the second largest city in South Korea. It's located in the South.

   A: What time are you going to Busan?
   B: I will go at 5:50.
   A: Who are you going with?
   B: I am going with my parents.

2. **Polite conversation between office workers.**

   A: 이 커피 마셨어요?
   B: 네, 마셨어요.
   A: 이 커피는 제 것이었어요.
   B: 죄송해요.

   죄송해요 means "I'm sorry". The verb is 죄송하다. A more polite version is 죄송합니다.

A: Did you drink this coffee?
B: Yes, I did.
A: This coffee was mine.
B: Sorry.

3. Polite conversation between friends.

A: 어제 파티에 누구랑 갔어요?
B: 친구랑 갔어요.
A: 재미있었어요?
B: 네, 아주 재미있었어요.

A: Who did you go to the party with yesterday?
B: I went with a friend.
A: Was it fun?
B: Yes, it was very fun.

11 Conversation 대화 E-K

1. Polite conversation between friends.

A: Did you watch TV on Wednesday?
B: Yes, I watched a lot!
A: What did you watch?
B: I watched Running Man.

런닝맨 (Running Man) is a popular South Korean variety TV show.

A: 수요일에 텔레비전을 봤어요?
B: 네, 많이 봤어요.
A: 뭐 봤어요?
B: 런닝맨 봤어요.

2. Polite conversation between friends.

A: Did you go to the convenience store yesterday?
B: Yes, I did.
A: What did you buy?
B: I bought some water and bread.

A: 어제 편의점에 갔어요?

B: 네, 갔어요.

A: 뭐 샀어요?

B: 물하고 빵을 샀어요.

3. Polite conversation between friends.

A: Will you buy a computer next week?

B: I already bought it last week.

A: How much was it?

B: It was 1,750,000 won.

A: 다음 주에 컴퓨터 살 거예요?

B: 지난주에 이미 샀어요.

A: 얼마였어요?

B: 백칠십오만 원이었어요.

11 Sentence Building 문장 만들기

In each lesson we will build on a previous sentence. Watch it grow and transform each time new concepts are introduced.

5 월 5 일에 콜라 두 병을 이미 샀어요.
I already bought 2 bottles of cola on May 5th.

NOTE: As weird as this completed sentence is, it showcases the new grammar learned in this lesson.

Compare how the sentence has changed from the prior lessons:

Lesson 8: 제 어머니는 가방이 없어요.
My mother doesn't have a bag.

Lesson 9: 콜라 두 병과 물 세 잔을 주세요.
2 bottles of cola and 3 cups of water please.

Lesson 10: 내일 콜라 두 병을 살 거예요.
I will buy 2 bottles of cola tomorrow.

11 Workbook Area

❑ A11-1. Reading comprehension

At your current level, you should understand all of the grammar and words in the following sections. If you are struggling to understand them, review this and prior lessons.

New words for this comprehension: 생일 선물 (birthday present)

① 이번 주 목요일은 준호의 생일이에요.

② 준호의 생일은 1 월 4 일이에요.

③ 올해 스물네살이에요.

④ 저 컴퓨터는 준호의 생일 선물이에요.

Dialogue

A: 준호 씨의 생일이 언제예요?

B: 이번 주 목요일이에요.

A: 생일 파티에 갈 거예요?

B: 네, 누나랑 갈 거예요.

❑ A11-2. Reading comprehension questions

Answer the following questions about the reading comprehension in the prior section.

1. 준호는 몇 살이에요?

____

2. 준호의 생일 선물은 침대예요?

____

3. 준호의 생일은 금요일이에요?

____

❑ A11-3. Date challenge

Write the complete date using only 한글.

1.

2.

3.

4.

5.

6.

❑ A11-4. Time challenge

Write the complete time using only 한글.

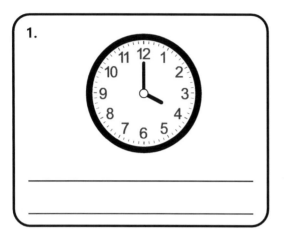

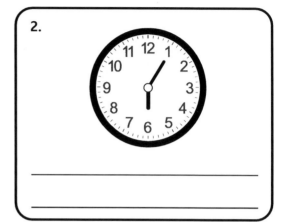

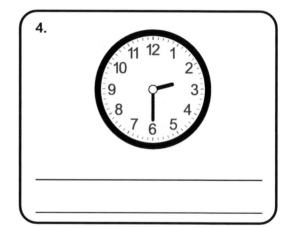

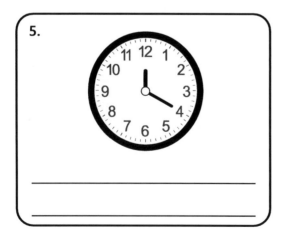

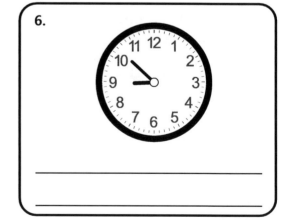

1.

2.

3.

4.

5.

6.

❑ A11-5. Korean translation

Translate the following conversation into English.

1.
A: 설날에 뭐를 먹었어요? B: 떡을 먹었어요. A: 맛있었어요? B: 아니요. 진짜 맛없었어요.
A:
B:
A:
B:

❑ A11-6. English translation

Translate the following conversation into Korean.

1.
A: Are you coming to my wedding ceremony next month? B: Yes, I will go with my girlfriend. What day of the month is it? A: It's the 15th at 3 pm. B: I will eat a lot at the wedding ceremony.
A:
B:
A:
B:

NOTE: We ran out of space in the beginning of Lesson 11. Please excuse the location of these very important phrases.

11 New Phrases 새로운 어구

1. **어때요?**
   How is it?

2. **어땠어요?**
   How was it?

   Both of these phrases are very commonly asked in Korea. We will use them in lesson 12 and beyond to ask "how" something is or was.

11 Vocabulary Builder

■ Group L: times of the day 시간대

아침	morning
오전	before noon, AM
오후	afternoon, PM
점심	afternoon, lunch
저녁	evening
늦은 밤	late night
새벽	dawn

■ Group M: school words 학교의 단어

과학	science
수업	class
교실	classroom
역사	history
수학	math
문학	literature
생물	biology

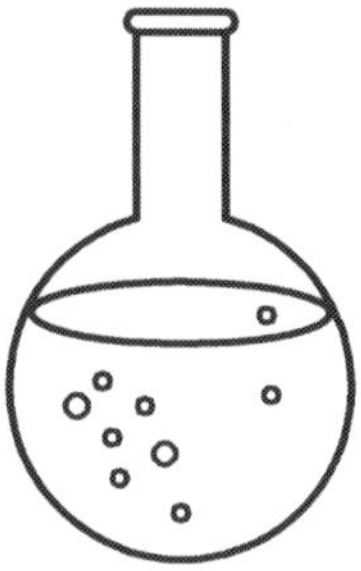

Lesson 12:

Descriptive verbs part II

12

Before This Lesson

1. Review the BASIC form taught in section 6-4.

Lesson Goals

1. Learn how to use descriptive verbs to directly modify nouns.
2. Learn how to do basic comparisons of objects and people.

From The Teachers

1. NOTE! The New Phrases section of Lesson 11 is on the PRIOR page as we ran out of space!
2. Using descriptive verbs to modify is a very powerful grammar structure. Learn this well and your Korean will dramatically improve.

Lesson Highlights

12-4.
다르다, 같다, 비슷하다

12-10.
Directly modifying with descriptive verbs

12-13.
The "inclusion" marker
도 (also, too)

12 New Words 새로운 단어

아마	maybe, probably
핸드폰	cell phone
돈	money
콘서트	concert
길	road, street
가족	family
장소	place

12 New Descriptive Verbs 새로운 형용사

Verb	Basic	English	Type
시끄럽다	시끄러워	to be loud	ㅂ irregular
조용하다	조용해	to be quiet	하다
길다	길어	to be long	regular
짧다	짧아	to be short	regular
다르다	달라	to be different	르 irregular
같다	같아	to be the same	regular
비슷하다	비슷해	to be similar	하다
필요하다	필요해	to need	하다
필요없다	필요없어	to not need	regular
가깝다	가까워	to be close	ㅂ irregular
멀다	멀어	to be far	regular

12 Descriptive Verb Usage 형용사 사용법

❑ 12-1. 시끄럽다 (to be loud)

시끄럽다 is a ㅂ irregular verb. It conjugates like the other ㅂ irregulars taught in section 7-1. The item, place, or person that is loud is marked with a topic or subject marker.

to be loud		remove 다		remove ㅂ add 워
시끄럽다	→	시끄럽	→	시끄러워

Example sentences

1. 미국 사람은 시끄러워요.
   Americans are loud.
2. 어제 이 방은 시끄러웠어요.
   This room was loud yesterday.
3. 아마 이 영화는 시끄러울 거예요.
   This movie will probably get loud.
4. 시끄러워!
   You're loud!

In the casual form this can be translated as "Shut Up!"

❑ 12-2. 조용하다 (to be quiet)

조용하다 is a 하다 verb, so to make the BASIC form, you just change the 하 to a 해. The item, place, or person that is quiet is marked with a topic or subject marker.

to be quiet		remove 다		하 changes to 해
조용하다	→	조용하	→	조용해

Example sentences

1. 여기가 아주 조용해요. It's very quiet here.
2. 제 동생이 진짜 조용해요. My siblings are really quiet.
3. 3 시에 이 장소가 조용할 거예요. At 3 o'clock this place will be quiet.
4. 어제 이 방은 조용했어요. Yesterday, this room was quiet.

❑ 12-3. 길다 (to be long), 짧다 (to be short)

The item that is long or short is marked with the subject marker 이/가 or topic marker 은/는.
NOTE: 짧다 ends with a ㅂ (비읍) but it is not ㅂ irregular. This "short" is not for height.

to be long		remove 다		basic form
길다	→	길	→	길어

to be short		remove 다		basic form
짧다	→	짧	→	짧아

Example sentences

1. 이 길은 너무 길어요. This road is very long.
2. 제 여자친구의 머리가 길어요. My girlfriend's hair is long.
3. 이 영화는 너무 짧아요. This movie is too short.
4. 당신의 다리가 짧아요. Your legs are short.

❑ 12-4. 다르다 (different), 같다 (same), 비슷하다 (similar)

다르다, 같다, and 비슷하다 are used to compare one or more items. The item being compared is marked with any of the three "and" markers, 와/과, 하고, 랑/이랑.

> NOTE 1: 다르다 is a 르 irregular verb. The BASIC form is 달라. Review section 9-2 to understand how to create the BASIC form for 르 irregulars.
>
> NOTE 2: 비슷하다 is pronounced 비스타다. BASIC form is pronounced 비스태.

다르다 (to be different)

A는 B와 달라요.
A is different from B.

A와 B는 달라요.
A and B are different.

A와 달라요.
It's different from A.

1. 영어는 한국어와 달라요.
   English is different from Korean.
2. 여자랑 남자는 달라요.
   Woman and men are different.
3. 이것하고 달라요.
   It's different than this.

같다 (to be the same)

A는 B와 같아요.
A is the same as B.

A와 B는 같아요.
A and B are the same.

A와 같아요.
It's the same as A.

1. 이것은 그것과 같아요.
   This and that are the same.
2. 제 차랑 제 누나 차는 같아요.
   My car and my older sister's car are the same.
3. 어제와 같아요.
   It's the same as yesterday.

비슷하다 (to be similar)

A는 B와 비슷해요.
A is similar to B.

A와 B는 비슷해요.
A and B are similar.

A와 비슷해요.
It's similar to A.

1. 일본어는 한국어하고 비슷해요.
   Japanese and Korean are similar.
2. 제 어머니하고 아버지는 비슷해요.
   My mother and father are similar.
3. 커피랑 비슷해요.
   It's similar to coffee.

Example conversation

1. A: 영화는 어땠어요? — A: How was the movie?
   B: 책과 달랐어요. — B: It was different from the book.
2. A: 핸드폰 어때요? — A: How is the cell phone?
   B: 컴퓨터하고 비슷해요. — B: It's similar to a computer.
3. A: 생일 파티는 어땠어요? — A: How was the birthday party?
   B: 크리스마스 파티랑 같았어요. — B: It was the same as the xmas party.

❑ 12-5. 필요하다 (to need), 필요없다 (to not need)

The thing that is needed or not needed is marked with subject marker 이/가 or when stressing 은/는 topic marker.

은 stresses that medicine was not needed today as opposed to other days.

Example sentences

1. 돈이 필요해요.
   I need money.
2. 작년에 진짜 돈이 필요했어요.
   I really needed money last year.
3. 오늘은 약이 필요없었어요.
   Today I didn't need medicine.
4. 시간이 필요해요.
   I need time.

❑ 12-6. 가깝다 (to be close), 멀다 (to be far)

가깝다 and 멀다 are used to describe distances. 가깝다 is a ㅂ (비읍) irregular. Another usage of the 에서 marker is to mean "to" and "from" a place only (not people or animals).

(place) 에서 가깝다
close to (place)

(place) 에서 멀다
far from (place)

Example sentences

1. 집이 가까워요? — Is your house close?
2. 학교가 우리 집에서 가까워요. — School is close to my house.
3. 집에서 회사가 멀어요. — It's far from my house to my work.
4. 병원이 공항에서 멀어요. — The hospital is far from the airport.

특별 정보 Special Information

에서 works with any place. It is commonly used with this style conversation.

A: 어디에서 왔어요? — Where are you from? (From where did you come?)
B: 미국에서 왔어요. — I am from America. (I came from America.)

12 New Action Verbs 새로운 동사

Verb	Basic	English	Type
하다	해	to do	하다
좋아하다	좋아해	to like	하다
싫어하다	싫어해	to dislike	하다
사랑하다	사랑해	to love	하다
공부하다	공부해	to study	하다

12 Verb Usage 동사 사용법

❑ 12-7. 하다 (to do)

This is the king of all verbs. A huge percentage of all Korean verbs are 하다 verbs. 하다 verbs can be descriptive or actions verbs. All by itself 하다 means, "to do". The thing you are doing is marked with the object marker 을/를.

(thing) 을/를 하다
to do a (thing)

Example sentences

1. 오늘 뭐해요?
   What are you doing today?

> 뭐해? is a common way to ask "What are you doing" or "What will you do?

2. 지금 숙제를 해요.
   I am doing my homework now.

❑ 12-8. 좋아하다 (to like), 싫어하다 (to dislike), 사랑하다 (to love)

The person, thing, place that you like, dislike, or love, is marked with the object marker 을/를.

(person, thing, place) 을/를 좋아하다
to like (person, thing, place)

Example sentences

1. 제가 진짜 한국어를 좋아해요.
   I really like Korean (language).
2. 제 부모님을 사랑해요.
   I love my parents.
3. 고양이하고 개를 너무 좋아해요.
   I really like cats and dogs.
4. 야채를 싫어해요.
   I dislike vegetables.
5. 너를 정말 사랑했어.
   I really loved you.
6. 선생님은 월요일을 싫어해요.
   Teacher dislikes Monday.

❑ 12-9. 공부하다 (to study)

The thing being studied is marked with 을/를 object marker. The place where you study is marked with the event location marker 에서.

(place) 에서 (thing)을/를 공부하다
to study a (thing) at a (place)

Example sentences

1. 저는 매일 한국어를 공부해요.
   I study Korean everyday.
2. 학교에서 일본어를 공부하지 않았어요.
   I didn't study Japanese in school.

12 Grammar 문법

❍ 12-10. Directly modifying with descriptive verbs

In order to use a descriptive verb to directly modify, you must add ㄴ/은, or in the case of ㅂ irregulars, 운 to the stem. NOTE: 르 irregulars act like regular verbs when modifying. An additional ㄹ is not added.

regular descriptive NO 받침

싸다 to be cheap	싼~ a cheap~
크다 to be big	큰~ a big~
비싸다 to be expensive	비싼~ an expensive~
빠르다 to be fast	빠른~ a fast~

Example sentences

1. 싼 핸드폰을 싫어해요.
   I dislike cheap cell phones.
2. 이 가게에 비싼 것이 많아요.
   There are a lot of expensive things at this store.
3. 저는 빠른 차를 좋아해요.
   I like fast cars.

것 means "thing" (section 7-6)

regular descriptive WITH 받침

같다 to be the same	같은~ the same~
좋다 to be good	좋은~ good~
작다 to be small	작은~ a small~
많다 to be many	많은~ many~

Example sentences

1. 우리 학교에 좋은 사람이 많아요.
   There are a lot of good people at our school.
2. 많은 사람은 만화책을 좋아해요.
   Many people like comic books.
3. 그 가게에는 작은 의자가 많아요.
   That store has many small chair.

하다 descriptive

조용하다 to be quiet	조용한~ a quiet~
착하다 to be kind	착한~ a kind~

Example sentences

1. 어제 조용한 장소에 있었어요. Yesterday, I was in a quiet place.
2. 착한 여자친구가 필요해요. I need a kind girlfriend.

❍ 12-11. Directly modifying with ㅂ irregular descriptive verbs

ㅂ irregular , since they are irregular, are converted a bit differently than other descriptive verbs. Instead of converting ㅂ into 워, it's converted into 운 to make the direct modifier.

ㅂ irregular descriptive	
춥다 to be cold	추운~ a cold~
맵다 to be spicy	매운~ spicy~

Example sentences

1. 뜨거운 국은 너무 맛있어요.
   Hot soup is very delicious.

   Don't make the common mistake of using 은. You must use 운 for ㅂ irregulars.

2. 저는 매운 음식을 좋아해요.
   I like spicy food.

3. 제 아버지는 차가운 커피를 진짜 싫어해요.
   My father really dislikes cold coffee.

4. 쉬운 시험을 좋아해요.
   I like easy tests.

❍ 12-12. Special case direct modifiers

Any time the stem of a descriptive verb ends with a ㄹ (리을) 받침, then the ㄹ is just changed to a ㄴ (니은). We will officially learn 길다 (to be long) in the next lesson but it's used here to show the pattern.

regular descriptive WITH ㄹ 받침	
달다 to be sweet	단~ a sweet~
길다 to be long	긴~ a long~

Example sentences

1. 저는 단 차를 정말 싫어해요.
   I really dislike sweet tea.

   Remember 차 can mean "tea" and "car"

2. 긴 머리의 여자를 좋아해요.
   I like long haired girls.

Another special case is when the descriptive verb ends with 있다 or 없다. With these types you simply add 는 to the stem.

~있다 ~없다 descriptive

재미있다	재미있는~	맛없다	맛없는~
to be interesting	an interesting~	to be tasteless	tasteless~

Example sentences

1. 제 친구의 학교에 재미있는 선생님이 많아요.
   There are a lot of interesting teachers at my friend's school.
2. 저 식당에 맛없는 음식이 많았어요.
   There was a lot of tasteless food at that restaurant over there.

Here 저 does not mean "I" because it's directly in front of a noun.

특별 정보 Special Information

Only **descriptive** verbs can be used to directly modify using the patterns taught above. In "Korean From Zero! book 2" modifying with **action** verbs will be introduced.

12-13. The "inclusion" marker 도 (also, too)

The marker 도 means "too" or "also". When it's used, it replaces or is added to marker.

Replace 은/는 with 도	Replace 이/가 with 도	Replace 을/를 with 도
저는 학생이에요. I am a student.	5시가 좋아요. 5 o'clock is good.	야채를 좋아해요. I like vegetables.
저도 학생이에요. I too am a student.	7시도 좋아요. 7 o'clock is also good.	과일도 좋아해요. I also like fruit.

Example conversation

1. A: 내년에 한국에 갈 거예요. — Next year I am going to Korea.
   B: 진짜요?! 저도 갈 거예요. — Really?! I am going too.
2. A: 햄버거 주세요. 콜라도 주세요. — A hamburger please. A coke also.
   B: 알겠습니다. — Understood.

Add 도 to location markers	Add 도 to time markers	Add 도 to event location marker
한국**에** 갈 거예요. I will go to Korea.	**1월에** 갈 거예요. I will go in January.	공항**에서** 일해요. I work at the airport.
일본에**도** 갈 거예요. I will also go to Japan.	**3**월에**도** 갈 거예요. I will also go in March.	가게에서**도** 일해요. I also work at the store.

Example conversation

1. A: 다음 주에 영국에 갈 거예요. 독일에도 갈 거예요.
   B: 프랑스에도 갈 거예요?
   A: 네. 갈 거예요.

   A: Next week I will go to England. I will go to Germany also.
   B: Will you go to France also?
   A: Yes. I will go.

❍ 12-14. 것 (thing, stuff)

We first introduced 것 in section 7-6. However, we haven't done much else with it. This grammar point is specifically just to remind you that 것 means "thing". The thing can be physical like a book or non-physical like an idea.

Example sentences

1. 이 가게에는 재미있는 것이 많아요.
   There are many interesting things in this store.
   (에는 stresses in THIS store.)

2. 저는 매운 것을 매일 먹어요.
   I eat spicy things everyday.

3. 이 식당에 다른 것이 있어요?
   Are there other things at this restaurant?
   (다른 means "different" but is better translated as "other".)

4. 이 책하고 그 책이 같은 것이에요.
   This book and that book are the same thing.

5. 제 가족은 단 것을 좋아해요.
   My family likes sweet things.

6. 필요한 것이 있어요?
   Is there anything you need?
   (Here it sounds better to translate 것 as "anything".)

12 Question and Answer 질문과 대답

1. **어제 싸이의 콘서트는 어땠어요?**
   How was PSY's concert yesterday?

   정말 재미있었어요.
   It was really fun.

   너무 시끄러웠어요.
   It was too loud.

   소녀시대의 콘서트와 비슷했어요.
   It was similar to Girl's Generation's concert.

   > 소녀시대 (Girl's Generation) is a popular South Korean girl pop group.

2. **파티에 맛있는 것이 있었어요?**
   Was there anything delicious at the party?

   케이크가 정말 맛있었어요.
   The cake was really delicious.

   단 것이 많았어요.
   There were a lot of sweet things.

   맥주가 맛있었어요. 너무 많이 마셨어요!
   The beer was delicious. I drank way too much.

   > 너무 by itself means "too" or "very", but in combination with 많이 means "excessively" or "too much".

3. **한국어 많이 공부했어요?**
   Did you study Korean a lot?

   네, 이미 많이 했어요.
   Yes, I already did a lot.

   아니요, 저녁에 공부 할 거예요.
   No, I'm going to study in the evening.

4. **아침에 뭐 먹었어요?**
   What did you eat in the morning?

   물 마셨어요.
   I drank some water.

단 빵하고 차가운 우유하고 떡을 먹었어요.
I ate sweet bread, cold milk, and rice cakes.

매운 것을 먹었어요. 차가운 커피도 마셨어요.
I ate some spicy things. I drank some cold coffee too.

12 Conversation 대화 K-E

1. Polite conversation at an electronics store.

A: 컴퓨터 필요해요?
B: 아니요, 필요 없어요. 저는 이미 삼성 컴퓨터가 있어요.
A: 그럼.. 뭐가 필요해요?
B: 저는 큰 텔레비전이 필요해요.

A: Do you need a computer?
B: No, I don't need one. I already have a Samsung computer.
A: Well then .. what do you need?
B: I need a big television.

2. Polite conversation between friends at the office.

A: 책상 위에 과일이 많이 있어요. 먹을 거예요?
B: 네, 먹을 거예요. 맛있어요?
A 귤하고 바나나는 정말 달아요.
B: 그럼, 바나나를 주세요.

A: There is a lot of fruit on the desk. Are you going to eat them?
B: Yes, I'll eat them. Are they delicious?
A: The tangerines and bananas are really sweet.
B: Ok then, give me the bananas.

흠 is the Korean way to say "hmmm".

3. Polite conversation between friends.

A: 저는 다음 주에 파리에 가요. 필요한 것이 있어요?
B: 흠... 저는 프랑스 책이 필요해요. 저는 다음 달에 프랑스어를 공부할 거예요.
A: 프랑스어는 쉬워요?
B: 아니요, 정말 어려워요. 프랑스어는 한국어와 많이 달라요.

A: I'm going to Paris next week. Is there anything you need?
B: Hmm.. I need a French book. I will study French next month.
A: Is French easy?
B: No, it's really difficult. It's very different from Korean.

12 Conversation 대화 E-K

1. Polite conversation between friends planning to go to a party.

A: My older sister needs a boyfriend.
B: Maybe there will be a nice man at the party. What time are you going?
A: I will go at 5 o'clock. Who will you go with?
B: I'll go with my older sister and a friend.

A: 제 누나는 남자친구가 필요해요.
B: 아마 파티에 좋은 남자가 있을 거예요. 몇 시에 갈 거예요?
A: 5 시에 갈 거예요. 누구랑 갈 거예요?
B: 누나하고 친구랑 갈 거예요.

2. Polite conversation at a real estate office.

A: Is this apartment the same as that apartment over there?
B: No, they are different apartments.
A From here, are schools close?
B: No, it's really far from the school.

A: 이 아파트는 저 아파트와 같아요?
B: 아니요, 다른 아파트예요.
A: 여기에서 학교는 가까워요?
B: 아니요, 정말 멀어요.

"From location marker" is 에서. Also as long as the markers remain with their words they can be moved around like 학교 is in this sentence.

3. Polite conversation between friends.

A: What did you do yesterday?
B: I went to the hospital. I needed medicine.
A: Are you okay now?
B: Yes, I am okay. I need some hot water and a quiet place.

A: 어제 뭐 했어요?

B: 병원에 갔어요. 약이 필요했어요.

A: 지금은 괜찮아요?

B: 네, 괜찮아요. 저는 뜨거운 물과 조용한 장소가 필요해요.

12 Sentence Building 문장 만들기

In each lesson we will build on a previous sentence. Watch it grow and transform each time new concepts are introduced.

제 친구가 저하고 다른 핸드폰을 샀어요.
My friend bought a different cell phone than me.

Compare how the sentence has changed from the prior lessons:

Lesson 9: 콜라 두 병과 물 세 잔을 주세요.
2 bottles of cola and 3 cups of water please.

Lesson 10: 내일 콜라 두 병을 살 거예요.
I will buy 2 bottles of cola tomorrow.

Lesson 11: 5 월 5 일에 콜라 두 병을 이미 샀어요.
I already bought 2 bottles of cola on May 5th.

12 Workbook Area

❑ A12-1. Reading comprehension

At your current level, you should understand all of the grammar and words in the following sections. If you are struggling to understand them, review this and prior lessons.

New words for this comprehension: 새롭다 (to be new, ㅂ irregular)

① 김준호 씨는 새로운 가구가 필요해요.
② 돈이 많이 없어요.
③ 가게에는 싼 가구가 많이 있어요.
④ 김준호 씨는 비싼 가구를 싫어해요.

Dialogue

A: 언제 큰 침대를 살 거예요?
B: 몰라요. 저는 지금 돈이 없어요.
A: 저 가게에 싼 가구가 많이 있을 거예요.
B: 지금 갈 거예요?
A: 아니요. 저는 오늘 수업이 있어요.

❑ A12-2. Reading comprehension questions

Answer the following questions about the reading comprehension in the prior section.

1. 김준호 씨는 에어컨이 필요해요?

____

2. 가게에는 싼 가구가 없어요?

____

3. 김준호 씨는 오늘 가게에 갔어요?

____

❑ A12-3. Fill in the blank

For each number in the Korean sentence, write the appropriate Korean word to match the English translation.

1. ①에는 ②음식이 많이 ③요.
There is a lot of spicy food in Korea.

① __________ ② __________ ③ __________

2. 저① ②친구가 ③해요.
I need a quiet friend.

① __________ ② __________ ③ __________

3. ①은 ② ③요.
Fruit is too expensive.

① __________ ② __________ ③ __________

4. ① 사람② 미국 사람은 너무 ③요.
Chinese people and Americans are too loud.

① __________ ② __________ ③ __________

5. 제 ①은 ② 고양이를 ③해요.
My younger sister likes cute cats.

① __________ ② __________ ③ __________

6. 내 ①는 ②요.
My legs are short.

① __________ ② __________

7. ①는 공항② ③요.
The school is far from the airport.

① __________ ② __________ ③ __________

8. 제 ①친구는 ②요.
My boyfriend is kind.

① ____________ ② ____________

9. 제 ①은 단 ②을 ③해요.
My parents dislike sweet things.

① ____________ ② ____________ ③ ____________

10. 거울 ①에 ② 가방이 있어③.
There is a big bag behind the mirror.

① ____________ ② ____________ ③ ____________

12 Vocabulary Builder

■ Group N: more foods 더 많은 음식

삼각김밥	triangle-shaped gimbap
불고기	roast meat (fire meat)
갈비	ribs
닭갈비	chicken ribs
치킨	chicken
포도	grapes
수박	watermelon
배	pear
치즈	cheese

Lesson 13:

Giving and Receiving

13

Before This Lesson

1. Review the verb 보다 (to see). Learn its various conjugations.

Lesson Goals

1. To learn how the giving and receiving verbs work and how to use the associated new particles.

From The Teachers

1. Pay special attention to the "Special Information" sections.

Lesson Highlights

13-1.
받다 (to receive)

13-2.
주다 (to give)

13-6.
The giving markers
한테, 에게

13-8.
Trying to do something

13 New Words 새로운 단어

전화	phone, phone call
전화번호	phone number
꽃	flowers
거짓말	a lie
그냥	just; just because
빨리	quickly; hurry up
미팅	meeting

13 New Action Verbs 새로운 동사

Verb	Basic	English	Type
받다	받아	to receive, to get	regular
주다	줘	to give	regular
전화하다	전화해	to phone	하다
알다	알아	to know	regular
모르다	몰라	to not know	르 irregular

13 Verb Usage 동사 사용법

❑ 13-1. 받다 (to receive, to get)

The item being received is marked with the object marker 을/를. 받다 is a regular verb, and since the vowel in the stem is ㅏ the BASIC form is 받아.

(item) 을/를 받다
to receive (item)

Example sentences

1. 크리스마스에 선물을 많이 받을 거예요.	I will get many presents on Christmas.
2. 꽃을 받았어요.	I received flowers.
3. 내일 돈을 받아요.	I will get money tomorrow.
4. 사탕 두개를 받았어요.	I received 2 pieces of candy.

❑ 13-2. 주다 (to give)

The item being given is marked with the object marker 을/를. 주다 is a regular action verb, and since the vowel in the stem is ㅜ the BASIC form is 줘.

주다 is the verb used to create 주세요 taught in section 9-5. 주다 is used in some form or other in many other patterns. In this lesson, we use 주다 simply to mean "give", "gave" etc.

Example sentences

1. 크리스마스에 선물을 많이 줄 거예요. — I will give many presents on Christmas.
2. 책을 줬어요. — I gave a book.
3. 돈을 줬어요. — I gave money.
4. 사탕 두 개 줬어요. — I gave 2 pieces of candy.

❑ 13-3. 전화하다 (to make a phone call)

전화하다 is only "making a phone call" and not "receiving one".

Example sentences

1. 전화했어요. — I called.
2. 내일 전화할 거예요. — I'll call tomorrow.
3. 지금 전화해요. — I'm calling now. / I'll call now.

The meaning changes based on the context of the conversation.

특별 정보 Special Information

To "get a phone call" can be 받다 (to receive) or 오다 (to come). To answer the phone is 받다 (to receive) but never 대답하다 (to answer).

Example sentences

1. 전화를 받았어요. — I answered the phone.
2. 전화가 왔어요. — A phone call came.
3. 전화를 받을 거예요. — I will answer the phone.

❑ 13-4. 알다 (to know)

The item that is known is marked with 을/를. Previously we learned the polite version of 알다 in lesson 9 as the phrase 알겠습니다. The casual form is 알았어. 알았어 is past tense because you have "understood" new information that you previously didn't know.

Example sentences

1. 알아요.	I know.
2. 알았어요.	I have understood. / Got it. / Okay.
3. 선생님의 이름을 알아요?	Do you know teacher's name?
4. 수업 시간을 알아요?	Do you know the time of the class?

❑ 13-5. 모르다 (to not know)

모르다 is a 르 irregular verb. The pattern to make the BASIC form is as follows.

르 irregular BASIC form rule

remove 다 **르 changes to 라** **add ㄹ before 라**

to not know → BASIC rule #5 → BASIC form

모르 → 모라 → 몰라

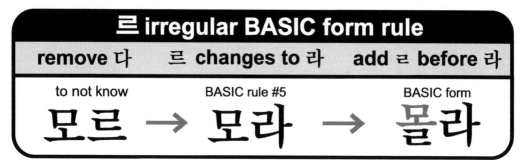

We have previously learned 몰다 as the phrase 몰라요 (I don't know). Now we can conjugate for more variety of usage.

Example sentences

1. 몰라요.	I don't know.
2. 몰랐어요.	I didn't know.
3. 선생님의 이름을 몰랐어요.	I didn't know teacher's name.
4. 그 사람을 몰라요.	I don't know that person.

특별 정보 Special Information

More grammar is required to fully use 알다 and 모르다. The next book in this series will cover phrases like "I don't know who is coming.", and "I know where to go". etc.

Also, even though 알다 and 모르다 are companion verbs, they are NOT the same type. Don't accidentally say 알라 instead of the correct 알아. Also, you can't say 몰아 since 몰라 is the correct conjugation. If you say these wrong, you might not be understood.

13 Grammar 문법

13-6. The giving markers 한테, 에게

When giving something "to" someone you mark the person you are giving the item to with 한테 or 에게. 에게 is more for written conversations. 한테 is best when speaking.

Example sentences

1. 친구한테 돈을 줬어요.	I gave money to a friend.
2. 남자친구한테 떡을 줄 거예요.	I will give rice cakes to my boyfriend.
3. 제 아버지에게 선물을 줬어요.	I gave a present to my father.
4. 선생님에게 사과를 줬어요.	I gave an apple to my teacher.

13-7. The receiving markers 한테서, 에게서

When receiving something "from" someone you mark the person you are receiving from with 한테서 or 에게서. 에게서 is more for written Korean. 한테서 is best when speaking.
NOTE: In conversation you might hear Koreans drop the 서 from 한테서 and 에게서.
In this book we do not drop the 서 to avoid confusion.

Example sentences

1. 친구한테서 돈을 받았어요.	I received money from a friend.
2. 남자친구한테서 떡을 받을 거예요.	I will get rice cakes from my boyfriend.
3. 제 아버지에게서 선물을 받았어요.	I received a present from my father.
4. 선생님에게서 사과를 받았어요.	I received an apple from my teacher.
5. 친구한테서 전화 받았어요.	I got a phone call from my friend.

13-8. Trying to do something BASIC +보다

You can combine any verb with 보다 (to see) to make "try and do" verb combinations.

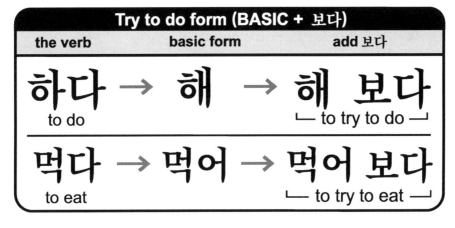

Try to do form (BASIC + 보다)

the verb	basic form	add 보다
하다 → (to do)	해 →	해 보다 (to try to do)
먹다 → (to eat)	먹어 →	먹어 보다 (to try to eat)

With this pattern it's MUCH easier to consider the new combined verb as a NEW verb. Then you can conjugate it into all of its various forms as you which. The good news is you already know how to conjugate 보다 (to see) from lesson 11.

Example sentences (future tense)

1. 먹어 볼 거예요. — I will try to eat it.
2. 가 볼 거예요. — I will try to go.
3. 마셔 볼 거예요. — I will try to drink it.
4. 해 볼 거예요. — I will try to do it.
5. 와 볼 거예요. — I will try to come.

Example sentences (past tense)

1. 먹어 봤어요. — I tried to eat it.
2. 가 봤어요. — I tried to go.
3. 마셔 봤어요. — I tried to drink it.
4. 해 봤어요. — I tried to do it.
5. 와 봤어요. — I tried to come.

특별 정보 Special Information

Koreans often use the BASIC + past tense of 보다 to say "Have you ~".

Example sentences

1. 일본에 가 봤어요? — Have you gone to Japan?
2. 김밥을 먹어 봤어요? — Have you eaten gimbap?
3. 역사를 공부해 봤어요? — Have you studied history?

Example Q&A

1. 한국에서 뭐를 먹어 봤어요?
In Korea what have you eaten?

치즈 닭갈비하고 김밥을 먹어 봤어요.
I have eaten cheese chicken ribs and gimbap.

치즈 닭갈비 is quite tasty, we recommend you try it!

배랑 수박이랑 치킨을 먹어 봤어요.
I have eaten pears, watermelons, and chicken.

❍ 13-9. Command form using BASIC form

The BASIC form of any verb without 요 on the end can be very rude. With friends it's just casual, but be very careful to not drop the 요. If the 요 is missing, you might be considered rude, especially when speaking to elders.

Example sentences

1. 먹어!	Eat!
2. 가!	Go!
3. 마셔!	Drink!
4. 해 봐!	Try to do it!
5. 와!	Come!
6. 사!	Buy it!
7. 먹어 봐!	Try to eat it!

Adding the 요 makes every one of the sentences above polite enough to use with everyday people. NOTE: If an elder says this form to you, it's not necessarily rude, but just casual. SUMMARY: If you want to be safe add 요.

❍ 13-10. Quick rules for casual Korean

Here are some simple ways you can speak casual (반말). Dropping markers is okay too!

1. 이에요 / 예요 becomes 이야 / 야.

1. 미국 사람이야.	I'm American.
2. 어디야?	Where is it?
3. 누구야?	Who are you?

2. 아니에요 becomes 아니야. (이/가 marker can be dropped)

1. 고양이 아니야.	It's not a cat.
2. 미국 사람 아니야.	I'm not American.
3. 아니야!	It's not!

3. 요 is dropped after verbs.

1. 많이 먹었어.	I ate a lot.
2. 언제 와?	When are you coming?
3. 숙제 했어?	Did you do your homework?
4. 너 사랑해.	I love you.
5. 뭐해?	What's up?

4. 거예요 becomes 거야

1. 돈 줄 거야. — I'll give you some money.
2. 내일 갈 거야? — Are you going tomorrow?
3. 내 파티 올 거야? — Are you coming to my party?

5. Use BASIC form as a command (learn the polite way in section 15-8)

1. 빨리해! — Do it quickly!
2. 그냥 마셔. — Just drink it.
3. 먹어 봐. — Try and eat it.
4. 와. — Come.

6. 것 becomes 거

1. 이거 뭐야? — What's this?
2. 이거 누구 거야? — Whose is this?
3. 그거 너무 재미있어. — That's very interesting.

7. Use casual versions of words

1. 응 — yeah, yes
2. 아니 — no
3. 흠 — hmm, well
4. 야! — hey! (rude)

13 Question and Answer 질문과 대답

1. **준호의 전화를 받았어요?**
Did you receive Junho's phone call?

네, 받았어요. 준호는 저에게 새벽에 전화했어요.
Yes, I got it. He called me at dawn.

네, 받았어요. 준호에게 제 전화번호를 줬어요?
Yes, I got it. Did you give Junho my phone number?

2. **부모님한테서 뭐 받았어요?**
What did you receive from your parents?

저에게 정말 큰 티비를 줬어요.
They gave me a really big TV.

티비 is short for "television".

많은 돈을 받았어요.
I received a lot of money.

Admit it… you are jealous!

선물요? 부모님한테서 맛있는 떡을 받았어요.
A present? I received delicious rice cakes from my parents.

You can just add 요 after a noun in place of 이에요.

3. **이것을 먹어 봤어요?**
Did you try to eat this?

네, 먹어 봤어요. 정말 매웠어요.
Yes, I tried it. It was really spicy.

네. 먹어 봤어요? 맛없어요.
Yes. Did you try it? It's tasteless.

4. **영어 공부해 볼 거예요?**
Are you going to try to study English?

네, 할 거예요. 친구한테서 영어 책을 받았어요.
Yes, I will. I received an English language book from my friend.

저는 작년에 영어 공부를 해 봤어요.
I tried to study English last year.

13 Conversation 대화 K-E

1. Polite conversation between friends.

A: 생일에 선물 많이 받았어요?

B: 네, 많이 받았어요. 꽃도 받았어요.

A: 누가 꽃을 줬어요?

B: 남자친구가 줬어요.

A: Did you get a lot of gifts on your birthday?

B: Yes, I got a lot. I also got flowers.

A: Who gave you the flowers?

B: My boyfriend gave them to me.

2. Casual conversation between mother and son.

A: 약 먹었어?

B: 응, 먹었어.

A 거짓말. 지금 먹어.

B: 약 싫어!

A: 그냥 먹어!

Remember "take" for medicine is 먹다.

A: Did you take your medicine?

B: Yeah I did.

A: That's a lie. Take it now.

B: I hate medicine!

A: Just take it!

With enough emotion 싫어 means "hate" instead of "dislike.

3. Casual conversation between friends.

A: 준호 생일 선물 살 거야?

B: 응, 오늘 살 거야. 선물 샀어?

A: 응, 이미 샀어. 저 가게에 귀여운 거 많이 있어. 가 봐.

B: 고마워.

A: Are you gonna buy Junho's birthday gift?

B: Yes, I'll buy it today. Did you buy a gift?

A: Yes, I already did. There are a lot of cute things in that store over there. Try going.

B: Thanks.

13 Conversation 대화 E-K

1. Polite conversation between friends.

A: Did you call to your parents?
B: Yes, I did. They are coming here tomorrow.
A: Tomorrow? You have a meeting with me tomorrow!
B: Oh, I didn't know.

A: 부모님한테 전화했어요?
B: 네, 했어요. 부모님이 여기에 내일 올 거예요.
A: 내일요? 내일 저랑 미팅 있어요!
B: 아, 몰랐어요.

2. Polite conversation at the office.

A: Did you drink this coffee?
B: Yes. Whose is it?
A: It's mine. I got it from George.
B: I am sorry.

A: 이 커피 마셨어요?
B: 네. 누구 것이에요?
A: 제 것이에요. 조지한테서 받았어요.
B: 미안해요.

This is a common way to say "sorry".

3. Polite conversation between friends.

A: Have you been to that restaurant?
B: Yes, I've been. That place was too loud. I don't like it.
A: Really? I like it there. I ate many delicious rice cakes there.

A: 그 레스토랑에 가 봤어요?
B: 네, 가 봤어요. 그 장소는 너무 시끄러웠어요. 싫어요.
A: 정말요? 저는 좋아해요. 거기에서 맛있는 떡을 많이 먹었어요.

13 Sentence Building 문장 만들기

In each lesson we will build on a previous sentence. Watch it grow and transform each time new concepts are introduced.

제 친구가 어머니한테서 다른 핸드폰을 받았어요.
My friend received a different cell phone from his mother.

Compare how the sentence has changed from the prior lessons:

Lesson 10: 내일 콜라 두 병을 살 거예요.
I will buy 2 bottles of cola tomorrow.

Lesson 11: 5 월 5 일에 콜라 두 병을 이미 샀어요.
I already bought 2 bottles of cola on May 5th.

Lesson 12: 제 친구가 저하고 다른 핸드폰을 샀어요.
My friend bought a different cell phone than me.

13 Workbook Area

❑ A13-1. Reading comprehension

At your current level, you should understand all of the grammar and words in the following sections. If you are struggling to understand them, review this and prior lessons.

① 남동생이 저에게 전화했어요.

② 저는 수업이 있었어요.

③ 지금은 오후 4 시예요.

④ 8 시에 미팅이 있어요.

Dialogue

A: 전화했어? 수업이 있었어.

B: 나 너의 학교에 일곱 시 반에 갈 거야. 나랑 같이 밥 먹을 거야?

A: 아니. 나 여덟 시에 미팅이 있어.

B: 알았어. 전화해.

❑ A13-2. Reading comprehension questions

Answer the following questions about the reading comprehension in the prior section.

1. 미팅은 몇 시에 있어요?

____

2. 지금은 7 시 30 분이에요?

____

3. 누가 전화했어요?

____

❑ A13-3. Fill in the blank

For each number in the Korean sentence, write the appropriate Korean word to match the English translation.

1. ①은 여자친구② 꽃을 ③요.
   My younger brother gave flowers to his girlfriend.

   ① ____________________ ② ____________________ ③ ____________________

2. 저는 저의 선생님① 생일 ②을 ③요.
   I received a birthday gift from my teacher.

   ① ____________________ ② ____________________ ③ ____________________

3. ①에 너② ③했어.
   I called you in the morning.

   ① ____________________ ② ____________________ ③ ____________________

4. 리키씨가 ①에 나② 기린을 ③요.
   Ricky gave me a giraffe last week. (Where do these guys live???)

   ① ____________________ ② ____________________ ③ ____________________

5. ①것을 먹어 ② 거예요.
   I will try to eat spicy things.

   ① ____________________ ② ____________________

6. ①.
   Buy it. * use only one hangul!

   ① ____________________

7. ① 맥주② ③ 볼 거예요?
   Will you try to drink this beer?

   ① ____________________ ② ____________________ ③ ____________________

8. 제 여자①가 저② 돈을 ③ 줬어요.
My girlfriend gave me money a lot.

① ____________ ② ____________ ③ ____________

9. 저는 ① 조지② 책을③ 거예요.
I will receive a book from George tomorrow.

① ____________ ② ____________ ③ ____________

10. 저는 ① ②를 먹어 ③요.
I already tried that meat.

① ____________ ② ____________ ③ ____________

❑ A13-4. Korean translation

Translate the following conversation into English.

1.
A: 다음 주에 누나랑 런던에 가요. B: 비행기표 이미 샀어요? A: 아니요, 부모님이 어제 돈을 줬어요. 오늘 살 거예요.
A:
B:
A:

13 Doodle Area

Use this area to draw something awesome. Seriously! Or maybe write some uber complicated sentences. Or… maybe play tic tac toe with a Korean friend you just met.

❑ Awesome drawing area!

❑ Complicated sentences I made!

K: ______________________ E: ______________________

K: ______________________ E: ______________________

K: ______________________ E: ______________________

K: ______________________ E: ______________________

❑ Tic Tac Toe with my Korean friends!

Lesson 14:

Negative tense

14

Before This Lesson

1. Know how to make past tense and future tense verbs.

Lesson Goals

1. Learn how to create the negative tense of verbs and then conjugate into the past and future tenses.

From The Teachers

1. In this lesson we learn the long awaited negative tense. Since there is "past negative", "future negative" and, "present negative", you will actually be learning three new tenses. This might seem overwhelming, but it isn't if you consider you are simply building off of the original negative verb.

Lesson Highlights

14-1.
Making negative verbs with 지 않다

14-5.
Shall I? Shall we? ~(으)ㄹ 까

14-6.
Let's ~자, (으)ㅂ시다

14 New Words 새로운 단어

일	work
회사	company
시간	time, hour
날	day
공원	park
호텔	hotel
식사	meal
아침밥 (밥 can be removed)	breakfast
점심밥 (밥 can be removed)	lunch
저녁밥 (밥 can be removed)	dinner

14 New Action Verbs 새로운 동사

Verb	Basic	English	Type
일하다	일해	to work	하다
쉬다	쉬어	to take a break, rest	regular
도착하다	도착해	to arrive	하다
출발하다	출발해	to depart	하다

14 Verb Usage 동사 사용법

❑ 14-1. Making negative verbs with 지 않다

Any verb can be made into its negative form by adding 지 않다 to its stem.

action verbs

가다 to go	가지 않다 to <u>NOT</u> go
하다 to do	하지 않다 to <u>NOT</u> do
먹다 to eat	먹지 않다 to <u>NOT</u> eat
사다 to buy	사지 않다 to <u>NOT</u> buy

It's VERY important to treat the 지 않다 verb as a NEW verb. If you treat it as a new verb, then you automatically know how to make all the tenses you already know.

For example, let's conjugate the new verb 가지 않다 (to not go).

> The pronunciation of the 않아 is 아나.

Example conjugations (가지 않다)

1. 내일 가지 않아요. (simple future / BASIC) — I won't go tomorrow.
2. 학교에 가지 않아요. (simple present / BASIC) — I don't go to school.
3. 가지 않을 거예요. (future) — I won't go.
4. 가지 않았어요. (past) — I didn't go.

It doesn't matter if the verb is a descriptive, action, ㅂ irregular, 하다, or even 르 irregular verb. The pattern to make the negative verb is always just (STEM + 지 않다). Let's look at a negative descriptive verb conjugation.

descriptive verbs

춥다 to be cold	춥지 않다 to NOT be cold	싸다 to be cheap	싸지 않다 to NOT be cheap
덥다 to be hot	덥지 않다 to NOT be hot	작다 to be small	작지 않다 to NOT be small

Example conjugations (춥지 않다)

1. 내일 춥지 않아요. (simple future / BASIC) — It won't be cold tomorrow.
2. 지금 춥지 않아요. (simple present / BASIC) — It's not cold now.
3. 춥지 않을 거예요. (future) — It won't be cold.
4. 춥지 않았어요. (past) — It wasn't cold.

Now, let's see how a negative 하다 descriptive verb conjugates.

Example conjugations (필요 않다)

1. 내일 필요하지 않아. (simple future / BASIC) — It won't need it tomorrow.
2. 지금 필요하지 않아. (simple present / BASIC) — I don't need it now.
3. 필요하지 않을 거예요. (future) — I won't need it.
4. 필요하지 않았어요. (past) — I didn't need it.

❑ 14-2. 일하다 (to work), 쉬다 (to take a break, to rest)

The time that you work or take a break at is marked with the time marker 에. The place that you work or take a break at is marked with the event location marker 에서.

(time) 에 (place) 에서 일하다
to work at a (place) at (time)

(time) 에 (place) 에서 쉬다
to take a break at a (place) at (time)

합니다 is more formal than the 해요 form.

Example sentences

1. 저는 병원에서 일합니다.	I work at a hospital.
2. 내일 4 시에 일하지 않을 거예요.	I won't work tomorrow at 4 o'clock.
3. 호텔에서 쉬어요.	I am resting at the hotel.
4. 공원에서 쉴 거예요.	I will take a break in the park.

For verbs with ㅜㅣ as the vowel, add 어 to make the basic form.

❑ 14-3. 도착하다 (to arrive)

The place you arrive is marked with the location marker 에, and the time is marked with the time marker 에.

(time) 에 (place) 에 도착하다
to arrive at a (place) at (time)

Example sentences

1. 공항에 3 시 반에 도착할 거예요.	I will arrive at the airport at 3:30.
2. 제 친구가 어젯밤에 도착하지 않았어요.	My friend didn't arrive last night.

❑ 14-4. 출발하다 (to depart)

The place you depart is marked with the "from location marker" 에서, and the time is marked with the time marker 에.

(time) 에 (place) 에서 출발하다
to depart from a (place) at (time)

Example sentences

1. 세 시 반에 공항에서 출발할 거예요. — I'll depart from the airport at 3:30.
2. 제 친구가 어젯밤에 출발하지 않았어요. — My friend didn't depart last night.

14 Grammar 문법

❍ 14-5. Shall I? Shall we? ~(으)ㄹ까

The (으)ㄹ까 pattern means, "Shall we" or "Shall I" depending on the context. If a verb has a 받침, you add 을까 and without a 받침 you add ㄹ (리을) to the stem and then add 까. This is a great way to make suggestions.

하다	→	하	→	할까요?
to do		stem		Shall I/we do?

먹다	→	먹	→	먹을까요?
to eat		stem		Shall I/we eat?

Example sentences

1. 아침밥 같이 먹을까요?	Shall we eat breakfast together?
2. 어디까지 갈까요?	How far shall we go?
3. 두 시에 시작할까요?	Shall we start at 2 o'clock?
4. 세 시부터 쉴까요?	Shall we take a break at 3 o'clock?
5. 몇 시에 갈까요?	What time shall we go?
6. 뭐를 살까요?	What shall I buy?
7. 누구한테 줄까요?	Whom shall I give it to?
8. 몇 시부터 출발할까요?	From what time should we depart?
9. 누구한테 전화할까요?	Who shall I call?
10. 몇 분 수영할까요?	How many minutes shall we swim?
11. 책을 읽을까요?	Shall I read a book?
12. 누구한테서 받을까요?	From whom shall I receive it?

특별 정보 Special Information

The (으)ㄹ까 pattern is commonly used when talking to oneself or thinking. In this case it is better translated as "I wonder if I should…" NOTE: You don't need 요 in your thoughts since you don't need to be polite to yourself.

1. 지금 먹을까? — I wonder if I should eat now.
2. 일할까? — I wonder if I should work.
3. 공부할까? — I wonder if I should study.

14-6. Let's ~자, ~(으)ㅂ시다

The "Let's do" form is created by adding 자 to any stem. The more polite version is made by adding 읍시다 after verb stems with 받침, or if the stem doesn't have a 받침 add ㅂ(비읍) to the bottom of the stem, then add 시다.

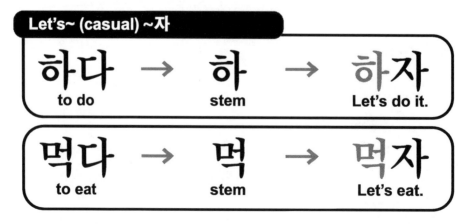

Let's~ (more polite) ~(으) ㅂ시다

하다 (to do) → 하 (stem) → 합시다 (Let's do it.)

먹다 (to eat) → 먹 (stem) → 먹읍시다 (Let's eat.)

NOTE: The 읍시다 form is polite, however it can be considered rude when speaking to an elder since it sounds more like a command. With someone above you in status it will be more polite to ask them if they would like to go instead instead of saying "let's go".

Let's~ (casual) ~자

하다 (to do) → 하 (stem) → 하자 (Let's do it.)

먹다 (to eat) → 먹 (stem) → 먹자 (Let's eat.)

Example sentences (polite)

1. 점심밥을 먹읍시다.	Let's eat lunch.
2. 같이 공부합시다.	Let's study together.
3. 영화를 봅시다.	Let's watch a movie.
4. 맛있는 것을 삽시다.	Let's buy tasty food.
5. 어머니한테 전화합시다.	Let's call mom.

Example sentences (casual)

1. 점심밥을 먹자.	Let's eat lunch.
2. 같이 공부하자.	Let's study together.
3. 영화를 보자.	Let's watch a movie.
4. 맛있는 것을 사자.	Let's buy tasty food.
5. 어머니한테 전화하자.	Let's call mom.

❍ 14-7. About something ~에 대해

에 대해 is a combination of the 에 particle and the verb 대하다. 에 대해 means "about" or "in regards to". Just add this after any noun and it means "about" that noun. It's very useful with the new verbs we learned in the last lesson. 에 대해 replaces 을/를 in the sentence.

Example sentences

1. 차**에 대해** 몰라요.	I don't know **about** cars.
2. 여자**에 대해** 몰라!	I don't know **about** girls!
3. 그 영화**에 대해** 몰랐어요.	I didn't know **about** that movie.
4. 싸이**에 대해** 알아요?	Do you know **about** PSY?
5. 네 여자친구**에 대해** 알아요.	I know **about** your girlfriend.
6. 이 책**에 대해** 알아요?	Do you know **about** this book?

❍ 14-8. Going to work

일 means "work" but 일 isn't a "place" to go to. So you when you say "I am at work" or "I am going to work" you should not use 일. Instead you will say 회사 (company) in it's place.

Example sentences

1. 아침 일곱시에 **회사**에 가요.	I go to work (company) at 7 in the morning.
2. 지금, **회사**에 있어요.	Now, I am at work (company).

14 Question and Answer 질문과 대답

1. **내일 뭐해?**
   What are you doing tomorrow?

   친구랑 도서관에서 공부할 거야.
   I am going to study with my friend at the library.

   > 거야 is the casual way to say 거예요. It's only used with friends.

   나는 거울을 살 거야.
   I am going to buy a mirror.

   내일 공항에서 일할 거야.
   I am going to work at the airport tomorrow.

2. **이 커피 필요해요?**
   Do you need this coffee?

   아니요, 그 커피는 너무 써요. 저는 쓴 커피를 싫어해요.
   No, that coffee is too bitter. I dislike bitter coffee.

   아니요, 그 커피는 매우 뜨거워요. 저는 차가운 커피가 필요해요.
   No, that coffee is very hot. I need a cold coffee.

   네, 필요해요. 고마워요.
   Yes, I need it. Thank you.

3. **오늘 몇 시에 제주도에 도착해요?**
   What time do you arrive on Jeju Island today?

   > 제주도 is a popular resort island in the southern part of South Korea.

   아마 여섯 시에 도착할 거예요.
   Maybe I will arrive at 6:00 pm.

   오늘 가지 않아요. 제주도에 비가 많이 와요.
   I'm not going today. It is raining a lot on Jeju Island.

   저는 오늘 제주도에 가지 않아요. 다음 주에 가요.
   I'm not going to Jeju Island today. I'm going next week.

4. **이 작은 핸드폰은 얼마예요?**
How much is this small cell phone?

몰라요. 아마 그 핸드폰은 너무 비쌀 거예요.
I don't know. Maybe that cell phone will be (is probably) too expensive.

In this case ㄹ 거예요 is not "future" but instead is assumptive.

그 핸드폰은 싸지 않을 거예요.
That cellphone is probably not (will not be) cheap.

오십오만 원이에요.
It's 550,000 Won.

5. **누구랑 한국어 공부할 거예요?**
Who will you study Korean with?

일본인 친구랑 같이 공부할 거예요.
I'll study with my Japanese friend.

Like 사람, 인 can be added to a country to say "person of that country".

혼자서 공부할 거예요.
I will study by myself.

혼자서 is a handy word you can use to explain that you are doing something "by yourself".

한국어 학교에서 다른 사람이랑 공부할 거예요.
I'll study with other people at a Korean language school.

6. **오늘 밤에 뭐 먹을 거예요?**
What are you going to eat tonight?

먹지 않아요. 2 시에 많이 먹었어요.
I'm not going to eat. I ate a lot at 2 o'clock.

이미 먹었어요.
I already ate.

7. **누구를 사랑해요?**
Who do you love?

소녀시대를 사랑해요. 싸이도 좋아해요.
I love Girls' Generation. I also like PSY.

제 부모님을 너무 사랑해요.
I really love my parents.

8. **몇 시에 공원에 갈까요?**
What time shall we go to the park?

한 시에 가자.
Let's go at 1 o'clock.

지금 갈까요?
Shall we go now?

11 시에 출발합시다.
Let's depart at 11 o'clock.

지금 공원에 가지 않아요. 저는 쉴 거예요.
I'm not going to go to the park now. I'll take a break.

9. **점심밥을 먹었어요?**
Did you eat lunch?

아니요, 먹지 않았어요. 같이 먹을까요?
No, I didn't eat. Shall we eat together?

아니요, 먹지 않았어요. 오늘 점심밥을 먹지 않을 거예요. 아침밥을 너무 많이 먹었어요.
No, I didn't. I'm not going to eat lunch today. I ate too much for breakfast.

14 Conversation 대화 K-E

1. **Polite conversation between college classmates.**
A: 준호랑 백화점에서 일했어요?
B: 네, 우리는 작년에 같이 일했어요.
A: 준호가 그 일을 좋아했어요?
B: 아니요, 싫어했어요. 지금 준호는 공항에서 일해요.

A: Did you work at the department store with Junho?
B: Yes, we worked together last year.
A: Did he like the work?
B: No, he disliked it. Now he is working at the airport.

2. Polite conversation between a returning exchange student and a friend.

A: 저는 미국 친구와 영국 친구가 있어요.
B: 미국 사람이랑 영국 사람은 달라요?
A: 네, 정말 달라요. 미국 사람은 정말 시끄러워요.
B: 영국 사람은 시끄럽지 않아요?
A: 아니요, 매우 조용해요.

A: I have American and English friends.
B: Are Americans and English people different?
A: Yes, they are really different. Americans are really loud.
B: Aren't English people loud?
A: No, they are very quiet.

3. Polite conversation between a couple on vacation.

A: 호텔에 몇 시에 갈 거예요?
B: 흠.. 9 시에 출발할까요?
A: 좋아요. 지금 저녁밥을 먹읍시다.
B: 어디에 갈까요? (pointing on a map) 저기에 갈까요?
A: 알았어요.

좋아요 is a really common way to say "Okay" or "Sounds good" etc.

A: What time are we going to the hotel?
B: Hmm.. Shall we depart at 9 pm?
A: That's good. Let's eat dinner now.
B: Where shall we go? (pointing on a map) Shall we go there?
A: Got it.

14 Conversation 대화 E-K

1. Polite conversation between two friends on the phone.

A: There are too many people at CGV movie theater.
B: Are you going to go to a different movie theater?
There is a good movie theater next to the bank.
A: I already went. That theater also had many people.
B: Well then… (so…) What are you going to do?
A: I will swim at the pool.

CGV is a popular movie theatre chain in South Korea.

A: CGV 영화관에 사람이 너무 많아요.
B: 다른 영화관에 갈 거예요?
은행 옆에 좋은 영화관이 있어요.
A: 이미 갔어요. 그 영화관도 사람이 많이 있어요.
B: 그럼... 뭐 할 거예요?
A: 수영장에서 수영할 거예요.

2. A casual breakup conversation between two soon to be ex-lovers.

A: I don't love you. We are too different.
B: Even now (now too) I love you a lot!
A: I already have a different boyfriend.
He is a really funny man.
We will go to Korea together next year.

A: 너를 사랑하지 않아. 우리는 너무 달라.
B: 나 지금도 너 많이 사랑해!
A: 벌써 다른 남자친구가 있어.
재미있는 사람이야.
우리는 내년에 같이 한국에 갈거야.

지금도 is better translated as "even now".

이야 is the casual form for 이에요.

거야 is casual for 거예요

3. Polite conversation between friends.

A: Did you watch that movie?
B: No, I didn't watch it.
A: My older brother gave me movie tickets. Shall we watch the movie today?
B: Sounds good.

A: 그 영화 봤어요?
B: 아니요, 보지 않았어요.
A: 저의 오빠가 저에게 영화표를 줬어요. 오늘 같이 영화 볼까요?
B: 좋아요.

14 Sentence Building 문장 만들기

In each lesson we will build on a previous sentence. Watch it grow and transform each time new concepts are introduced.

제 친구가 어머니한테서 다른 핸드폰을 받지 않았어요.
My friend didn't get a different cell phone from his mother.

Compare how the sentence has changed from the prior lessons:

Lesson 11: 5 월 5 일에 콜라 두 병을 이미 샀어요.
I already bought 2 bottles of cola on May 5th.

Lesson 12: 제 친구가 저하고 다른 핸드폰을 샀어요.
My friend bought a different cell phone than me.

Lesson 13: 제 친구가 어머니한테서 다른 핸드폰을 받았어요.
My friend received a different cell phone from his mother.

14 Workbook Area

❑ A14-1. Reading comprehension

At your current level, you should understand all of the grammar and words in the following sections. If you are struggling to understand them, review this and prior lessons.

New words for this comprehension: 일 (work), 회사 (company, work)

① 일요일에는 회사에 가지 않아요.

② 친구랑 공원에 갈 거예요.

③ 오늘은 춥지 않아요.

④ 오전 11 시에 출발할 거예요.

Dialogue

A: 오늘 회사에 갈 거예요?

B: 아니요, 오늘은 회사에 가지 않아요.

A: 공원 갈까요?

B: 좋아요. 오전 11 시에 출발할까요?

❑ A14-2. Reading comprehension questions

Answer the following questions about the reading comprehension in the prior section.

1. 몇 시에 공원에 가요?

____

2. 오늘은 추워요?

____

3. 몇 시에 회사에 가요?

____

❑ A14-3. Fill in the blank

For each number in the Korean sentence, write the appropriate Korean word to match the English translation.

1. ① ②에 가③.
   Let's go to the park together.

   ① ____________ ② ____________ ③ ____________

2. 저녁밥 ① 선생님② 먹을③요?
   Shall we eat dinner with the teacher?

   ① ____________ ② ____________ ③ ____________

3. 제 ①은 ②6 시에 도착하지 ③요.
   My family didn't arrive at 6 pm.

   ① ____________ ② ____________ ③ ____________

4. ① 호텔② ③요.
   I am resting at the hotel now.

   ① ____________ ② ____________ ③ ____________

5. ① 도서관② 공부③.
   Let's study at the library together.

   ① ____________ ② ____________ ③ ____________

6. 이 ①는 ② 않아요.
   This coffee isn't hot.

   ① ____________ ② ____________

7. ① 공원② 같이 ②요?
   Shall we take a break together at that park over there?

   ① ____________ ② ____________ ③ ____________

8. 친구의 ①에 대해 ②요.
I don't know about my friend's family.

① ____________ ② ____________

9. 이것을 해 ①?
Shall we try to do this?

① ____________

10. ① 4 시② ③하자.
Let's depart at 4 pm.

① ____________ ② ____________ ③ ____________

11. ①에서 호주② 많이 ③해요.
In school I am studying a lot about Australia.

① ____________ ② ____________ ③ ____________

12. ①일은 ②하지 않③.
I am not going to work tomorrow.

① ____________ ② ____________ ③ ____________

❑ A14-4. Korean translation

Translate the following conversation into English.

1.
A: 어머니는 몇 시에 학교에 도착해요? B: 몰라요. 어머니한테 전화했어요? A: 아니요, 전화하지 않았어요. B: 지금 전화합시다.
A:
B:
A:
B:

❑ A14-5. English translation

Translate the following conversation into Korean.

1.
A: I don't know about American history. Do you know? B: I don't know (anything). We are studying about China in school now. A: Is China interesting? B: No, it isn't interesting.
A:
B:
A:
B:

14 Vocabulary Builder

■ Group O: other body parts 더 많은 몸의 부분

손가락	finger
어깨	shoulder
무릎	knee
팔꿈치	elbow
턱	chin
배	stomach
등	back

■ Group P: famous cities 유명한 도시

뉴욕	New York, USA
로스앤젤레스	Los Angeles, USA
라스베가스	Las Vegas, USA
도쿄	Tokyo, Japan
파리	Paris, France
런던	London, England
베를린	Berlin, Germany
방콕	Bangkok, Thailand
베이징	Beijing, China
마닐라	Manila, Philippines
오타와	Ottawa, Canada
퀘벡	Quebec, Canada

Lesson 15:

Can and Can't do

15

Before This Lesson

1. Know word groups O (other body parts) and P (famous cities).

Lesson Goals

1. Learn how to conjugate ㄷ (디귿) irregular verbs.
2. Learn how to ask someone to do an action in a nice way.
3. Learn how to say "I can do" and "I can't do" form.

From The Teachers

1. The ㄷ irregular verbs introduced in this lesson are some of the most common verbs within the ㄷ irregular type of verbs.

Lesson Highlights

15-9.
To and from
(부터 / 까지)

15-11.
ㄹ/을 수(가) 있다,
ㄹ/을 수(가) 없다
(Can do and can't do)

15 New Words 새로운 단어

바다	ocean
수영장	swimming pool
이름	name
대학교	college
음악	music
소리	sound
이메일	e-mail
다	everything, all
아까	just now, just a moment ago
질문	question
대답	reply
엄마	my mother, mom
아빠	my father, dad

15 New Action Verbs 새로운 동사

Verb	Basic	English	Type
수영하다	수영해	to swim	하다
읽다	읽어	to read	regular
시작하다	시작해	to start, to begin	하다
묻다	물어	to ask	ㄷ irregular
듣다	들어	to listen, hear	ㄷ irregular
걷다	걸어	to walk	ㄷ irregular
대답하다	대답해	to answer, reply	하다
배우다	배워	to learn	regular
질문하다	질문해	to ask a question	하다

15 Verb Usage 동사 사용법

❑ 15-1. 수영하다 (to swim)

Swimming is an event. So the event location marker 에서 is used to mark where you swim.

Example sentences

1. 오전 10 시에 수영장에서 수영했어요.
   I swam at the pool at 10 am.

2. 다음 주에 가족이랑 바다에서 수영할 거예요.
   Next week I will swim in the ocean with my family.

❑ 15-2. 읽다 (to read)

The item being read is marked with the object marker 을/를.

Example sentences

1. 저는 책하고 잡지를 많이 읽어요.
   I read a lot of books and magazines.

2. 오늘 도서관에서 친구하고 같이 소설을 읽을 거예요.
   Today I will read a novel at the library together with my friend.

3. 만화책을 읽지 않아요.
   I don't read comic books.

4. 지금 대학교에서 일본에 대해 읽어요.
   I am reading about Japan in college now.

❑ 15-3. 시작하다 (to start)

Starting will use a variety of times. The time is marked with the time marker 에.

Example sentences

1.	학교가 아침 9 시에 시작해요.	School starts at 9 in the morning.
2.	일은 몇 시에 시작할 거예요?	What time does your work start?
3.	학교가 저녁 4 시에 시작해요.	School starts at 4 in the evening.
4.	영화가 5 시 반에 시작했어요.	The movie started at 5:30.

❑ 15-4. ㄷ irregulars, 묻다 (to ask), 듣다 (to listen, hear)

묻다 (to ask) and 듣다 (to listen) are ㄷ irregular verbs. The ㄷ (디귿) 받침 changes to the ㄹ (리을) for many of the conjugations. The thing you are listening to is marked with 을/를 but if you are listening to a person they are marked with 에게 / 한테.

ㄷ irregular BASIC form

	remove 다	change ㄷ to ㄹ	add 어
묻다 (to ask)	묻	물	물어
듣다 (to listen)	듣	들	들어

Example sentences

1. 우리 선생님이 제 가족에 대해 물었어요.
   Our teacher asked about my family.
2. 매일 방 안에서 음악을 들어요.
   I listen to music everyday in my room.
3. 수업에서 선생님에게 들을 거예요.
   I will listen to the teacher in class.
4. 선생님한테 숙제에 대해 물어봤어요.
   I asked the teacher about the homework.
5. 아까 큰 소리를 들었어요.
   Just now I heard a big (loud) sound.

> 물어보다 is a verb that means "to ask". It is NOT 묻다 + 보다 taught in section 13-8 so no space is required.

> Normally, future tense is just STEM + ㄹ/을 거예요. But ㄷ irregular stems must first switch the ㄷ to ㄹ to make the stem.

❑ 15-5. 걷다 (to walk)

걷다 is also a ㄷ irregular.

ㄷ irregular BASIC form

to walk	remove 다	change ㄷ to ㄹ	add 어
걷다	걷	걸	걸어

Example sentences

1. 진짜 걸었어요? — Did you really walk?
2. 친구하고 걸을 거예요. — I will walk with a friend.

특별 정보 Special Information

The BASIC form of 걸어 is used to mean "by foot" or "walk" in front of motion verbs such as 가다 (to go) and 오다 (to come) etc.

Example sentences

1. 친구가 걸어 올 거예요. — My friend will come by foot.
2. 어제 제 집에 걸어 갔어요. — Yesterday, I walked to my house.
3. 오늘 학교에 걸어 갔어요. — Today I walked to school.

❑ 15-6. 대답해다 (to answer)

The thing you are answering is marked with the marker 에. 대답하다 is not used to "answer" the phone.

Example sentences

1. 준호씨가 선생님의 질문에 대답하지 않았어요.
   Junho didn't answer the teacher's question.

2. 다음 주까지 대답할 거예요.
   I will answer by next week.

3. 제 질문에 대답해 주세요. (Taught in section 15-10.)
   Please answer my question.

특별 정보 Special Information

There are other verbs used for "to answer" that you might hear:
답신하다 (to reply), 답장하다 (to respond to email / texts etc.)

Also remember that you can use 질문 (question) and 대답 (reply, answer) as nouns.

Example sentences

1. **질문**이 있어요? — Do you have any **questions**?
2. **대답**은 어려워요. — The **answer** is difficult.
3. 이메일에 다 **답장**했어요. — I **replied to** all of my emails.

❑ 15-7. 배우다 (to learn)

The thing you are learning is marked with the object marker 을/를. If you are learning "about" something use ~에 대해 to mark the subject you are learning about.

Example sentences

1. 한국어를 배워요. — I'm learning Korean.
2. 내년에 한글을 배울 거예요. — I will learn hangul next year.
3. 대학교에서 일본에 대해 배웠어요. — I learned about Japan in college.
4. 인도에 대해 아직 배우지 않았어요. — I haven't learned about India yet.

❑ 15-8. 질문하다 (to ask a question)

If you are asking a question "about" something use ~에 대해 (section 14-7) to mark the subject you are asking about. In section 15-4 you learn how to ask questions with 물어보다. In everyday Korean it's more common to use 물어보다. Note there is no space in 물어보다.

As you learn more Korean, you will realize there are several ways to say what you want to say. Here are a few ways to let someone know you have a question.

질문할 거예요.	I will ask a question.
물어 볼 거예요.	I will (try to) ask.
질문이 있어요.	I have a question.

Now let's look at past tense:

질문했어요.	I asked a question.
물어봤어요.	I asked.
질문이 있었어요.	I had a question.

The person you are asking a question to is marked with 에게 or 한테.

(person) 에게 / 한테 질문하다
to ask a question to a (person)

Example sentences

1. 선생님한테 질문했어요. — I asked a question to my teacher.
2. 아빠에게 질문할 거예요. — I will ask my father.

15 Grammar 문법

❍ 15-9. To and from (부터 / 까지)

The Korean version "to" and "from, until" work exactly like their English counterparts. The only difference is that they come after the place or time. So instead of saying "from Seoul" you say "Seoul from". They can be used one at a time, or together.

Examples (locations)

1. 서울부터 부산까지	from Seoul to Pusan
2. 집부터 학교까지	from home to school
3. 직장부터 여기까지	from the workplace to here

Examples (time)

1. 6 시부터 8 시까지	from 6 o'clock to 8 o'clock
2. 금요일부터 일요일까지	from Friday to Sunday
3. 1 월부터 5 월까지	from January to May

까지 can be translated as "as far as", "up to" etc. The time and location marker 에 is used with an exact destination or time. 까지 shows progression to the final time or location.

Example Q&A

1. **어디까지 갈 거예요?**
   How far are you going?

   서울까지 갈 거예요.
   I am going to Seoul.

   > If 에 was used here then the person would be going only to Seoul. Using 까지 means there might be other cities along the way.

   이미 뉴욕까지 갔어요.
   I already went up to New York.

2. **몇 시까지 일해요?**
   What time are you working until?

   5 시 반까지 일해요.
   I work until 5:30.

   > Work is UNTIL 5:30. If 에 is used, the EXACT time of the work is 5:30 and there isn't work done before.

   10 시 45 분까지 일해요.
   I work until 10:45.

부터 is translated as “from”, and can be used after times and locations.

Example Q&A

1. **언제부터 시작할 거예요?**
   From when are you going to start?

   1 시부터 시작할 거예요.
   I'll start from 1 o'clock.

   화요일부터 시작할 거예요.
   I will start from Tuesday.

2. **어디부터 어디까지 갔어요?**
   From where to where did you go?

   베를린부터 런던까지 갔어요.
   I went from Berlin to London.

   뉴욕부터 로스앤젤레스까지 갔어요.
   I went from New York to Los Angeles.

3. **월요일에 몇 시부터 몇 시까지 일할 거예요?**
   From what time until what time will you work on Monday?

   아직 몰라요. 아마 아침 3 시부터 6 시까지 예요.
   I don't know yet. I will probably be at work from 3:00 to 6:00.

특별 정보 Special Information

When saying “from a (place)” or “from a (time)”, both 부터 and 에서 can be used. Koreans however normally use 에서 more with places and 부터 more with times. To sound natural you should also use 에서 with locations instead of 부터.

Example Q&A

1. **어디에서 왔어요?** — **Where are you from?**
   미국에서 왔어요. — I am from America.

2. **집에서 왔어요?** — **Did you come from your house?**
   네, 아까 왔어요. — Yes, I came just now.

❍ 15-10. Please do this

In section 9-5 you learned how to ask for things using 주세요 and in section 13-10 you learned the casual way to make a command. Now we will learn the polite way to ask someone to do something. The pattern is BASIC + 주세요. 을/를 is not required.

(BASIC form) 주세요.
Please (verb).

Example sentences

1. 가 주세요.	Please go.
2. 와 주세요.	Please come.
3. 사 주세요.	Please buy it.
4. 해 주세요.	Please do it.
5. 먹어 주세요.	Please eat it.

❍ 15-11. ㄹ/을 수(가) 있다, ㄹ/을 수(가) 없다 (Can do and can't do)

The 수 portion of 할 수 있다 (can do) and 할 수 없다 (can't do) means "ability" or "possibility". If the stem of the verb does not have a 받침 then you add ㄹ to it, and if there is a 받침 then you add 을 after it. NOTE: The 가 is often dropped.

(STEM + ㄹ/을) 수 있다
I can (verb).

(STEM + ㄹ/을) 수 없다
I can't (verb).

First let's see how we can apply this pattern to some action verbs.

Example sentences

1. 언제 한국에 올 수 있어요?
   When can you come to Korea?
2. 수영할 수 있어요?
   Can you swim?
3. 12 시까지 도착할 수 있어요?
   Can you arrive by 12 o'clock?
4. 4 시부터 시작할 수 없었어요.
   I couldn't start at 4 o'clock.
5. 제 예쁜 얼굴을 볼 수 있어요?
   Can you see my pretty face?
6. 매운 것을 먹을 수 있어요?
   Can you eat spicy things?
7. 내일 오전 5 시에 일할 수 없어요.
   I can't work tomorrow at 5 am.
8. 조용한 소리를 들을 수가 없어요.
   I can't hear quiet sounds.

특별 정보 Special Information

The rules for modifying the stem of verbs to create the ~수 있다 / ~수 없다 verb form is exactly the same as creating the future tense verbs. These rules are covered in section 10-4 and 10-5. Another simple way to create this pattern is:

(future tense) MINUS 거예요 PLUS 수 있다

1. 할 거예요.	I will do it.
할 수 있어요.	I can do it.
할 수 없어요.	I can't do it.
2. 갈 거예요.	I will go.
갈 수 있어요.	I can go.
갈 수 없어요.	I can't go.
3. 물을 거예요.	I will ask.
물을 수 있어요.	I can ask.
물을 수 없어요.	I can't ask.

NOTE: It's possible to use this form with descriptive verbs, and you might even hear it used. However, typically Koreans would say "I think it will be cold" or "it might be cold", instead of "it can be cold" or "it could be cold" with descriptive verbs.

❍ 15-12. Doing things well 잘~

You can add 잘 before any verb to say that it's done well. Or if you use the negative form how well you don't to something. With a 하다 verb the 잘 must be directly in front of the 하다.

Example sentences

1. 제 여동생이 공부 잘 해요.	My younger sister is studying well.
2. 박민수는 수영 잘 해요.	Minsu Park swims well.
3. 숙제를 잘 할 수 없었어요.	I couldn't do the homework well.
4. 수학에 대해 잘 몰라요.	I don't know math well.
5. 잘 먹었어요.	I ate well.

Before eating it's polite to say, 잘 먹겠습니다 (I will eat well).
After eating you say, 잘 먹었습니다 (I ate well).

특별 정보 Special Information

When you speak Korean to Koreans for the first time, no matter how bad your Korean is you will likely hear one of these phrases.

한국어 잘 하시네요. (very polite)	You are good at Korean.
한국어 잘 해요. (polite)	You are good at Korean.
한국어 잘 해. (casual)	You are good at Korean.

잘 하다 means "you are skilled" or "you are good" in this case. You might hear it after you play guitar for someone or after you sing at the 노래방. 노래방 means "song room" and is the Korean word for "karaoke".

15 Question and Answer 질문과 대답

1. **선생님에게 질문했어요?**
Did you ask a question to the teacher?

물어봤어요 would have also been acceptable.

네, 물어봤어요. 선생님이 어제 저에게 대답해 줬어요.
Yes, I asked. She answered (to) me yesterday.

아니요, 할 수 없었어요.
오전 8 시부터 오후 9 시까지 역사와 문학과 생물 수업이 있었어요.
No, I couldn't.
I had history, literature, and biology classes from 8 am to 9 pm.

2. **이 한국어 책을 읽을 수 있어요?**
Can you read this Korean book?

"for me" is commonly translated as 나에게 or 저에게. (한테 too)

네, 다 읽을 수 있어요. 그 책은 나에게 쉬워요.
Yes, I can read everything. That book is easy for me.

아니요, 읽을 수 없어요. 저에게 너무 어려워요.
No, I can't read it. It is too difficult for me.

아니요, 저는 내일부터 한국어를 공부할 거예요.
No, I will study Korean from tomorrow.

3. **언제 수영장에 갈 거예요??**
When are you going to the swimming pool?

벌써 왔어요.
I already came. (I'm already here.)

If you said 벌써 있어요 it would mean "I already have" instead of "I am already here."

이번주는 갈 수 없어요. 일요일까지 비가 많이 올 거예요.
I can't go this week. It's probably going to rain a lot until Sunday.

몰라요. 오늘은 가지 않을 거예요.
I don't know. Today I won't be going.

4. **이름 물어봤어요?**
Did you ask her name?

네, 했어요. 이름이 너무 길었어요.
Yes, I did. Her name is too long.

이름을 들을 수 없었어요.
I couldn't hear her name.

네, 했어요. 그녀의 이름이 진짜 귀여워요.
Yes, I did. Her name is really cute.

커피빈 (Coffee Bean) is a popular coffee shop in South Korea.

5. **준호의 생일 파티는 커피빈에서 9 시에 시작할 거예요. 같이 갈까요?**
Junho's birthday party is starting at 9 o'clock at the Coffee Bean.
Shall we go together?

저는 갈 수 없어요. 커피빈은 우리집에서 너무 멀어요.
I can't go. Coffee Bean is too far from my house.

우리 is often used to mean "my". It can also mean "we" even without the 의 particle.

지금 준호의 생일 선물을 살 거예요. 준호는 제 생일에 떡을 줬어요.
I am going to buy Junho's birthday gift now. Junho gave me rice cakes on my birthday.

네, 갈 수 있어요.
Yes, I can go.

6. **수학 수업을 몇 시에 시작해요?**
What time do you start your math class?

아마 3 시에 시작 할 거예요. 수업 갈 거예요?
Maybe it will start at 3 o'clock. Are you going to the class?

지금 선생님한테 물어볼 거예요.
I am going to ask my teacher now.

3 시에 시작해요.
It starts at 3 o'clock.

몰라요. 같이 선생님에게 물어봐요.
I don't know. Let's ask to the teacher together.

15 Conversation 대화 K-E

1. Polite conversation between friends.

A: 이 바나나 우유를 선아한테서 받았어요.
B: 맛이 어땠어요?
A: 마실 수 없었어요. 선아는 저에게 너무 단 우유를 줬어요.
B: 저는 단 것을 좋아해요. 우유를 저에게 주세요.

A: I got this banana milk from Seonah.
B: How did it taste?
A: I couldn't drink it. She gave me really sweet milk.
B: I like sweet things. Please give it to me.

2. Polite conversation between two girls who HAVE TO GO!

A: 저 화장실에 갈 수 없어요. 사람이 너무 많아요.
B: 도서관 안에 화장실이 있어요. 같이 갑시다.
A 고마워요. 화장지 있어요?
B: 아니요, 없어요. 제가 살까요?

화장지 and 휴지 mean "toilet paper". 휴지 can also mean "facial tissue"

A: I can't go to that restroom over there. There are too many people.
B: There is a restroom inside of the library. Let's go together.
A: Thank you. Do you have toilet paper?
B: No, I don't. Shall I buy some?

3. **Polite conversation between college students.**

A: 이 책 읽었어요? 이 책은 진짜 재미있는 책이에요.
B: 아니요, 읽을 수 없었어요. 시간이 없었어요. 다음 주까지 시험이 세 개 있어요.
A: 공부 많이 했어요?
B: 네, 했어요. 오늘부터 수학 공부를 시작할 거예요.

A: Did you read this book? It's a really interesting book.
B: No, I couldn't read it. I didn't have time. I have three tests (by) next week.
A: Did you study a lot?
B: Yes, I did. I'll start math studies (from) today.

15 Conversation 대화 E-K

1. **Polite conversation between a friend and a shy girl.**

A: How was Junho's birthday party?
B: I am not going. People asked me too many questions.
A: What did they ask?
B: They asked me my age and name.

A: 준호의 생일 파티는 어땠어요?
B: 가지 않을 거예요. 사람들이 저에게 너무 많이 물어봤어요.
A: 뭐를 물어봤어요?
B: 나이하고 이름을 물어봤어요.

나이 means "age".

2. **Polite conversation between a friend and a man without a car.**

A: Did you really walk from the hospital to the department store by foot?
B: Yes. I just now arrived at the department store.
A: Are you going to walk to the hospital by foot again?
B: No, I can't do it. It is too far.

A: 정말 병원에서 백화점까지 걸어 갔어요?
B: 네. 저는 아까 백화점에 도착했어요.
A: 다시 병원에 걸어 갈 거예요?
B: 아니요, 할 수 없어요. 너무 멀어요.

다시 means "again".

3. Polite conversation between a friend and a lonely man.

A: Did you ask for her phone number?
B: Yes, I did. I just now called her.
A: Did she answer it?
B: No, she didn't answer.

A: 그녀의 전화번호를 물어봤어요?
B: 네, 물어봤어요. 아까 전화했어요.
A: 그녀가 받았어요?
B: 아니요, 받지 않았어요.

받다 means "receive", but sounds more natural to translate as, "answer". 대답하다 is only used for answering questions.

15 Sentence Building 문장 만들기

In each lesson we will build on a previous sentence. Watch it grow and transform each time new concepts are introduced.

제 친구가 어머니한테서 다른 핸드폰을 받을 수 없었어요.
My friend couldn't get a different cell phone from his mother.

Compare how the sentence has changed from the prior lessons:

Lesson 12: 제 친구가 저하고 다른 핸드폰을 샀어요.
My friend bought a different cell phone than me.

Lesson 13: 제 친구가 어머니한테서 다른 핸드폰을 받았어요.
My friend received a different cell phone from his mother.

Lesson 14: 제 친구가 어머니한테서 다른 핸드폰을 받지 않았어요.
My friend didn't get a different cell phone from his mother.

15 Workbook Area

❑ A15-1. Reading comprehension

At your current level, you should understand all of the grammar and words in the following sections. If you are struggling to understand them, review this and prior lessons.

New words in this comprehension: 독일어 (German language), 독일어공부 (German studies)

① 아까 친구한테 전화했어요.

② 제가 다음 달에 한국에서 베를린까지 갈 거예요.

③ 지난달부터 독일어 공부를 시작했어요.

④ 지금도 독일어는 저한테 너무 어려워요.

Dialogue

A 씨: 저는 오후 3 시까지 베를린에 도착할 수 없어요.

B 씨: 몇 시에 도착해요?

A 씨: 몰라요. 아마 5 시에 도착할 거예요.

B 씨: 알았어요.

❑ A15-2. Reading comprehension questions

Answer the following questions about the reading comprehension in the prior section.

1. A 씨는 오후 3 시에 베를린에 도착할 거예요?

____

2. A 씨는 언제부터 독일어 공부를 시작했어요?

____

3. A 씨는 어디부터 어디까지 갈 거예요?

____

❑ A15-3. Fill in the blank

For each number in the Korean sentence, write the appropriate Korean word to match the English translation.

1. ① 5 시② 영화가 ③요.
   At 5 pm the movie started.

   ① ____________ ② ____________ ③ ____________

2. 제 ①은 ②에 ③ 거예요.
   My class will start before noon.

   ① ____________ ② ____________ ③ ____________

3. ①는 나에게 ②을 ③봤어요.
   He asked me my birthday.

   ① ____________ ② ____________ ③ ____________

4. 선생님① 이메일을 ②요.
   I received an e-mail from my teacher.

   ① ____________ ② ____________

5. 그① 전화②를 ③요.
   I couldn't give my number to him.

   ① ____________ ② ____________ ③ ____________

6. 어제 ①을 ②요.
   I listened to music yesterday.

   ① ____________ ② ____________

7. 이 ①를 ② 있어요?
   Can you drink this beer?

   ① ____________ ② ____________

8. 사랑①요.
   I can't love you.

   ① ____________________

9. ①은 ②에 집에 ③ 거예요.
   My parents will come to my house late (at) night.

   ① ____________________ ② ____________________ ③ ____________________

10. 이 ① 길은 남자친구② 같이 ③요.
    I walked this long street with my boyfriend.

    ① ____________________ ② ____________________ ③ ____________________

❑ A15-4. Korean translation

Translate the following conversation into English.

1.
A: 오늘 친구랑 바다에 갈 거예요. 같이 갈 거예요? B: 몇 시에 갈 거예요? A: 2 시에 갈 거예요. B: 저는 갈 수 없어요. 수업이 1 시에 시작해요.
A:
B:
A:
B:

❑ A15-5. English translation

Translate the following conversation into Korean.

1.
A: What are you doing now? B: I am listening to PSY's music. A: I really like PSY. His music is really interesting. Can you give me the music? B: Yes, I can give.
A:
B:
A:
B:

15 Vocabulary Builder

■ Group Q: office words 사무실 단어

연필	pencil
가위	scissors
명함	business card
스테이플러	stapler
종이	paper
테이프	tape
자	ruler
노트북	laptop computer
계산기	calculator
사장님	president (of company)
편지	a letter

Lesson 16:

Not being able to do

16

Before This Lesson

1. Know vocabulary group: Q (office words).
2. Review section 14-1 on 지 않다.

Lesson Goals

1. Learn how to say how an action was accomplished with the "by means marker".
2. Learn how to distinguish between "can't do" and "unable to do".
3. Learn the difference between "present tense" and "ongoing present tense".

From The Teachers

1. In this lesson we teach shorter versions of grammar you already know. Knowing more than one way to say something is important, as each person you meet will have their own speech preferences.

Lesson Highlights

16-3.
처음 (first time, the beginning)

16-5.
Ongoing present tense form ~고 있다 (~ing)

16-12.
~(으)로 by which means marker

16-14.
Unable to do form ~지 못하다

16 New Words 새로운 단어

아직	not yet
일찍	early
늦게	late
처음	first time
다시	again
노래	song
사진	photograph, picture
지하철	subway
기차	train
택시	taxi
자동차	automobile
할머니	grandmother
할아버지	grandfather

16 Word Usage 단어 사용법

❑ 16-1. 아직 (still, not yet)

아직 means "still" or "not yet" and is placed somewhere before the verb. The opposite of 아직 is 이미 or 벌써 (already).

1. 저는 아직 차가 없어요.	I don't have a car yet.
2. 부모님은 아직 도착하지 않았어요.	My parents haven't arrived yet.
3. 불고기 아직 있어요?	Is there still bulgogi (roast meat)?
4. 아직 한국어를 공부해요.	I still study Korean.
5. 아직 시작 하지 않았어요.	I haven't started yet.
6. 뉴욕 아직 추워요?	Is New York still cold?

❑ 16-2. 일찍 (early), 늦게 (late)

일찍 and 늦게 come somewhere before the verb.

Examples

1. 학교에 일찍 갈 거예요. — I will go to school early.
2. 선물을 일찍 받았어요. — I received my present early.
3. 도쿄에서 늦게 출발했어요. — I departed Tokyo late.
4. 늦게 왔어요. 죄송합니다. — I came late. I'm sorry.
5. 늦게 밥을 먹었어요. — I ate dinner late.
6. 오늘 일찍부터 늦게까지 일했어요. — I worked from early until late today.

❑ 16-3. 처음 (first time, the beginning)

There are a few ways you can use 처음 in a sentence.

처음 – the first time, the first

1. 오늘은 처음이에요. — Today is the first time.
2. 이 김밥은 처음이에요. — This gimbap is my first.
3. 처음은 어려워요. — The first time is difficult.

처음에 – in the beginning…, at first…

1. 처음에 어려웠어요. — In the beginning it was difficult.
2. 처음에 좋았어요. — At first it was good.
3. 처음에 재미있었어요. — In the beginning it was fun.

처음부터 – from the beginning…, from the start

1. 처음부터 어려웠어요. — From the beginning it was difficult.
2. 처음부터 좋았어요. — From the start it was good.
3. 처음부터 재미있었어요. — From the beginning it was fun.

처음으로 – for the first time

1. 처음으로 먹었어요. — I ate it for the first time.
2. 처음으로 봤어요. — I saw it for the first time.
3. 처음으로 들었어요. — I heard it for the first time.

Examples

1. 5 월에 처음으로 한국에 갔어요.
   I went to Korea for the first time in May.

2. 제가 이 노래를 처음으로 들어요.
   I'm hearing this song for the first time.

3. 오늘 바다에서 처음으로 수영했어요.
   Today I swam in the ocean for the first time.

특별 정보 Special Information

Often 처음 will be used without the following 으로.

Example sentences

1. 처음 봤어요.	It's the first time I saw it.
2. 처음 들어요.	It's the first time I heard it.
3. 처음 왔어요.	It's the first time I came.

❑ 16-4. 다시 (again)

This works like the English word "again" except that you put it in front of the verb.

Examples

1. 내년에 한국에 다시 갈 거예요.	I am going to Korea again next year.
2. 다시 하자!	Let's do it again!
3. 다시 와 주세요.	Please come again.
4. 다시 물어봐요.	Try to ask again.
5. 어머니한테서 다시 전화를 받았어요.	I got a call from mother again.

16 New Phrases 새로운 어구

1. 배고파요.
I'm hungry.

2. 배가 불러요.
I'm full.

3. 괜찮아요.
It's okay. / I'm okay.

4. 물론이에요.
Of course.

16 New Action Verbs 새로운 동사

Verb	Basic	English	Type
타다	타	to ride	regular
내리다	내려	to get off	regular
자다	자	to sleep	regular
일어나다	일어나	to wake up	regular
말하다	말해	to speak, tell, talk	하다
보내다	보내	to send	regular
쓰다	써	to write	regular
쓰다	써	to use	regular

16 Verb Usage 동사 사용법

❑ 16-5. Ongoing present tense form ~고 있다 (~ing)

The present tense is easily created just by using the BASIC form of a verb. To say "I am doing an action right now" then you will use the ~고 있다 pattern. This pattern is created by adding~고 있다 directly to the stem. After adding ~고 있다 you can then conjugate the verb into various tenses.

(verb stem) + 고 있다
(verb stem) ing

Example sentences

1. 먹고 있어요.	I am eating.
2. 먹고 있었어요.	I was eating.
3. 먹고 있지 않아요.	I am not eating.
4. 먹고 있지 않았어요.	I was not eating.
5. 일하고 있어요.	I am working.
6. 일하고 있었어요.	I was working.
7. 일하고 있지 않아요.	I am not working.
8. 일하고 있지 않았어요.	I was not working.

특별 정보 Special Information

As you learn more Korean you will learn more than one way to say the same thing. For example all of the sentences below mean basically the same thing.

1. 제가 지금 먹어요.	I am eating now.
2. 제가 지금 먹고 있어요.	I am eating now.
3. 제가 지금 먹는 중이에요.	I am in the middle of eating now.

Over time and with more experience you will choose which sentence best suits your situation. One thing that can be said about 먹어요 vs 먹고 있어요 is that there is no ambiguity with 먹고 있어요. Depending on the context 먹어요 can mean "I will eat.", "I am eating", and even "Eat (command)." However, 먹고 있어요 can only mean "I am eating."

❑ 16-6. 타다 (to ride)

The mode of transportation by which you are riding is marked with the object marker 를.

Example sentences

1. 아직 택시를 타고 있어요.
   I'm still riding in a taxi.

2. 여기까지 자전거를 탔어요.
   I rode a bicycle (up to) here.

3. 제가 다음 주에 처음으로 비행기를 탈 거예요.
   I am going to ride an airplane for the first time next week.

4. 내일 이 시간에 비행기를 타고 있을 거예요.
   Tomorrow at this time, I will be riding in an airplane.

❑ 16-7. 내리다 (to get off)

Use the "from location marker" 에서 to mark the mode of transportation that you are getting off of.

(mode of transportation) 에서 내리다
to get off of (mode of transportation)

Example sentences

1. 버스에서 내렸어요.
   I got off of the bus.

2. 지금 비행기에서 내리고 있어요.
   I am getting off of the plane right now.

3. 강남역에서 내릴 거예요.
   I will get off at Gangnam station.

   The 에서 in this sentence is the "event location" marker and NOT the "from location marker".

4. 기차에서 내립시다.
   Let's get off of the train.

❑ 16-8. 자다 (to sleep), 일어나다 (to wake up)

The time that you wake up, or sleep is marked with the time marker 에. The place that you sleep is marked with 에서.

Example sentences

1. 어제 여동생은 몇 시에 잤어요?
   What time did your little sister sleep yesterday?

2. 아까까지 차에서 자고 있었어요.
   Up until just a moment ago I was sleeping in my car.

3. 저는 오늘 너무 늦게 일어났어요.
   Today I woke up too late.

4. 토요일에 몇 시에 일어날 거예요?
   What time will you wake up on Saturday?

❑ 16-9. 말하다 (to speak, to tell, to talk)

The thing you are talking about is marked with 을/를. The person you are speaking with is marked with any of the three "with" words taught in 11-2. The person who you are telling something to do is marked with 에게 / 한테.

Example sentences

1. 친구랑 말해요.
   I'm talking with a friend.

2. 사장님에게 말했어요?
   Did you tell the president?

3. 선생님한테 말해 봐요.
   Try telling the teacher.

4. 버스에서 많이 말해요.
   I talk a lot on the bus.

5. 매일 한국어를 말해요.
   I speak Korean everyday.

특별 정보 Special Information

SUMMARY: 말하다 isn't used for describing the ability to speak a language. 말하다 is more about physical act of speaking, than it is about ability to speak. With language you use 하다 to say "do" a language.

1. 일본어를 할 수 있어요?
   Can you speak (do) Japanese?

2. 리키는 한국어를 할 수 있어요.
   Ricky can speak (do) Korean.

❑ 16-10. 보내다 (to send)

The item being sent is marked with, you guessed it, the object marker 을/를. The person being sent the item is marked with 한테 or 에게.

send (something) to (someone)
(someone) 한테(something) 을/를 보내다

Example sentences

1. 할아버지한테 사진을 보냈어요.
   I sent pictures to my grandfather.

2. 남동생한테 돈을 보낼 거예요.
   I will send money to my younger brother.

3. 준호 씨에게 이메일을 보낼까요?
   Shall I send an email to Junho?

❑ 16-11. 쓰다 (to write), 쓰다 (to use)

Both of these verbs are exactly the same in terms of how they are used and which particles are used. The only difference is their meaning. The thing you are writing or using is marked with the object marker 을/를. The person you are writing to is marked with 한테 or 에게.

write (something) to (someone)
(someone) 한테(something) 을/를 쓰다

use (something)
(something) 을/를 쓰다

Example sentences (쓰다 to write)

1. 매달 할머니한테 편지를 써요.
   I write a letter to my grandmother every month.

2. 이메일을 선생님에게 아직 쓰지 않았어요.
   I didn't write an email to teacher yet.

Example sentences (쓰다 to use)

1. 이 노트북을 쓸 수 있어요?
   Can I use this laptop?

2. 계산기를 쓰지 않았어요.
   I didn't use a calculator.

16 Grammar 문법

16-12. ~(으)로 by which means marker

This marker is VERY handy! It's used to mark the method, or tool that was used to do something with. If there is no 받침 OR if the 받침 is ㄹ you just add 로. For all other 받침 you add 으로.

no 받침	with 받침	with (ㄹ) 받침
차로 by car	트럭으로 by truck	지하철로 by subway

Example sentences (transportation)

1. 버스**로** 갈 거예요. — I will go **by** bus.
2. 비행기**로** 갈 거예요. — I will go **by** airplane.
3. 택시**로** 갈 거예요. — I will go **by** taxi.
4. 지하철**로** 갈 거예요. — I will go **by** subway.
5. 이메일**로** 보냈어요. — I sent it **by** email.

Example sentences (methods)

1. 카드**로** 샀어요. — I bought it **with** my credit card.
2. 젓가락**으로** 먹었어요. — I ate **with** chopsticks.
3. 연필**로** 썼어요. — I wrote it **with** a pencil.
4. 눈**으로** 봤어요. — I saw it **with** my eyes.
6. 핸드폰**으로** 전화했어요. — I called **with** my cell phone.

Example sentences (languages)

1. 영어**로** 말해 주세요. — Please speak **in** English.
2. 한국어**로** 말해 주세요. — Please speak **in** Korean.
3. 일본어**로** 말해 주세요. — Please speak **in** Japanese.

❍ 16-13. ~들 Plurals in Korean

들 is added to nouns to make them plural. However, when it's obvious from the context, 들 is not needed. 들 is most commonly added after people but can be used after objects also. All of the following words CAN be plural OR singular WITHOUT the 들, however, adding 들 makes it clear that there is more than one.

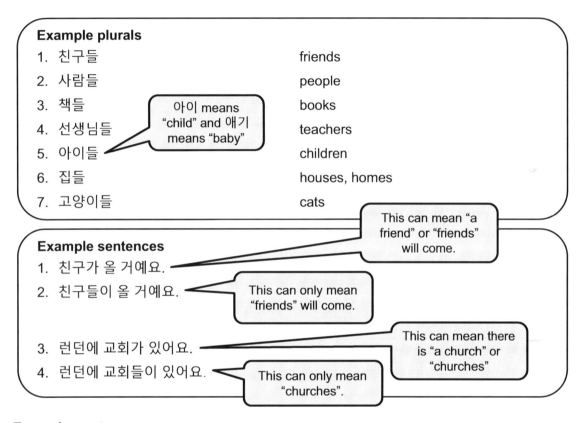

Example plurals

1. 친구들 — friends
2. 사람들 — people
3. 책들 — books
4. 선생님들 — teachers
5. 아이들 — children
6. 집들 — houses, homes
7. 고양이들 — cats

아이 means "child" and 애기 means "baby"

Example sentences

1. 친구가 올 거예요.
2. 친구들이 올 거예요.
3. 런던에 교회가 있어요.
4. 런던에 교회들이 있어요.

This can mean "a friend" or "friends" will come.

This can only mean "friends" will come.

This can mean there is "a church" or "churches"

This can only mean "churches".

Example sentences

1. 고양이들이 귀여워요. — The cats are cute.
2. 이 집들은 예뻐요. — These houses are pretty.
3. 그 여자들은 한국 사람입니다. — Those girls are Korean.
4. 대학생들이 숙제가 많아요. — College students have a lot of homework.
5. 이 강아지들은 너무 시끄러워요. — These puppies are too loud.
6. 이 연필들이 길어요. — These pencils are long.

❍ 16-14. Unable to do form ~지 못하다

In lesson 15 you learned how to say "can" and "can't do". Now we will learn a much stronger form of "can't do". ~지 못하다 (pronounced 모타다) means that you are unable to do something. There is perhaps a physical barrier that prevents you from doing it.

For example, you have no legs, therefore you are "UNABLE to walk" (**걷지 못해요**). If your mom doesn't let you go to a party, then you "CAN NOT go" (**갈 수 없어요**), but there isn't a physical limitation. The pattern is very similar to the 지 않다 (won't, don't do) form.

STEM + 지 못하다	
가다 to go	가지 못하다 unable to go
먹다 to eat	먹지 못하다 unable to eat
하다 to do	하지 못하다 unable to do
자다 to sleep	자지 못하다 unable to sleep
보다 to see	보지 못하다 unable to see

1. **Polite conversation at a concert with many tall people.**
   A: 볼 수 있어요? — Can you see?
   B: 보지 못해요. (pronounced 모태요) — I'm unable to see.

2. **Polite conversation with a person who hasn't learned to ride a bicycle.**
   A: 자전거를 탈 수 있어요? — Can you ride a bicycle?
   B: 타지 못해요. — I'm unable to ride.

❍ 16-15. Contracted versions of 지 못하다 and 지 않다

There are shorter versions that are commonly used for ~지 못하다 (unable to) and ~지 않다 (won't, don't) forms. The short versions are 못 and 안. They are added directly in front of the 다 form of the verb. Then all you do is treat it as a NEW verb and follow all the patterns and rules you already know. Simple!

	안 (won't, don't)	못 (unable)
가다 to go	안 가다 won't, don't go	못 가다 unable to go
먹다 to eat	안 먹다 won't, don't eat	못 먹다 unable to eat
하다 to do	안 하다 won't, don't do	못 하다 unable to do
자다 to sleep	안 자다 won't, don't sleep	못 자다 unable to sleep
보다 to see	안 보다 won't, don't see	못 보다 unable to see

⟨!⟩ 특별 정보 Special Information ⟨!⟩

Even though in the prior section we taught distinct differences between ㄹ 수 없다 (can not) and 못 + verb (unable) actual usage if among Koreans doesn't follow such clear lines. For example, it's more common to just say 못 해요 to say you can't do something than 할 수 없어요.

Examples (안)

1. 오늘 안 먹었어요.
   I didn't eat today.

2. 안 자요.
   I won't sleep.

3. 저는 지하철을 안 탈 거예요.
   I will not ride the subway.

4. 숙제를 안 해요.
   I didn't do my homework.

Examples (못)

1. 오늘 못 먹었어요.
   Today I couldn't eat.

2. 못 자요.
   I can't sleep.

3. 저는 지하철을 못 타요.
   I can't ride the subway.

4. 숙제를 못 해요.
   I couldn't do my homework.

IMPORTANT! 안 and 못 contractions can NOT be used with descriptive verbs. Descriptive verbs can only use ~지 못하다 (unable to) and ~지 않다.

ALSO IMPORTANT! When using the contracted 안 and 못 with 하다 verbs they must come directly before the 하다 and never before the full verb.

안 / 못 Placement Rule

Action Verbs 안	Action Verbs 못
수영 **안** 하다 **won't / don't swim**	수영 **못** 하다 **can't swim**
공부 **안** 하다 **won't / don't study**	공부 **못** 하다 **can't study**
대답 **안** 하다 **won't / don't answer**	대답 **못** 하다 **can't answer**

Examples (안)

1. 금요일에 출발 **안** 해요.
   I **won't** depart on Friday.

2. 너를 사랑 **안** 해.
   I **don't** love you.

Examples (못)

1. 세 시에 도착 **못** 했어요.
   I **couldn't** arrive at 3:00.

2. 전화가 없어요. 전화 **못** 해요.
   I don't have a phone. I **can't** call.

특별 정보 Special Information

SUMMARY: Proper usage of ~지 않다 and ~지 못하다 is important.
It's important to understand the difference between "not doing something" and "not being able to do something". In English, we might say "I didn't see you yesterday" and no one would be offended. However, the form ~지 않다 / 안~ implies "chose not to".

So, if you say 어제 보지 않았어요 to a friend, you are saying "I chose not to see you yesterday". The better phrase is, 어제 보지 못했어요 (I couldn't see you yesterday").

Examples (my choice)

1. 일 하지 않았어요.
   I didn't work.

2. 전화 안 했어요.
   I didn't call.

3. 이메일을 안 보내요.
   I won't send the email.

Examples (not my choice)

1. 일 하지 못했어요.
   I couldn't work.

2. 전화 못 했어요.
   I couldn't call.

3. 이메일을 못 보내요.
   I can't send the email.

❍ 16-16. Bonus ~고 있다 examples

Since we taught the "ongoing present tense" form at the beginning of the lesson, you might need a quick review. Here are some bonus examples.

Example sentences

1. 아이들은 자고 있어요.
   The children are sleeping.

2. 제 친구들이 버스를 타고 있어요.
   My friends are riding the bus.

3. 지금 어머니하고 티비를 보고 있어요.
   Right now I am watching TV with my mother.

4. 다섯 시까지 일하고 있었어요.
   I was working until 5:00.

Notice how the ~고 있다 pattern is now past tense.

5. 제 여자친구는 할아버지의 노트북을 쓰고 있어요.
   My girlfriend is using my grandfather's laptop computer.

6. 지금 친구들이랑 맛있는 것을 먹고 있어요.
   Right now I am eating delicious things with my friends.

16 Question and Answer 질문과 대답

1. **저에게 사진 보냈어요?**
Did you send a picture to me?

아직 보내지 않았어요. 다음 주에 보낼 거예요.
I didn't send it yet. I will send it next week.

보낼 수 없었어요. 아침에 진짜 늦게 일어났어요.
I couldn't send it. I woke up really late in the morning.

네, 사진과 선물을 같이 보냈어요.
Yes, I sent a picture and a present together.

2. **버스를 탔어요?**
Did you ride a bus?

아니요, 타지 못했어요. 어제 늦게 잤어요.
No, I wasn't able to ride it. I slept late yesterday.

아니요, 오늘은 택시 탈 거예요.
No, I'll take a taxi today.

네, 지금 타고 있어요. 저는 학교에 일찍 도착할 거예요. 이 버스가 일찍 출발했어요.
Yes, I am riding one now. I will arrive at school early. This bus departed early.

3. **우리 선생님한테 편지를 쓸까요?**
Shall we write a letter to our teacher?

저는 어제 썼어요.
I wrote it yesterday.

지금 쓰고 있어요.
I'm writing it now.

이미 선생님에게 이메일로 보냈어요.
I already sent it to her by email.

지금 쓰자!
Let's write it now!

4. **저는 비행기에서 내렸어요. 어디예요? 공항에 올 거예요?**
   I got off the airplane. Where are you? Are you going to come to the airport?

   지금 가고 있어요. 공항 앞에서 먹을까요?
   I am going now. Shall we eat in front of the airport?

   지하철을 탔어요. 5 시에 도착 할 거예요.
   I rode the subway. I will arrive at 5 pm.

   지금 차가 없어요. 공항에 못 가요.
   I don't have a car right now. I'm unable to go the airport.

5. **뭐해요?**
   What are you doing?

   동생들하고 물고기에 대해 배우고 있어요.
   I am learning about fish with my younger siblings.

   그냥 티비를 보고 있어요.
   I'm just watching TV.

   오늘 강남에 가요. 지금 버스를 타고 있어요.
   I am going to Gangnam today. I am riding a bus now.

> 강남 is a famous section of Seoul known for its wealth and plastic surgery centers.

16 Conversation 대화 K-E

1. **Polite conversation between students studying Korean.**
   A: 저는 내일 한국에 가요. 한국에 가 봤어요?
   B: 네, 가 봤어요.
   A: 언제 갔어요?
   B: 2010 년에 처음으로 갔어요.

> The past tense of BASIC + 보다 form, taught in section 13-8, can also be translated as "Have you ever (verb)ed" depending on the context.

   A: I am going to Korea tomorrow. Have you been to Korea?
   B: Yes, I have been.
   A: When did you go?
   B: I went for the first time in 2010.

2. **Polite conversation between friends.**

A: 오늘 밤에 나랑 같이 조지의 결혼식에 갈 수 있어요?

B: 아니요, 가지 못해요. 아침 일찍 수업이 있어요. 조지에게 이미 말했어요.

A: 알았어요.

A: Can you go to George's wedding ceremony with me tonight?

B: No, I am unable to go. I have a class early in the morning. I already told George.

A: Okay.

16 Conversation 대화 E-K

1. **Casual conversation between classmates working on a school project.**

A: Can I use your laptop?

B: No, I am using it right now. Ask George.

A: George, are you going to use your laptop now? My laptop is at home. Can I use yours?

C: Yes, you can. Are you going to send an email to your teacher?

A: No, I will send it to my mother.

A: 네 노트북을 쓸 수 있어?

B: 아니, 지금 내가 쓰고 있어. 조지한테 물어봐.

A: 조지야, 지금 노트북 쓸 거야? 내 노트북은 집에 있어. 네 것을 쓸 수 있어?

C: 응, 써. 선생님한테 이메일 보낼 거야?

A: 아니, 내 어머니한테 보낼 거야.

In casual speech 야 without 받침 and 아 with 받침 is added after names.

Because this is a casual conversation you can use 네 것 to say "yours".

2. **Polite conversation between friends.**

A: Can you read this Japanese?

B: No, I am unable to read it. I am still studying Japanese. I am going to Japan next year.

A: Is it your first time?

B: No, I went to Japan last year too.

A: Do you have time now? Shall we study with my Japanese friends?

B: Really? Of course.

A: 이 일본어를 읽을 수 있어요?
B: 아니요, 못 읽어요. 저는 아직 일본어를 공부하고 있어요. 내년에 일본에 갈 거예요.
A: 처음이에요?
B: 아니요, 작년에도 갔어요.
A: 지금 시간이 있어요? 제 일본인 친구들이랑 공부 할까요?
B: 정말요? 물론이에요.

3. Polite conversation between a boyfriend and girlfriend.

A: Are you sleeping?
B: No, I'm not sleeping.
A: I had a nightmare for the first time. Can you come to my house?
B: I have work from early tomorrow. I'm unable to go.

A: 자고 있어요?
B: 아니요, 안 자요.
A: 처음으로 악몽을 꿨어요. 제 집에 올 수 있어요?
B: 내일 일찍부터 일이 있어요. 못 가요.

The verb "to have a dream or nightmare" is 꾸다. It's conjugated like 주다.

16 Sentence Building 문장 만들기

In each lesson we will build on a previous sentence. Watch it grow and transform each time new concepts are introduced.

제 친구가 처음으로 자전거를 타고 있어요.
My friend is riding a bicycle for the first time.

Compare how the sentence has changed from the prior lessons:

Lesson 13: 제 친구가 어머니한테서 다른 핸드폰을 받았어요.
My friend received a different cell phone from his mother.

Lesson 14: 제 친구가 어머니한테서 다른 핸드폰을 받지 않았어요.
My friend didn't get a different cell phone from his mother.

Lesson 15: 제 친구가 어머니한테서 다른 핸드폰을 받을 수 없었어요.
My friend couldn't get a different cell phone from his mother.

16 Workbook Area

❑ A16-1. Reading comprehension

At your current level, you should understand all of the grammar and words in the following sections. If you are struggling to understand them, review this and prior lessons.

New words for this comprehension: 기차표 (train ticket), 아이스크림 (ice cream)

① 제 남자친구는 저한테 기차표를 보냈어요.

② 아침 일찍 부산에 기차로 갔어요.

③ 오늘 처음으로 남자친구하고 닭갈비를 먹을 거예요.

④ 오늘 밤에도 같이 먹을 거예요.

Dialogue

A 씨: 몇 시에 닭갈비 먹을까요?

B 씨: 아침 8 시 15 분에 부산에 도착할 거예요.

A 씨: 오늘 밤에 단 것도 먹읍시다!

B 씨: 좋아요. 아이스크림 먹읍시다.

❑ A16-2. Reading comprehension questions

Answer the following questions about the reading comprehension in the prior section.

1. A 씨는 부산에서 뭐를 처음으로 먹을 거예요?

____

2. A 씨랑 B 씨는 오늘 밤에 뭐를 먹을 거예요?

____

3. A 씨는 몇 시에 부산에 출발했어요?

____

❑ A16-3. Fill in the blank

For each number in the Korean sentence, write the appropriate Korean word to match the English translation.

1. 지하철① 학교에 ② 거예요.
   I will go home by subway.

   ① ____________ ② ____________

2. 고양이①이 ②에 ③ 있어요.
   There are a lot of cats at home.

   ① ____________ ② ____________ ③ ____________

3. 저는 ①를 못 ②요.
   I am unable to ride in an airplane.

   ① ____________ ② ____________

4. ①에 ② ③요.
   I slept late last night.

   ① ____________ ② ____________ ③ ____________

5. 제가 ① 한국어를 못 ②요.
   I am unable to read Korean yet.

   ① ____________ ② ____________

6. ①에 ② 해③요.
   Please answer your email.

   ① ____________ ② ____________ ③ ____________

7. ①를 ② ③요?
   Are you unable to eat fish?

   ① ____________ ② ____________ ③ ____________

8. ① ②를 안 ③.
I won't use these scissors.

① ____________ ② ____________ ③ ____________

9. ①부터 ②를 좋아③요.
From the start I liked him.

① ____________ ② ____________ ③ ____________

10. 친구①② ③ 있어요.
I am talking to my friends

① ____________ ② ____________ ③ ____________

❑ A16-4. Korean translation

Translate the following conversation into English.

1.
A: 어디에서 내렸어요? B: 아직 안 내렸어요. 지금도 버스를 타고 있어요. A: 여기에 늦게 도착할 거예요? B: 네, 아마 3 시에 도착할 거예요.
A:
B:
A:
B:

16 Vocabulary Builder

■ Group R: sports 스포츠

스포츠	sports
탁구	ping pong, table tennis
농구	basketball
축구	soccer
야구	baseball
배구	volleyball
수영	swimming
태권도	tae kwon do
스타크래프트	StarCraft

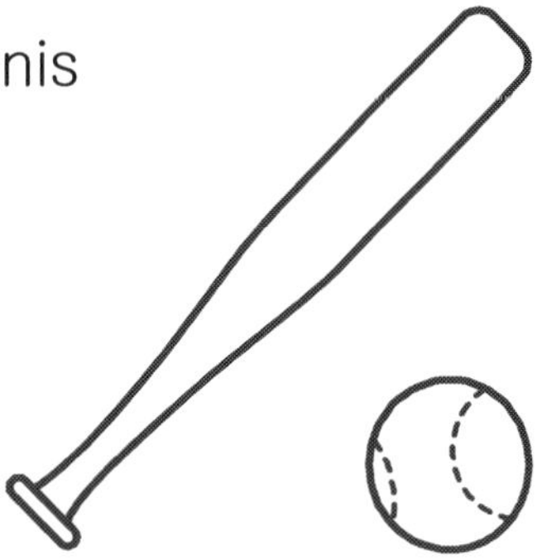

StarCraft is a popular PC game that is even broadcast on TV in South Korea.

■ Group S: colors 색깔

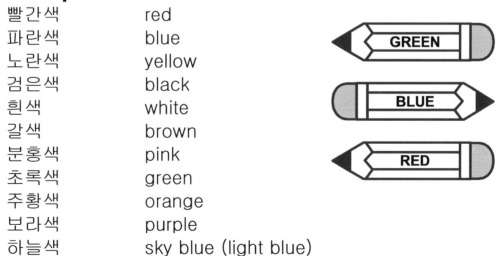

빨간색	red
파란색	blue
노란색	yellow
검은색	black
흰색	white
갈색	brown
분홍색	pink
초록색	green
주황색	orange
보라색	purple
하늘색	sky blue (light blue)

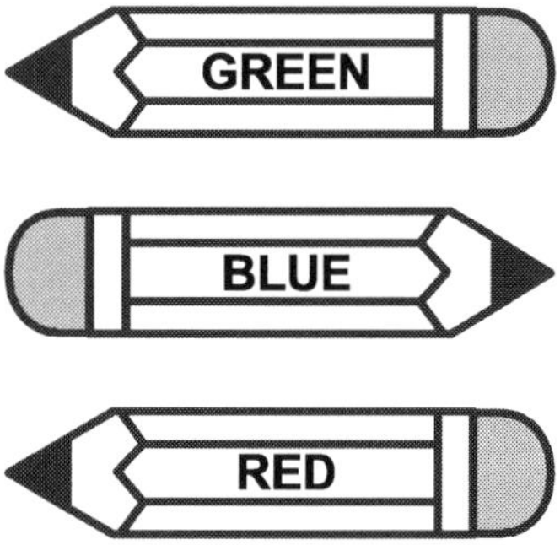

16 Learning Korean Resource List

KoreanFromZero.com

There is a 100% free course of this book on the site. Also check out our YouTube channel.
http://www.koreanfromzero.com / http://www.youtube.com/KoreanFromZero

Naver Korean Dictionary

One of the best online K-E and E-K dictionaries.
http://endic.naver.com

Korean YouTuber: Deeva Jessica

Deeva Jessica is a fantastic listening resource. She tells interesting stories in Korean and her "Saturday Mystery" series is well known amongst many Koreans.
https://www.youtube.com/deevajessica

Lesson 17:

Wanting and Colors

Before This Lesson

1. Learn the words in vocabulary groups: R (sports) and S (colors)
2. Review the counters you have learned in prior lessons.

Lesson Goals

1. Learn how to say all tenses of the “want to” verb form.
2. Learn how to use Korean colors as nouns and like adjectives.

From The Teachers

1. This is the last lesson! Congratulations on making it all the way! Many people quit, where you have persevered. Good job! 수고 하셨습니다!

17

Lesson Highlights

17-1.
어느~ (which), 무슨~ (what), 어떤~ (what kind of)

17-11.
Korean color usage

17-13.
Wanting to ~고 싶다

17-14.
Sentence connector words

17 New Words 새로운 단어

무슨	what~
어느	which~
어떤	what kind of~, what type of~
별로	not so~ much
더	more
색깔	color
동물	animal
시합	sports game, match
와인	wine
교육	education
노래방	singing room (karaoke)
노래	song
딸	daughter
아들	son
공	ball
치마	skirt
역	station (train etc.)
최근	recently

17 Word Usage 단어 사용법

❑ 17-1. 어느~ (which), 무슨~ (what), 어떤~ (what kind of)

All of these words require a noun directly after them.

Example sentences

1. **무슨** 색깔을 좋아해요? — **What** color do you like?
2. **무슨** 음식을 싫어해요? — **What** foods do you dislike?
3. **어떤** 동물을 좋아해요? — **What kind of** animals do you like?
4. **어떤** 것을 샀어요? — **What type of** things did you buy?
5. **어느** 식당에 갔어요? — **Which** restaurant did you go to?
6. **어느** 것이 싸요? — **Which** one is cheap?

특별 정보 Special Information

In Korean the "one" pronoun is 것. 것 also means "thing"

1. 매운 **것**을 주세요. — Give me the spicy **one** please.
2. 비싼 **것**을 좋아해요. — I like expensive **things**.
3. **어느** 것을 좋아해요? — Which **one** do you like?

❑ 17-2. 별로 (not so~ much, not that much)

별로 is used before negative tense action and descriptive verbs to say, "not so much" or "not that often". It isn't with positive tenses. 별로 lowers the frequency or amount if the verb.

Example sentences

1. 오늘은 **별로** 춥지 않아요. — Today isn't **so** cold.
2. 나는 사과를 **별로** 좋아하지 않아요. — I don't like apples **that much**.
3. 미국에는 **별로** 안 가요. — I don't go to America **that often**.
4. 농구 시합을 **별로** 안 봐요. — I don't watch basketball matches **often**.
5. 파티에서 선물을 **별로** 받지 않았어요. — I didn't get **that many** presents at the party.

❑ 17-3. 더 (more)

Add 더 in front of any verb to say "did more" or "will do more".

Example sentences

1. 물 **더** 주세요. — **More** water please.
2. 과일을 **더** 샀어요. — I bought **more** fruit.
3. 친구들이 **더** 왔어요. — **More** friends came.
4. 고양이가 **더** 필요해요. — I need **more** cats.
5. **더** 필요했어요. — I needed **more**.

Counter words can also be added to the sentence.

Example sentences

1. 와인 **한 잔** 더 주세요. — **One** more **glass** of wine please.
2. 과일을 **세 개** 더 샀어요. — I bought **three** more **pieces** of fruit.
3. 친구들 **다섯 명**이 더 왔어요. — **Five** more friends came.
4. 고양이 **두 마리**가 더 필요해요. — I need **two** more cats.
5. **5 분**이 더 필요했어요. — I needed **five** more **minutes**.

17 New Descriptive Verbs 새로운 형용사

Verb	Basic	English	Type
중요하다	중요해	to be important	하다
아프다	아파	to be sick, to hurt	regular
슬프다	슬퍼	to be sad	regular
기쁘다	기뻐	to be happy	regular
배고프다	배고파	to be hungry	regular
배부르다	배불러	to be full	르 irregular

17 Descriptive Verb Usage 형용사 사용법

❑ 17-4. 중요하다 (to be important)

The item that is important is marked with the topic 은/는 or subject marker 이/가.

Example sentences

1. 친구들은 너무 중요해요. Friends are very important.
2. 부모님은 아이에게 중요해요. Parents are important to children.
3. 한국 사람에게 교육이 중요해요. For Koreans education is important.
4. 학교에 중요한 사람이 올 거예요. An important person is coming to school.
5. 스타크래프트가 중요하지 않아요. StarCraft isn't important.

WE REQUIRE MORE MINERALS!

❑ 17-5. 아프다 (to be sick, to hurt)

In Korean, "being sick" and, "hurting" are the same word. The item that hurts is marked with the topic or subject marker.

Example sentences

1. 제 머리가 아파요. My head hurts.
2. 아까 제 눈이 진짜 아팠어요. My eyes really hurt just now.
3. 제 할아버지는 아파요. My grandfather is sick.
4. 몸이 아파! My body hurts!
5. 팔꿈치가 아주 아파요. My elbow hurts a lot.
6. 저는 수요일까지 아팠어요. I was sick until Wednesday.

❑ 17-6. 기쁘다 (happy), 슬프다 (sad)

These verbs can only be used to describe your own emotional state. In KFZ! book 2 we will learn how to use these verbs to describe other people's emotional state using phrases like "He looks happy" or "I think she is happy" etc.

Example sentences

1. 저는 오늘 정말 기뻐요.	I'm really happy today.
2. 저는 지난주부터 슬퍼요.	I am sad since last week.
3. 어제 기뻤어요.	I was happy yesterday.
4. 아마 다음 주부터 제가 슬플 거예요.	I'll probably be sad from next week.

❑ 17-7. 배고프다 (to be hungry), 배부르다 (to be full)

배고프다 (to be hungry) is a regular verb but 배부르다 (to be full) is a 르 irregular.
NOTE: Review section 6-4 BASIC rule #5 for both of these verbs.

르 irregular BASIC form rule

remove 다	르 changes to 러	add ㄹ before 러
to be full	BASIC rule #5	BASIC form
배부르	배부러 →	배불러

Example sentences

1. 아침부터 배불러요.	I'm full since morning.
2. 배고파!	I'm hungry!
3. 어제 정말 배고팠어요.	I was really hungry yesterday.

17 New Action Verbs 새로운 동사

Verb	Basic	English	Type
연습하다	연습해	to practice	하다
노래하다	노래해	to sing	하다
만나다	만나	to meet	regular
놀다	놀아	to play, hang out	regular

17 Verb Usage 동사 사용법

❑ 17-8. 연습하다 (to practice), 노래하다 (to sing)

The song you sing, or thing you practice is marked with the object marker 을/를.

Example sentences

1. 저는 이 노래를 많이 연습했어요.
   I practiced this song a lot.
2. 제 아버지는 노래 잘 해요.
   My father sings well.
3. 저는 공원에서 매일 야구를 연습해요.
   I practice baseball everyday in the park.
4. 이 노래를 노래해 주세요.
   Please sing this song.

❑ 17-9. 만나다 (to meet)

The person you are meeting with is marked with one of any of the three "with" markers 하고, 랑/이랑, 와/과 learned in section 11-3.

Example sentences

1. 어디에서 만날까요?
   Where shall we meet?
2. 처음에 어디에서 만났어요?
   Where did you meet the first time?
3. 내일 남자친구의 부모님하고 처음으로 만날 거예요.
   Tomorrow I will meet with my boyfriend's parents for the first time.
4. 다음 주 화요일에 선생님이랑 몇 시에 만날 수 있어요?
   What time can you meet with the teacher next Tuesday?

❑ 17-10. 놀다 (to play, hang out)

놀다 is not used to "play" a musical instrument. It's used to "play", "hang out", or "get together" with friends. You can use any of the "with" markers to say who you will play with.

[person]와/과 놀다
to play / hang out with [person]

Example sentences

1. 할아버지는 아이들과 놀고 있어요.
   Grandfather is playing with the children.

2. 어제 친구하고 새벽까지 놀았어요.
   Yesterday I hung out with friends until dawn.

3. 제 딸들은 친구의 집에서 놀고 있었어요.
   My daughters were playing at a friends house.

4. 내일 놀자.
   Let's hang out tomorrow.

5. 다음 주에 친구랑 놀고 싶어요.
   Next week I want to hang out with my friends.

The "want to" form is taught in section 17-13.

17 Grammar 문법

17-11. Korean color usage

The color words are in Group S of the Vocabulary Builder section. The 색 part means "color". The colors are all listed in their noun form, but some colors have multiple forms and versions. To keep it simple we will start by using the noun forms only.

Example sentences (colors as nouns)

1. 나는 초록색을 좋아해요.
   I like green.

2. 제 차가 파란색이에요.
   My car is blue.

3. 축구공은 검은색과 흰색이에요.
   Soccer balls are black and white.

You can use "and" between colors.

4. 이 사과는 빨간색이 아닙니다.
   This apple isn't red.

5. 아까 갈색 물고기 두 마리가 있었어요.
   Just now there were two brown fish.

Noun versions of the colors can be put in front of any noun to change the color of the noun.

Example sentences (noun colors as modifiers)

1. 빨간색 차를 좋아해요. — I like red cars.
2. 초록색 사과가 써요. — Green apples are bitter.
3. 분홍색 치마가 필요해요. — I need a pink skirt.
4. 보라색 포도가 맛있어요. — Purple grapes taste good.
5. 어제 하늘색 자전거를 탔어요. — Yesterday I rode a light blue bicycle.

Example conversation

A: 오늘 재미있는 택시를 탔어요. 색깔이 진짜 예뻤어요!
B: 그 택시는 무슨 색깔이었어요?
A: 분홍색하고 노란색이었어요.
B: 저도 금요일에 비슷한 택시를 탔어요.

A: Today I rode in an interesting taxi. The colors were really beautiful.
B: What color was that taxi?
A: It was pink and yellow.
B: I also rode in a similar taxi on Friday.

특별 정보 Special Information

Red, blue, yellow, black and white all have a special native Korean versions.

Native Korean	English	Modifier version
빨갛다	red	빨간
파랗다	blue	파란
노랗다	yellow	노란
까맣다, 검다	black	까만, 검은
하얗다, 희다	white	하얀, 흰

Example sentences

1. 우리 대학교 앞에 빨간 차가 많아요.
   There are a lot of red cars in front of my college.

2. 병원에 하얀 것이 많아요.
   There are a lot of white things in hospitals.

3. 지난 주 토요일에 검은 컴퓨터를 샀어요.
   I bought a black computer last Saturday.

❍ 17-12. Please don't do this ~지 마세요

In section 15-9 we learned "Please do." ~지 마세요 means the opposite, "Please don't do."

(STEM) + 지 마세요.
Please (verb).

Example sentences

1. 가지 마세요. Please don't go.
2. 오지 마세요. Please don't come.
3. 사지 마세요. Please don't buy it.
4. 하지 마세요. Please don't do it.
5. 먹지 마세요. Please don't eat it.

특별 정보 Special Information

~지 마세요 is polite, but you can make it casual / strong / rude by dropping the 세요.

Example sentences

1. 가지 마! Don't go!
2. 먹지 마! Don't eat it!
3. 자지 마! Don't sleep!
4. 보지 마! Don't look!

❍ 17-13. Wanting to ~고 싶다

Have you wanted to say "I want to eat.", or "I want to play."? Well now you can! This form is created by adding ~고 싶다 after the verb STEM.

STEM + 고 싶다 (Want to do~)			
가다 to go	→ 가고 싶다 to want to go	주다 to give	→ 주고 싶다 to want to give
먹다 to eat	→ 먹고 싶다 to want to eat	배우다 to learn	→ 배우고 싶다 to want to learn
하다 to do	→ 하고 싶다 to want to do	사다 to buy	→ 사고 싶다 to want to buy

Just like with prior verb tense changes, we are going to consider STEM + 고 싶다 as a completely new verb. Using the patterns we know, we can now make future, past, negative tenses of the 고 싶다 portion.

Conjugating ~고 싶다 (Want to do~)

Positive Forms	Negative Forms
하고 싶어요. **I want to do.**	하고 싶지 않아요. **I don't want to do.**
하고 싶었어요. **I wanted to do.**	하고 싶지 않았어요. **I didn't want to do.**

Example sentences

1. 단 것을 먹고 싶어요.	I want to eat something sweet.
2. 맥주를 마시고 싶지 않아요.	I don't want to drink beer.
3. 어제 영화를 보고 싶었어요.	I wanted to see a movie yesterday.
4. 전화를 받고 싶지 않았어요.	I didn't want to answer the phone.
5. 진짜 자고 싶어요!	I really want to sleep.
6. 강남역에서 내리고 싶어요.	I want to get off at Gangnam station.
7. 작년부터 한국어 배우고 싶었어요.	I wanted to learn Korean from last year.

특별 정보 Special Information

In Korea, the verb 원하다 means, "to want a~". It is used when you want a noun. For example, "I want money." etc. However, this structure is not as broadly used in Korean as it is in English. Many students of Korean assume 원하다 is used like the English "I want a~".

This is not the case. 원하다 has a much deeper meaning. It's more like a "hoping for" or "longing for" something. Typically when English speakers say, "I want a car", Koreans will say 차를 사고 싶어요 (I want to buy a car.) instead. You should fight the instinct to say "I want a~" and instead use the most appropriate verb.

❍ 17-14. Sentence connector words

Welcome, to the last grammar section in the entire book! In this section we learn how to connect two sentences together. This is done by using a word in front of the second sentence that connects it to the first. Here are the words you need to know:

하지만	but, however
그리고	and then
그래서	so, therefore, that's why

These words are normally only said BETWEEN sentences. It's okay to have a pause if required after the connector word.

Example sentences

1. 배불러요. **하지만** 더 먹고 싶어요.
   I am full. **But** I want to eat more.

2. 일월에 처음으로 한국에 갔어요. **그리고**, 중국에도 갔어요.
   I went to Korea for the first time in January. **And then** I went to China too.

3. 최근 별로 공부하지 않았어요. **그래서** 제 성적이 안 좋아요.
   Recently I haven't studied much. **That's why** my grades aren't good.

17 Question and Answer 질문과 대답

1. **언제 조지를 만날 거예요?**
   When are you going to meet George?

   조지를 별로 만나고 싶지 않아요.
   I don't want to meet him that much.

   별로 should come just prior to the verb.

   어제 이미 만났어요. 우리는 치킨을 너무 많이 먹었어요. 그래서 케이크를 못 먹었어요.
   I already met him yesterday. We ate too much chicken. So we were unable to eat cake.

   만날 수 없었어요. 조지는 아파요. 그래서 다음 주에 만날 거예요.
   I couldn't meet him. He is sick. So I am going to meet him next week.

2. **축구를 연습하고 싶어요?**
   Do you want to practice soccer?

   네, 하고 싶어요. 하지만 이 장소는 너무 작아요.
   Yes, I want to practice. But this place is too small.

   별로 안 하고 싶어요. 저는 야구를 연습하고 싶어요.
   No, I don't want to that much. I want to practice baseball.

   아니요, 안 하고 싶어요. 아침밥을 못 먹었어요. 그래서 저는 너무 배고파요.
   아침밥이 중요해요.

   No, I don't want to. I was unable to eat breakfast. So I am really hungry.
   I need breakfast.

3. **너랑 놀고 싶어. 시간 있어?**
   I want to hang out with you. Do you have time?

   노래방에서 노래할 거예요. 같이 갈까요?
   I am going to sing at karaoke. Shall we go together?

   아니, 없어. 3 시에 중요한 농구 시합이 있어. 농구 연습할거야.
   하지만 4 시에는 같이 놀 수 있어.
   No, I don't. I have an important basketball game at 3 o'clock. I'll practice basketball.
   But, we can hang out together at 4 o'clock.

   응, 있어. 나 너무 배고파. 우리 점심밥 먹을까?
   Yes, I do. I am so hungry. Shall we eat lunch?

4. **저는 내일 영국에 가요. 그리고 프랑스도 갈 거예요. 너무 기뻐요.**
   I'm going to England tomorrow. And then, I will go to France too. I am very happy.

   언제 다시 올 거예요? 저도 같이 가고 싶어요.
   When are you going to come here again? I want to go there with you.

   영국이랑 프랑스에 비행기로 갈 거예요?
   Will you go to England and France by airplane?

   거기에서 뭐 할 거예요? 중요한 시합이 있어요?
   What are you going to do there? Do you have an important game?

5. 기분이 어때요?
How are you feeling?

기분 means "mood" or "feelings".

저는 돈이 없어요. 저녁밥을 먹을 수 없었어요. 그래서 너무 슬퍼요.
I don't have money. I couldn't eat dinner. So I am very sad.

저는 수학 시험에서 A를 받았어요. 그래서 정말 기뻐요.
I got an A on my math test. So I am really happy.

17 Conversation 대화 K-E

1. Polite conversation between friends at a chicken and beer restaurant.

A: 닭갈비 먹어 봤어요?
B: 아니요, 아직 안 먹어 봤어요. 정말 먹고 싶어요. 먹어 봤어요? 매워요?
A: 아니요, 별로 안 매워요.
B: 지금 먹을까요?

A: Did you try the chicken ribs?
B: No, I didn't try them yet. I really want to eat them. Did you try them? Are they spicy?
A: No, they weren't that spicy.
B: Shall we eat some now?

2. Polite conversation between friends in search of relief.

A: 화장실에 가고 싶어요. 어디에 화장실이 있어요?
B: 저 빨간 문이 화장실이에요. 하지만 그 화장실에 가지 마세요.
거기에 화장지가 없어요.
A: 오, 그럼 편의점은 어디에 있어요?
B: 저기에 있어요. 같이 갑시다. 저도 화장지가 필요해요.

A: I want to go to the bathroom. Where is the bathroom?
B: The red door over there is the bathroom. But don't go to that restroom.
There is no toilet paper there.
A: Oh, then where is a convenience store?
B: It's over there. Let's go together. I need toilet paper too.

3. Polite conversation between friends.

A: 오늘 일하고 싶지 않아요. 눈이 많이 오고 있어요.
B: 사장님한테 전화해 봐요.
아마 오늘 쉴 수 있을 거예요.
A: 지금 사장님은 제 전화를 받을 수 없어요. 방콕에 있어요.

A: I don't want to work today. It's snowing too much.
B: Try calling the president of your company.
Maybe you will be able to take a break today.
A: The president is unable to answer my call right now. He is in Bangkok.

17 Conversation 대화 E-K

1. Casual conversation between a hungry friend and a glutton.

A: I am not that full. I want to eat more.
B: You ate all my food. So I was unable to eat.
A: But I am still hungry. Let's buy delicious food at that store over there.
B: Buy it.

A: 나 별로 배부르지 않아. 더 먹고 싶어.
B: 네가 내 음식을 다 먹었어. 그래서 나는 못 먹었어.
A: 하지만 나는 아직 배고파. 저 가게에서 맛있는 음식을 사자.
B: 사 봐.

Remember that 네 is pronounced 니 when speaking.

2. Polite conversation between friends.

A: I am really hungry. I wasn't able to eat from morning until now.
B: Shall we eat dinner now?
A: I'm unable to eat now. My grandmother is coming to my home.
B: It's okay. Let's eat tomorrow.

A: 너무 배고파요. 아침부터 지금까지 먹지 못했어요.
B: 지금 저녁밥을 먹을까요?
A: 지금 못 먹어요. 할머니가 집에 올 거예요.
B: 괜찮아요. 내일 먹읍시다.

17 Workbook Area

❑ A17-1. Reading comprehension

At your current level, you should understand all of the grammar and words in the following sections. If you are struggling to understand them, review this and prior lessons.

New word for this comprehension: 완전히 (completely)

① 제 집은 서울에 있어요.

② 다음 주에 남자친구와 제주도에서 놀 거예요.

③ 서울하고 제주도는 완전히 달라요.

④ 제주도에는 착한 사람이 많아요.

⑤ 그리고 바다가 너무 예뻐요.

⑥ 제주도의 바다에서 수영하고 싶어요.

Dialogue

A 씨: 너 어디야?

B 씨: 지금 남자친구랑 비행기를 타고 있어. 아직 출발 안 했어.

A 씨: 부모님한테 말했어?

B 씨: 아니, 안 했어. 부모님한테 말하지 마.

❑ A17-2. Reading comprehension questions

Answer the following questions about the reading comprehension in the prior section.

1. 이 사람들은 어디에 가고 있어요?

____

2. 여자친구는 부모님한테 말했어요?

____

3. B 씨는 누구랑 같이 제주도에 가요?

____

Answer Key

❑ Lesson A: Hangul Matching

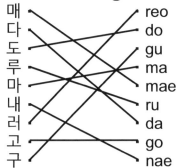

매	reo
다	do
도	gu
루	ma
마	mae
내	ru
러	da
고	go
구	nae

❑ Lesson B: Hangul Matching

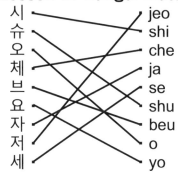

시	jeo
슈	shi
오	che
체	ja
브	se
요	shu
자	beu
저	o
세	yo

❑ Lesson C: Hangul Matching

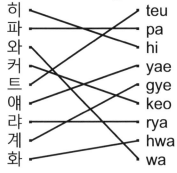

히	teu
파	pa
와	hi
커	yae
트	gye
얘	keo
랴	rya
계	hwa
화	wa

❑ Lesson D: Hangul Matching

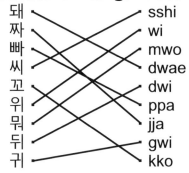

돼	sshi
짜	wi
빠	mwo
씨	dwae
꼬	dwi
위	ppa
뭐	jja
뒤	gwi
귀	kko

--- LESSON 2 ANSWERS ---

❑ A2-1. Korean VS Chinese number practice

1. 12 - Korean: 열둘 Chinese: 십이
2. 43 - Korean: 마흔셋 Chinese: 사십삼
3. 29 - Korean: 스물아홉 Chinese: 이십구
4. 55 - Korean: 쉰다섯 Chinese: 오십오
5. 16 - Korean: 열여섯 Chinese: 십육
6. 20 - Korean: 스물 Chinese: 이십

--- LESSON 3 ANSWERS ---

❑ A3-1. Korean VS Chinese number practice

1. 19 years old – 열아홉 살
2. 41 years old – 마흔한 살
3. 22 years old – 스물두 살
4. 20 years old – 스무 살
5. 36 years old – 서른여섯 살
6. 28 years old – 스물여덟 살
7. 5 years old – 다섯 살
8. 67 years old – 예순일곱 살

--- LESSON 4 ANSWERS ---

❑ A4-1. Questions to you

1. Are you Minsu Park?

   Possible answers
   A) 아니요
   B) 박민수가 아닙니다.

❑ A4-2. Sentence Jumble

1. 개입니다. / 개예요.
   책입니까? 책이에요?
   아니요. 차입니다. / 차예요.
2. 사과입니다. / 사과예요.
   바나나입니까? 바나나예요?
   아니요. 버스입니다. / 버스예요.

❑ A4-3. Picture question and answer

1. What is it?
   개입니다. / 개예요.

2. Is this a nose?
   아니요, 입입니다 / 입이에요.

3. Is this Minsu Park?
   아니요, 김준호 씨입니다 / 김준호 씨예요.

4. What is it? (this)
   사과입니다 / 사과예요.

--- LESSON 5 ANSWERS ---

❑ A5-1. Sentence Jumble

1. 이것은 버섯입니까? / 이것은 버섯이에요?
   그것은 고기가 아닙니다. /그것은 고기가 아니에요.
   야채는 뭐예요? / 야채는 뭐입니까?

2. 어느 나라 사람입니까 / 이에요?
   미국 사람입니다 / 이에요.
   한국 사람이 아닙니다 / 아니에요.

3. 이것은 오이가 아니에요.
   발은 다리가 아니에요.
   그것은 코예요.

❑ A5-2. Picture question and answer

1. What is this?
   이것은 고양이입니다.
   이것은 고양이예요.
   고양이예요.

2. Is this a cat?
   아니요, 귤입니다.
   아니요, 귤이에요.
   귤이에요.

3. What is it?
   강아지예요.
   강아지입니다.
   개예요.
   개입니다.

4. Is this a nose?
   아니요, 입입니다.
   아니요, 입이에요,
   아니요.

5. Is this meat?
   아니요, 과일이에요.
   아니요, 사과예요.

6. What is it?
   차예요.

❑ A5-3. Korean translation

1. A: What is this?
   B: That is meat.
   A: Is that a car over there?
   B: No, that's a bicycle.

❑ A5-4. English translation

1. A: 고양이예요?
   B: 아니요, 개예요.
   A: 박민수 씨예요?
   B: 아니요, 김민수예요.

--- LESSON 6 ANSWERS ---

❑ A6-1. Reading comprehension

① Bananas are fruit.
② Fruit is delicious.
③ Juice is sweet.
④ Melons are big.

A: Is it a banana?
B: No it's a tangerine.
A: Does it taste good?
B: Yes, it's sweet.

❑ A6-2. Reading comprehension questions

1. Is juice sweet?
   네, 달아요.
2. Are tangerines salty.
   아니요, 달아요.
3. Are melons small?
   아니요, 커요.

❑ A6-3. Sentence Jumble

Different verb conjugations are acceptable in answers.

1. 이 사람은 대학생입니다.
   저 과일은 맛있어요.
   그 선생님은 대학생이 아닙니다.
2. 이 양말은 비싸요.
   그 고기는 맛있어요.
   과일은 써요.
3. 이 바나나는 달아요.
   날씨가 좋아요.
   그 영화는 재미있어요.

❑ A6-4. Korean translation

1. A: What is this?
   B: That is pizza
   A: Is it delicious?
   B: No, it is salty.

❑ A6-5. English translation

1. A: 버섯이에요?
   B: 아니요, 멜론이에요.
   A: 달아요?
   B: 아니요, 써요.

❑ A6-6. Basic form drill

1.	A) 기쁘	B) ㅡ	C) 빠	D) 기뻐	E) rule 5
2.	A) 느리	B) ㅣ	C) no	D) 느려	E) rule 3
3.	A) 늦	B) ㅡ	C) yes	D) 늦어	E) rule 5

--- LESSON 7 ANSWERS ---

❑ A7-1. Reading comprehension

① My sibling's girlfriend's name is Jenny.
② Jenny is a college student.
③ She is English.
④ She is 20 years old.

A: Who is this girl?
B: It's my younger brother's girlfriend Jenny.
A: She's a foreigner? Which nationality is she?
B: She is English.

❑ A7-2. Reading comprehension questions

1. What nationality is Jenny?
   영국 사람이에요.
2. Is my sibling's girlfriend's name "Seona"?
   아니요. 제니예요.
3. Is Jenny 30 years old?
   아니요. 스무 살이에요.

❑ A7-3. Sentence Jumble

Different verb conjugations are acceptable in answers.

1. 제 성적은 나빠요.
   이 커피는 차가워요.
   이름이 뭐예요.

2. 그녀가 제 선생님입니다.
   제 남동생의 이름이 선호입니다.
   날씨가 더워요.

3. 그녀의 방이 작아요.
   제 어머니의 차는 도요타입니다.
   저 국은 맛있어요.

❑ A7-4. Korean translation

1. A: Is this coffee hot?
   B: No, it is cold.
   A: Is the weather hot?
   B: No, it is cold.

❑ A7-5. English translation

1. A: 이 잡지는 누구의 것이에요?
   B: 제 것이에요.
   A: 이 도요타는 누구의 것이에요?
   B: 제 친구의 차예요.

❑ A7-6. BASIC form drill

1.	A) 더럽	B) ㅂ	C) 워	D) 더러워	
2.	A) 슬프	B) ㅡ	C) 퍼	D) 슬퍼	E) rule 5
3.	A) 흐리	B) ㅣ	C) no	D) 흐려	E) rule 3
4.	A) 넓	B) ㅓ	C) yes	D) 넓어	E) rule 4
5.	A) 바쁘	B) ㅡ	C) 빠	D) 바빠	E) rule 5

--- LESSON 8 ANSWERS ---

❑ A8-1. Reading comprehension

① There is a banana next to the book.
② That book is Minsu's book.
③ Where is Minsu's magazine?
④ It's not in the bag.

A: Is the book on top of the chair?
B: No, it's not there.
A: Where is the magazine?
B: It's next to the apple.

❑ A8-2. Reading comprehension questions

1. Is the magazine next to the banana?
   아니요, 사과 옆에 있어요.
2. Is the magazine in the bag?
   아니요, 사과 옆에 있어요.
3. Whose book is this book?
   민수 씨의 책이에요.

❑ A8-3. Sentence Jumble

Different verb conjugations are acceptable in answers.

1. 제 양말은 책상 위에 있어요.
   그의 숙제는 쉬워요.
   네 오빠가 있어요.

2. 그녀는 병원에 있어요.
   귤은 의자 뒤에 있어요.
   선생님은 교실에 있어요?

3. 그의 누나는 어디에 있어요?
   너는 개가 있어?
   그녀는 숙제가 없어요.

❑ A8-4. Korean translation

1. A: Where is Seonhee's bag?
   B: It's next to the desk.
   A: Is this homework easy?
   B: No, it is hard.

❑ A8-5. English translation

1. A: 의자 있어요?
   B:아니요, 없어요.
   A: 어머니는 방에 있어요?
   B: 네, 있어요.

--- LESSON 9 ANSWERS ---

❑ A9-1. Reading comprehension

① Next to my school there is a movie theater.
② Kelly has 2 movie tickets.
③ 2 movie tickets is 17,000 won.
④ Popcorn is 5,000 won.

A: Hello.
B: 3 movie tickets please. How much is it?
A: It's 25,500 won.
B: 2 popcorns please.
A: Okay.

❑ A9-2. Reading comprehension questions

1. How many movie tickets does Jenny have?
   두 장 있어요.
2. How much is the popcorn?
   오천 원이에요.
3. Is there a movie theater next to the airport?
   아니요, 학교 옆에 있어요.

❑ A9-3. Sentence Jumble

Different verb conjugations are acceptable in answers.

1. 이 맥주는 맛없어.
   제 차는 빨라요. / 저의 차는 빨라요.
   물을 주세요.

2. 음식 오 인분을 주세요.
   제 아버지는 재미없어요.
   개가 열 마리 있어요.

3. 맥주가 있어요?
   이 학교에 백 명 있어요.
   네 남동생이 너무 귀여워요.

❑ A9-4. Korean translation

1. A: How much is one piece of candy?
   B: It's 1000 won.
   A: Give me 5 please.
   B: It's 5,000 won.

❑ A9-5. English translation

1. A: 이 김밥은 맛있어요?
   B: 아니요, 너무 짜요.
   A: 그럼, 계란 세개 주세요.
   B: 세 개 없어요. 두 개 있어요.

❑ A9-6. BASIC form drill

1.	A) 어렵	B) ㅂ	C) 워	D) 어려워	
2.	A) 빠르	B) ㅡ	C) 라	D) ㄹ	E) 빨라
3.	A) 머무르	B) ㅡ	C) 러	D) ㄹ	E) 머물러
4.	A) 입	B) ㅣ	C) yes	D) 입어	E) rule 3
5.	A) 가르치	B) ㅣ	C) no	D) 가르쳐	E) rule 3

--- LESSON 10 ANSWERS ---

❑ A10-1. Reading comprehension

① Ricky goes to Mexico every July.
② He has many friends and family in Mexico.
③ Ricky's father is Mexican.
④ Mexico is very beautiful.

A: Junho when will you go to Mexico?
B: I will go in July.
A: What day of the week will you go?
B: I will go on Monday.

❑ A10-2. Reading comprehension questions

1. When will Junho go to Mexico?
   월요일에 갈 거예요.
2. What nationality is Ricky's father?
   멕시코 사람이에요.
3. Who is there a lot of in Mexico?
   친구와 가족이 많아요.

❑ A10-3. Sentence Jumble

Different verb conjugations are acceptable in answers.

1. 제 친구는 금요일에 서울에 올 거예요.
   저는 내일 절에 갈 거예요.
   금요일과 토요일에 서울에 갔어요.

2. 십일월은 더울 거예요?
   이 국은 너무 뜨거워!
   제 친구의 집에 갔어요.

3. 어제 약국에 갔어요.
   매년 삼월에 어머니가 여기에 와요.
   이 숙제는 정말 어려워요.

❑ A10-4. Korean translation

1. A: When is your test?
   B: It's on Wednesday.
   A: Are your grades good now?
   B: No… they are bad.

❑ A10-5. English translation

1. A: 남동생은 몇 월에 호주에 갔어요?
   B: 십이월에 갔어요.
   A: 매년 십이월에 가요?
   B: 네, 매년 십이월과 오월에 가요.

--- LESSON 11 ANSWERS ---

❑ A11-1. Reading comprehension

① This Thursday is Junho's birthday.
② Junho's birthday is January 4.
③ This year he is 24 years old.
④ That computer over there is Junho's birthday present.

A: When is Junho's birthday?
B: It's this Thursday.
A: Will you be going to his party.
B: Yes, I will go with my older sister.

❑ A11-2. Reading comprehension questions

1. How old is Junho.
   스물네살이에요.
2. Is Junho's birthday present a bed?
   아니요. 컴퓨터예요.
3. Is Junho's birthday on Friday?
   아니요, 목요일이에요.

❑ A11-3. Date challenge

1. 천구백구십삼년 시월 삼십일일
2. 천구백팔십팔년 사월 오일
3. 천구백육십구년 칠월 이십일.
4. 이천년 일월 일일
5. 이천이십년 팔월 십오일
6. 이천십오년 오월 이십삼일

❑ A11-4. Time challenge

1. 네 시
2. 여섯 시 오 분
3. 일곱 시 오십 분
4. 두 시 삼십 분 / 두 시 반
5. 열두 시 이십 분
6. 여덟 시 오십이 분

❑ A11-5. Korean translation

1. A: What did you eat on New Year's Day
   B: I ate rice cakes.
   A: Did they taste good?
   B: No. They tasted really bad.

❑ A11-6. English translation

1. A: 다음 달에 제 결혼식에 올 거예요?
   B: 네, 여자친구하고 같이 갈 거예요. 며칠이에요?
   A: 십오일 오후 세 시예요.
   B: 결혼식에서 많이 먹을 거예요.

--- LESSON 12 ANSWERS ---

❑ A12-1. Reading comprehension

① Junho Kim needs new furniture.
② He doesn't have a lot of money.
③ At the store, there is a lot of cheap furniture.
④ Junho Kim doesn't like expensive furniture.

A: When are you buying a big bed?
B: I don't know. I don't have money now.
A: There is probably a lot of cheap furniture at that store over there.
B: Are you going now?
A: No. Today I have class.

❑ A12-2. Reading comprehension questions

1. Does Junho Kim need an air conditioner?
   아니요. 침대가 필요해요.
2. Is there not cheap furniture at the store.
   아니요. 싼 가구가 많이 있어요.
3. Did Junho Kim go to the store today?
   아니요. 수업이 있어요. / 수업에 갔어요. / 수업에 갈 거예요.

❑ A12-3. Fill in the blank

1. ① 한국 ② 매운 ③ 있어
2. ① 는 ② 조용한 ③ 필요
3. ① 과일 ② 너무 ③ 비싸
4. ① 중국 ② 하고 ③ 시끄러워
5. ① 여동생 ② 귀여운 ③ 좋아
6. ① 다리 ② 짧아
7. ① 학교 ② 에서 ③ 멀어
8. ① 남자 ② 착해
9. ① 부모님 ② 것 ③ 싫어
10. ① 뒤 ② 큰 ③ 요

--- LESSON 13 ANSWERS ---

❑ A13-1. Reading comprehension

① My younger brother called me.
② I had a class.
③ Now it's 4:00 in the afternoon.
④ I have a meeting at 8:00.

A: Did you call? I had a class.
B: I will go to your school at 7:30. Are you going to eat dinner with me?
A: No. I have a meeting at 8:00.
B: Understood. Call me.

❑ A13-2. Reading comprehension questions

1. What time is there a meeting?
   여덟 시에 미팅이 있어요.
2. Is it 7:30 right now?
   아니요. 아직 일곱 시가 아니에요. (We know this because he hasn't gone to the school yet.)
3. Who called?
   남동생이 전화했어요.

❑ A13-3. Fill in the blank

1. ① 남동생 ② 에게 or 한테 ③ 줬어
2. ① 에게서 ② 선물 ③ 받았어
3. ① 아침 ② 에게 or 한테 ③ 전화
4. ① 지난주 ② 에게 ③ 줬어
5. ① 매운 ② 볼
6. ① 사
7. ① 이 ② 를 ③ 마셔
8. ① 친구 ② 에게 ③ 많이
9. ① 내일 ② 에게서 ③ 받을
10. ① 이미 ② 고기 ③ 봤어

❑ A13-4. Korean translation

1. A: I will go to London with my older sister next week.
   B: Did you already buy an airline ticket?
   A: No, my parents gave me money yesterday. I will buy them today.

--- LESSON 14 ANSWERS ---

❑ A14-1. Reading comprehension

① On Sunday, I won't go to work.
② I will go to the park with a friend.
③ Today isn't cold.
④ We will depart at 11 am.

A: Are you going to work today?
B: No, today I'm not going to work.
A: Shall we go to the park?
B: Nice. Shall we depart at 11 am?

❑ A14-2. Reading comprehension questions

1. What time are they going to the park?
   11 시에 가요.
2. Is today cold?
   아니요. 춥지 않아요.
3. What time is he/she going to work?
   회사에 가지 않을 거예요.

❑ A14-3. Fill in the blank

1. ① 같이 ② 공원 ③ 자
2. ① 우리 ② 하고 / 랑 / 와 ③ 까
3. ① 가족 ② 오후 ③ 않았어
4. ① 지금 ② 에서 ③ 쉬어
5. ① 같이 ② 에서 ③ 하자 / 합시다
6. ① 커피 ② 뜨겁지
7. ① 저 ② 에서 ③ 쉴까
8. ① 가족 ② 몰라
9. ① 볼 까요
10. ① 오후 ② 에 ③ 출발
11. ① 학교 ② 에 대해 ③ 공부
12. ① 내 ② 일 ③ 을 거예요

❑ A14-4. Korean translation

1. A: What time is mother going to arrive at school?
   B: I don't know. Did you call mom?
   A: No, I didn't call her.
   B: Let's call her now.

❑ A14-5. English translation

1. A: 미국 역사에 대해 몰라요. 당신은 알아요?
   B: 몰라요. 지금은 학교에서 중국에 대해 공부해요.
   A: 중국은 재미있어요?
   B: 아니요, 재미없어요.

--- LESSON 15 ANSWERS ---

❑ A15-1. Reading comprehension

① I called my friend just now.
② Next month I will be going from Korea to Berlin.
③ From last month I started German language studies.
④ Even now, German is hard for me.

A: I can't arrive in Berlin by 3 pm.
B: What time will you arrive?
A: I don't know. I will probably arrive at 5:00.
B: Got it.

❑ A15-2. Reading comprehension questions

1. Will Mr. A arrive in Berlin at 3 pm.
   아니요. 도착할 수 없어요.
2. Since when did Mr. A start studying German?
   지난달부터 시작했어요.
3. From where to where is Mr. A going?
   한국부터 베를린까지 갈 거예요.

❑ A15-3. Fill in the blank

1. 오후 5 시에 영화가 시작해요.
2. 제 수업은 오전에 시작할 거예요.
3. 그는 나에게 생일을 물어봤어요.
4. 선생님한테서 이메일을 받았어요.
5. 그에게 전화번호를 줄 수 없었어요.
6. 어제 음악을 들었어요.
7. 이 맥주를 마실 수 있어요?
8. 사랑할 수 없어요.
9. 부모님은 늦은 밤에 집에 올 거예요.
10. 이 긴 길은 남자친구와 같이 걸었어요.

❑ A15-4. Korean translation

1. A: Today I'm going to the ocean with my friend. Will you go with me?
   B: What time are you going?
   A: I'm going at 2 o'clock.
   B: I can't go. My class starts at 1 o'clock.

❑ A15-5. Korean translation

1. A: 지금 뭐해요?
   B: 싸이의 음악을 들어요.
   A: 정말 싸이를 좋아해요. 그의 음악이 재미있어요. 저한테 음악을 줄 수 있어요?
   B: 네, 줄 수 있어요.

--- LESSON 16 ANSWERS ---

❑ A16-1. Reading comprehension

① My boyfriend sent me a train ticket.
② I went to Busan early morning by subway.
③ Today I will eat chicken ribs with my boyfriend for the first time.
④ We will eat together tonight also.

A: What time shall we eat chicken ribs?
B: I will arrive in Busan at 8:15 in the morning.
A: This evening let's eat something sweet too.
B: Sounds good. Let's eat ice cream.

❑ A16-2. Reading comprehension questions

1. What will Ms. A eat for the first time in Busan.
   닭갈비를 먹을 거예요.
2. What will Ms. A and Mr. B eat tonight?
   단 것을 먹을 거예요. / 아이스크림을 먹을 거예요.
3. What time did Ms. A depart from Busan?
   몰라요.

❑ A16-3. Fill in the blank

1. 지하철로 학교에 갈 거예요.
2. 고양이들이 집에 많이 있어요.
3. 저는 비행기를 못 타요.
4. 어젯밤에 늦게 잤어요.
5. 제가 아직 한국어를 못 읽어요.
6. 이메일에 대답해 주세요.
7. 물고기를 못 먹어요?
8. 이 가위를 안 쓸 거예요.
9. 처음부터 그를 좋아했어요.
10. 친구들에게 말하고 있어요.

❑ A16-4. Korean translation

1. A: Where did you get off at?
   B: I didn't get off yet. Even now I am riding on a bus.
   A: Are you going to arrive here late?
   B: I'll probably arrive at 3 o'clock.

--- LESSON 17 ANSWERS ---

❑ A17-1. Reading comprehension

① My house is in Seoul.
② Next week, I will play on Jeju island with my boyfriend.
③ Seoul and Jeju island are completely different.
④ On Jeju island there are a lot of kind people.
⑤ And, the beach is very pretty.
⑥ I want to swim at Jeju island's beach.

A: Where are you?
B: I'm on an airplane with my boyfriend. We haven't departed yet.
A: Did you tell your parents?
B: No, I didn't. Don't tell my parents.

❑ A17-2. Reading comprehension questions

1. Where are these people going?
   제주도에 가고 있어요.
2. Did the girlfriend tell her parents?
   아니요. 말하지 않았어요.
3. Who is Ms. B going with to Jeju island?
   남자친구랑 갈 거예요.

Verb Reference Guide

Dictionary Form
This is the form of the verb found in the dictionary. There are also uses for it in speaking and a variety of grammar structures use it.

Basic Form
From section 6-4 and above this is taught. It's the glue of many grammar structures in Korean. Without further conjugation it can be used "AS IS" to be a command, future tense, and also present tense based on the context of the sentence it's used in.

Verb Type
Action verbs are things that are "DONE". *Descriptive verbs* are adjectives. They describe characteristics of things.

English	Dictionary Form	Basic Form	Verb Type	Lesson
to answer	대답하다	대답해	action	15
to arrive	도착하다	도착해	action	14
to ask	묻다	물어	action	15
to be a lot, many	많다	많아	descriptive	8
to be bad	나쁘다	나빠	descriptive	6
to be big	크다	커	descriptive	6
to be bitter	쓰다	써	descriptive	6
to be black	검다	검은	descriptive	17
to be blue	파랗다	파란	descriptive	17
to be cheap	싸다	싸	descriptive	6
to be close	가깝다	가까워	descriptive	12
to be cold (weather)	춥다	추워	descriptive	7
to be cold to the touch	차갑다	차가워	descriptive	7
to be cute	귀엽다	귀여워	descriptive	9
to be different	다르다	달라	descriptive	12
to be difficult	어렵다	어려워	descriptive	8
to be easy	쉽다	쉬워	descriptive	8
to be expensive	비싸다	비싸	descriptive	6
to be far	멀다	멀어	descriptive	12
to be fast	빠르다	빨라	descriptive	9

to be full	배부르다	배불러	descriptive	17
to be good, nice	좋다	좋아	descriptive	6
to be happy	기쁘다	기뻐	descriptive	17
to be hot (weather)	덥다	더워	descriptive	7
to be hot to the touch	뜨겁다	뜨거워	descriptive	7
to be hungry	배고프다	배고파	descriptive	17
to be important	중요하다	중요해	descriptive	17
to be interesting, fun	재미있다	재미있어	descriptive	6
to be kind, nice	착하다	착해	descriptive	8
to be long	길다	길어	descriptive	12
to be loud	시끄럽다	시끄러워	descriptive	12
to be pretty, beautiful	예쁘다	예뻐	descriptive	8
to be quiet	조용하다	조용해	descriptive	12
to be red	빨갛다	빨간	descriptive	17
to be sad	슬프다	슬퍼	descriptive	17
to be salty	짜다	짜	descriptive	6
to be short	짧다	짧아	descriptive	12
to be sick, to hurt	아프다	아파	descriptive	17
to be similar	비슷하다	비슷해	descriptive	12
to be small	작다	작아	descriptive	6
to be spicy	맵다	매워	descriptive	8
to be sweet	달다	달아	descriptive	6
to be tasteless	맛없다	맛없어	descriptive	9
to be tasty, delicious	맛있다	맛있어	descriptive	6
to be the same	같다	같아	descriptive	12
to be uninteresting	재미없다	재미없어	descriptive	9
to be white	하얗	하얀	descriptive	17
to be white	희다	흰	descriptive	17
to be yellow	노랗다	노란	descriptive	17
to be, to exist, to have	있다	있어	action	8
to buy	사다	사	action	11
to come	오다	와	action	10
to depart	출발하다	출발해	action	14
to dislike	싫어하다	싫어해	action	12
to do	하다	해	action	12

to drink	마시다	마셔	action	11
to eat	먹다	먹어	action	11
to get off	내리다	내려	action	16
to give	주다	줘	action	13
to go	가다	가	action	10
to know	알다	알아	action	13
to learn	배우다	배워	action	15
to like	좋아하다	좋아해	action	12
to listen, hear	듣다	들어	action	15
to love	사랑하다	사랑해	action	12
to meet	만나다	만나	action	17
to need	필요하다	필요해	descriptive	12
to not exist, to not have	없다	없어	action	8
to not know	모르다	몰라	action	13
to not need	필요없다	필요없어	descriptive	12
to phone	전화하다	전화해	action	13
to play, hang out	놀다	놀아	action	17
to practice	연습하다	연습해	action	17
to read	읽다	읽어	action	15
to receive, to get	받다	받아	action	13
to ride	타다	타	action	16
to see, to watch	보다	봐	action	11
to send	보내다	보내	action	16
to sing	노래하다	노래해	action	17
to sleep	자다	자	action	16
to speak, tell, talk	말하다	말해	action	16
to start, to begin	시작하다	시작해	action	15
to study	공부하다	공부해	action	12
to swim	수영하다	수영해	action	15
to take a break	쉬다	쉬어	action	14
to use	쓰다	써	action	16
to wake up	일어나다	일어나	action	16
to walk	걷다	걸어	action	15
to work	일하다	일해	action	14
to write	쓰다	써	action	16

Glossary
E-K

1, one	하나, 일	90, ninety	아흔, 구십
2, two	둘, 이	afternoon	오후
3, three	셋, 삼	again	다시
4, four	넷, 사	air conditioning	에어컨
5, five	다섯, 오	airline ticket	비행기표
6, six	여섯, 육	airplane	비행기
7, seven	일곱, 칠	airport	공항
8, eight	여덟, 팔	America	미국
9, nine	아홉, 구	American person	미국 사람
10, ten	열, 십	and then	그리고
11, eleven	열하나, 십일	animal	동물
12, twelve	열둘, 십이	apartment	아파트
13, thirteen	열셋, 십삼	apple	사과
14, fourteen	열넷, 십사	April	사월
15, fifteen	열다섯, 십오	arm	팔
16, sixteen	열여섯, 십육	August	팔월
17, seventeen	열일곱, 십칠	Australia	호주
18, eighteen	열여덟, 십팔	Australian person	호주 사람
19, nineteen	열아홉, 십구	automobile	자동차
20, twenty	스물, 이십	baby	아기
21, twenty one	스물하나, 이십일	back	등
22, twenty two	스물둘, 이십이	bad	나쁘다
23, twenty three	스물셋, 이십삼	bag	가방
24, twenty four	스물넷, 이십사	ball	공
25, twenty five	스물다섯, 이십오	banana	바나나
26, twenty six	스물여섯, 이십육	Bangkok, Thailand	방콕
27, twenty seven	스물일곱, 이십칠	bank	은행
28, twenty eight	스물여덟, 이십팔	baseball	야구
29, twenty nine	스물아홉, 이십구	basketball	농구
30, thirty	서른, 삼십	bathroom	화장실
40, forty	마흔, 사십	bear	곰
50, fifty	쉰, 오십	beautiful	예쁘다
60, sixty	예순, 육십	bed	침대
70, seventy	일흔, 칠십	beer	맥주
80, eighty	여든, 팔십	before noon	오전

Beijing, China	베이징
Berlin, Germany	베를린
beverage (non-alcoholic)	음료수
bicycle	자전거
big	크다
biology	생물
birthday party	생일 파티
bitter	쓰다
black (noun)	검은색
black (verb)	검다
blue (noun)	파란색
blue (verb)	파랗다
body	몸
book	책
book store	서점
boy, man	남자
boyfriend	남자친구
bread	빵
breakfast	아침밥
brown	갈색
Buddhist temple	절
bus	버스
business card	명함
but, however	하지만
buttocks	엉덩이
cake	케이크
calculator	계산기
Canada	캐나다
Canadian person	캐나다 사람
candy	사탕
car	차
cat	고양이
cell phone	핸드폰
chair	의자
cheap	싸다
cheese	치즈
cherry	앵두
chicken	치킨
chicken ribs	닭갈비
child	아이
chin	턱
China	중국
Chinese person	중국 사람
Christmas	크리스마스
church	교회
class	수업
classroom	교실
coffee	커피
cola (Coke ®)	콜라
cola light (Diet Coke ®)	콜라 라이트
cold (weather)	춥다
cold to the touch	차갑다
college	대학교
college student	대학생
color	색깔
comic book	만화책
computer	컴퓨터
concert	콘서트
convenience store	편의점
cooked rice	밥
cooking	요리
country	나라
cucumber	오이
daughter	딸
dawn	새벽
day	날
day of birth	생일
December	십이월
delicious	맛있다
department store	백화점

desk	책상
difficult	어렵다
dinner	저녁밥. 밥
dog	개
dollar	달러
door	문
dragon	용
dream	꿈
ear	귀
early	일찍
easy	쉽다
education	교육
egg	계란
eight	여덟, 팔
eighteen	열여덟, 십팔
eighty	여든, 팔십
elbow	팔꿈치
elephant	코끼리
eleven	열하나, 십일
e-mail	이메일
emergency	응급
English person	영국 사람
etc	등등
euro (EU money)	유로
evening	저녁
every day	매일
every month	매달
every week	매주
every year	매년
everything, all	다
expensive	비싸다
eye	눈
face	얼굴
family	가족
father	아버지
February	이월
fifteen	열다섯, 십오
fifty	쉰, 오십
Filipino person	필리핀 사람
finger	손가락
first time	처음
fish	물고기
five	다섯, 오
flowers	꽃
food	음식
foot	발
forty	마흔, 사십
four	넷, 사
fourteen	열넷, 십사
France	프랑스
french fries	감자튀김
Friday	금요일
friend	친구
fruit	과일
furniture	가구
Germany	독일
giraffe	기린
girl, woman	여자
girlfriend	여자친구
good, nice	좋다
goodbye	안녕
grades	성적
grandfather	할아버지
grandmother	할머니
grapes	포도
green	초록색
hamburger	햄버거
hand	손
head, hair	머리
heart, mind	마음

here	여기
hippo	하마
history	역사
homework	숙제
hospital	병원
hot (weather)	덥다
hot to the touch	뜨겁다
hotel	호텔
hour	시간
house, home	집
how much?	얼마
hurry up	빨리
I (polite)	저, 제
I, me (casual)	나
India	인도
interesting, fun	재미있다
January	일월
Japan	일본
joke	농담
juice	주스
July	칠월
June	유월
Junho Kim (man's name)	김준호
just now, just a moment ago	아까
just; just because	그냥
karaoke (singing room)	노래방
kind, nice	착하다
knees	무릎
Korea	한국
Korean person	한국 사람
laptop computer	노트북
Las Vegas, USA	라스베가스
last month	지난달
last night	어젯밤
last week	지난주
last year	작년
late	늦게
late night	늦은 밤
leg	다리
letter	편지
library	도서관
lie	거짓말
light blue	하늘색
literature	문학
London, England	런던
Los Angeles, USA	로스앤젤레스
lots	많이
lots (verb form)	많다
lunch	밥, 점심밥
magazine	잡지
man	남자
mandarin orange	귤
Manila, Philippines	마닐라
many	많이
many (verb form)	많다
March	삼월
match	시합
math	수학
May	오월
maybe, probably	아마
me (casual)	나
me (polite)	저
meal	식사
meat	고기
meat (roasted)	불고기
medicine	약
meeting	미팅
melon	멜론
Mexico	멕시코
milk	우유

Minsu Park (man name)	박민수	October	시월
mirror	거울	older brother	오빠
Monday	월요일	older sister	누나
money	돈	one	하나, 일
more	더	orange	주황색
morning	아침	Ottawa, Canada	오타와
mother	어머니	our	우리의
mouse	쥐	over there	저기
mouth	입	paper	종이
movie	영화	parents	부모님
movie theater	영화관	Paris, France	파리
Mr., Mrs., Miss	~씨	park	공원
much	많이	party	파티
much (verb form)	많다	pear	배
mushroom	버섯	pen	펜
music	음악	pencil	연필
my	제, 내	penguin	펭귄
name	이름	person	사람
New Year's Day	설날	pharmacy	약국
New York, USA	뉴욕	Philippines	필리핀
next month	다음달	phone number	전화번호
next week	다음 주	phone, phone call	전화
next year	내년	photograph	사진
night, evening	밤	picture	사진
nightmare	악몽	ping pong	탁구
nine	아홉, 구	pink	분홍색
nineteen	열아홉, 십구	pizza	피자
ninety	아흔, 구십	place	장소
nonsense	옹알이	pollution	오염
nose	코	potato	감자
not so~ much	별로	present	선물
not yet	아직	president (of company)	사장님
November	십일월	pretty	예쁘다
now, right now	지금	PSY (Korean singer)	싸이
ocean	바다	puppy	강아지

purple	보라색
purse	가방
Quebec, Canada	퀘벡
question	질문
quickly	빨리
quite~	아주
ramen noodles	라면
really~	정말, 진짜
reason	이유
recently	최근
red (noun)	빨간색
red (verb)	빨갛다
restaurant	식당
ribs	갈비
rice (cooked)	밥
rice cakes	떡
road	길
roasted meat	불고기
room	방
ruler	자
salty	짜다
Saturday	토요일
school	학교
science	과학
scissors	가위
seaweed roll	김밥
September	구월
seven	일곱, 칠
seventeen	열일곱, 십칠
seventy	일흔, 칠십
shoes	신발
shoulder	어깨
singing room (karaoke)	노래방
six	여섯, 육
sixteen	열여섯, 십육
sixty	예순, 육십
skirt	치마
sky blue	하늘색
small	작다
snow	눈
so	그래서
so~	매우
soccer	축구
socks	양말
son	아들
song	노래
sound	소리
soup	국
spicy	맵다
sports	스포츠
sports game	시합
stapler	스테이플러
Starcraft	스타크래프트
station	역
stomach	배
store	가게
story	이야기
street	길
student	학생
subway	지하철
subway station	역
Sunday	일요일
sweet	달다
swimming	수영
swimming pool	수영장
table tennis	탁구
Tae kwon do	태권도
tangerine	귤
tape	테이프
tasty	맛있다

taxi	택시	to be happy	기쁘다
tea	차	to be hungry	배고프다
teacher	선생님	to be important	중요하다
teeth	이	to be long	길다
television	텔레비전	to be loud	시끄럽다
TV	티부이	to be quiet	조용하다
ten	열, 십	to be sad	슬프다
test, exam	시험	to be short	짧다
Thai person	태국 사람	to be sick, to hurt	아프다
Thailand	태국	to be similar	비슷하다
that	그것, 저것	to be tasteless	맛없다
that one	그것	to be the same	같다
that one over there	저것	to be uninteresting	재미없다
that's why	그래서	to begin	시작하다
there	거기	to buy	사다
therefore	그래서	to come	오다
thirteen	열셋, 십삼	to depart	출발하다
thirty	서른, 삼십	to dislike	싫어하다
this	이것	to do	하다
this month	이번달	to drink	마시다
this one	이것	to eat	먹다
this week	이번주	to exist, to have	있다
this year	올해	to get	받다
three	셋, 삼	to get off	내리다
Thursday	목요일	to give	주다
time	시간	to go	가다
to answer	대답하다	to know	알다
to arrive	도착하다	to learn	배우다
to ask	묻다	to like	좋아하다
to be close	가깝다	to listen, hear	듣다
to be cute	귀엽다	to love	사랑하다
to be different	다르다	to meet	만나다
to be far	멀다	to need	필요하다
to be fast	빠르다	to not exist, to not have	없다
to be full	배부르다	to not know	모르다

to not need	필요없다
to phone	전화하다
to play, hang out	놀다
to practice	연습하다
to read	읽다
to receive	받다
to ride	타다
to see	보다
to send	보내다
to sing	노래하다
to sleep	자다
to speak	말하다
to start	시작하다
to study	공부하다
to swim	수영하다
to take a break	쉬다
to talk	말하다
to tell	말하다
to use	쓰다
to wake up	일어나다
to walk	걷다
to watch	보다
to work	일하다
to write	쓰다
today	오늘
toes	발가락
together	같이
Tokyo, Japan	도쿄
tomorrow	내일
tonight	오늘 밤
too~	너무
tooth	이
train	기차
train station	역
travel	여행
triangle-shaped gimbap	삼각김밥
trip	여행
Tuesday	화요일
twelve	열둘, 십이
twenty	스물, 이십
two	둘, 이
umbrella	우산
United Kingdom	영국
vegetable	야채
very~	아주, 정말, 진짜, 매우, 너무
volleyball	배구
wallet	지갑
water	물
watermelon	수박
we	우리
weather	날씨
wedding	결혼식
Wednesday	수요일
what day of the week?	무슨 요일
what kind of~?	어떤
what type of~?	어떤
what~	무슨
when?	언제
where?	어디
which nationality?	어느 나라 사람
which~?	어느
white (noun)	흰색
white (verb)	하얗다, 희다
who?	누구
windows	창문
wine	와인
won (Korean money)	원
work	일
workplace	직장

yellow (noun)	노란색
yellow (verb)	노랗다
yen (Japanese money)	엔
yesterday	어제
yoga	요가
yogurt	요거트
you (casual)	너
you (polite, formal)	당신
younger brother	남동생
younger sibling	동생
younger sister	여동생
your	네

Glossary K-E

가게	store
가구	furniture
가깝다	to be close
가다	to go
가방	purse, bag
가위	scissors
가족	family
갈비	ribs
갈색	brown
감자	potato
감자튀김	french fries
강아지	puppy
같다	to be the same
같이	together
개	dog
거기	there
거울	mirror
거짓말	lie
걷다	to walk
검다	black
검은색	black
결혼식	wedding
계란	egg
계산기	calculator
고기	meat
고양이	cat
곰	bear
공	ball
공부하다	to study
공원	park
공항	airport
과일	fruit
과학	science
교실	classroom
교육	education
교회	church
구	9, nine
구십	90, ninety
구월	September
국	soup
귀	ear
귀엽다	to be cute
귤	tangerine/mandarin orange
그것	that / that one
그냥	just; just because
그래서	so, therefore, that's why
그리고	and then
금요일	Friday
기린	giraffe
기쁘다	to be happy
기차	train
길	road, street
길다	to be long
김밥	seaweed roll
김준호	Junho Kim (man's name)
꽃	flowers
꿈	dream
나	I, me (casual)
나라	country
나쁘다	bad
날	day
날씨	weather
남동생	younger brother
남자	man
남자친구	boyfriend
내년	next year
내리다	to get off
내일	tomorrow
너	you (casual)
너무	very (too~)
넷	4, four
노란색	yellow
노랗다	yellow
노래	song
노래방	singing room (karaoke)
노래하다	to sing
노트북	laptop computer
놀다	to play, hang out
농구	basketball
농담	joke
누구	who?
누나	older sister
눈	eye, snow
뉴욕	New York, USA

늦게	late
늦은 밤	late night
다	everything, all
다르다	to be different
다리	leg
다섯	5, five
다시	again
다음달	next month
다음 주	next week
달다	sweet
달러	dollar
닭갈비	chicken ribs
당신	you (polite, formal)
대답하다	to answer
대학교	college
대학생	college student
더	more
덥다	hot (weather)
도서관	library
도착하다	to arrive
도쿄	Tokyo, Japan
독일	Germany
돈	money
동물	animal
동생	younger sibling
둘	2, two
듣다	to listen, hear
등	back
등등	etc
딸	daughter
떡	rice cakes
뜨겁다	hot to the touch
라면	ramen noodles
라스베가스	Las Vegas, USA
런던	London, England
로스앤젤레스	Los Angeles, USA
마닐라	Manila, Philippines
마시다	to drink
마음	heart, mind
마흔	40, forty
만나다	to meet
만화책	comic book
많다	lots, many, much
많이	lots, many, much
말하다	to speak, tell, talk
맛없다	to be tasteless
맛있다	tasty, delicious
매년	every year
매달	every month
매우	very (so~)
매일	every day
매주	every week
맥주	beer
맵다	spicy
머리	head, hair
먹다	to eat
멀다	to be far
멕시코	Mexico
멜론	melon
명함	business card
모르다	to not know
목요일	Thursday
몸	body
무릎	knees
무슨	what~
무슨 요일	what day of the week?
문	door
문학	literature
묻다	to ask
물	water
물고기	fish
미국	America
미국 사람	American person
미팅	meeting
바나나	banana
바다	ocean
박민수	Minsu Park (man's name)
받다	to receive, to get
발	foot
발가락	toes
밤	night, evening
밥	dinner, lunch etc., cooked rice
방	room
방콕	Bangkok, Thailand

배	pear; stomach
배고프다	to be hungry
배구	volleyball
배부르다	to be full
배우다	to learn
백화점	department store
버섯 (버섣)	mushroom
버스	bus
베를린	Berlin, Germany
베이징	Beijing, China
별로	not so~ much
병원	hospital
보내다	to send
보다	to see, to watch
보라색	purple
부모님	parents
분홍색	pink
불고기	roast meat (fire meat)
비슷하다	to be similar
비싸다	expensive
비행기	airplane
비행기표	airline ticket
빠르다	to be fast
빨간색	red
빨갛다	red
빨리	quickly; hurry up
빵	bread
사	4, four
사과	apple
사다	to buy
사람	person
사랑하다	to love
사십	40, forty
사월	April
사장님	president (of company)
사진	photograph, picture
사탕	candy
삼	3, three
삼각김밥	triangle-shaped gimbap
삼십	30, thirty
삼월	March
새벽	dawn
색깔	color
생물	biology
생일	day of birth
생일 파티	birthday party
서른	30, thirty
서점	book store
선물	present
선생님	teacher
설날 (설랄)	New Year's Day
성적	grades
셋	3, three
소리	sound
손	hand
손가락	finger
수박	watermelon
수업	class
수영	swimming
수영장	swimming pool
수영하다	to swim
수요일	Wednesday
수학	math
숙제	homework
쉰	50, fifty
쉽다	easy
스물	20, twenty
스물넷	24
스물다섯	25
스물둘	22
스물셋	23
스물아홉	29
스물여덟	28
스물여섯	26
스물일곱	27
스물하나	21
스타크래프트	Starcraft
스테이플러	stapler
스포츠	sports
슬프다	to be sad
시간	time, hour
시끄럽다	to be loud
시월	October
시작하다	to start, to begin

시합	sports game, match
시험	test, exam
식당	restaurant
식사	meal
신발	shoes
싫어하다	to dislike
십	10, ten
십구	19, nineteen
십사	14, fourteen
십삼	13, thirteen
십오	15, fifteen
십육	16, sixteen
십이	12, twelve
십이월	December
십일	11, eleven
십일월	November
십칠	17, seventeen
십팔	18, eighteen
싸다	cheap
싸이	PSY (Korean singer)
쓰다	bitter, to use, to write
씨	Mr., Mrs., Miss
아기	baby
아까	just now, just a moment ago
아들	son
아마	maybe, probably
아버지	father
아이	child
아주	very~, quite~
아직	not yet
아침	morning
아침밥	breakfast
아파트	apartment
아프다	to be sick, to hurt
아홉	9, nine
아흔	90, ninety
악몽	nightmare
안녕	goodbye
알다	to know
앵두	cherry
야구	baseball
야채	vegetable
약	medicine
약국	pharmacy
양말	socks
어깨	shoulder
어느	which~
어느 나라 사람	which nationality?
어디	where?
어떤	what kind of~, what type of~
어렵다	difficult
어머니	mother
어제	yesterday
어젯밤	last night
언제	when?
얼굴	face
얼마	how much?
없다	to not exist, to not have
엉덩이	buttocks
에어컨	air conditioning
엔	yen (Japanese money)
여기	here
여덟	8, eight
여동생	younger sister
여든	80, eighty
여섯	6, six
여자	girl, woman
여자친구	girlfriend
여행	trip, travel
역	train station, subway station
역사	history
연습하다	to practice
연필	pencil
열	10, ten
열넷	14, fourteen
열다섯	15, fifteen
열둘	12, twelve
열셋	13, thirteen
열아홉	19, nineteen
열여덟	18, eighteen
열여섯	16, sixteen
열일곱	17, seventeen
열하나	11, eleven
영국	United Kingdom

영국 사람	English person
영화	movie
영화관	movie theater
예쁘다	pretty, beautiful
예순	60, sixty
오	5, five
오늘	today
오늘 밤	tonight
오다	to come
오빠	older brother
오십	50, fifty
오염	pollution
오월	May
오이	cucumber
오전	before noon
오타와	Ottawa, Canada
오후	afternoon
올해	this year
옹알이	nonsense
와인	wine
요가	yoga
요거트	yogurt
요리	cooking
용	dragon
우리	we
우리의	our
우산	umbrella
우유	milk
원	won (Korean money)
월요일	Monday
유로	euro (EU money)
유월	June
육	6, six
육십	60, sixty
은행	bank
음료수	beverage, drinks
음식	food
음악	music
응급	emergency
의자	chair
이	tooth, 2, two
이것	this, this one

이름	name
이메일	e-mail
이번달	this month
이번주	this week
이십	20, twenty
이십구	29, twenty-nine
이십사	24, twenty-four
이십삼	23, twenty-three
이십오	25, twenty-five
이십육	26, twenty-six
이십이	22, twenty-two
이십일	21, twenty-one
이십칠	27, twenty-seven
이십팔	28, twenty-eight
이야기	story
이월	February
이유	reason
인도	India
일	work, 1, one
일곱	7, seven
일본	Japan
일어나다	to wake up
일요일	Sunday
일월	January
일찍	early
일하다	to work
일흔	70, seventy
읽다	to read
입	mouth
있다	to exist, to have
자	ruler
자다	to sleep
자동차	automobile
자전거	bicycle
작년	last year
작다	small
잡지	magazine
장소	place
재미없다	to be uninteresting
재미있다	interesting, fun
저	I, me (polite)
저것	that, that one over there

저기	over there
저녁	evening
저녁밥	dinner
전화	phone, phone call
전화번호	phone number
전화하다	to phone
절	Buddhist temple
점심밥	lunch
정말	very, really~
조용하다	to be quiet
종이	paper
좋다	good, nice
좋아하다	to like
주다	to give
주스	juice
주황색	orange
중국	China
중국 사람	Chinese person
중요하다	to be important
쥐	mouse
지갑	wallet
지금	now, right now
지난달	last month
지난주	last week
지하철	subway
직장	workplace
진짜	very, really~
질문	question
집	house, home
짜다	salty
짧다	to be short
차	car
차	tea
차갑다	cold to the touch
착하다	kind, nice
창문	windows
책	book
책상	desk
처음	first time
초록색	green
최근	recently
축구	soccer
출발하다	to depart
춥다	cold (weather)
치마	skirt
치즈	cheese
치킨	chicken
친구	friend
칠	7, seven
칠십	70, seventy
칠월	July
침대	bed
캐나다	Canada
캐나다 사람	Canadian person
커피	coffee
컴퓨터	computer
케이크	cake
코	nose
코끼리	elephant
콘서트	concert
콜라	cola (Coke ®)
콜라 라이트	cola light (Diet Coke ®)
퀘벡	Quebec, Canada
크다	big
크리스마스	Christmas
타다	to ride
탁구	ping pong, table tennis
태국	Thailand
태국 사람	Thai person
태권도	Tae kwon do
택시	taxi
턱	chin
테이프	tape
텔레비전	television, TV
토요일	Saturday
티부이	TV
파란색	blue
파랗다	blue
파리	Paris, France
파티	party
팔	arm, 8, eight
팔꿈치	elbow
팔십	80, eighty
팔월	August

펜	pen
펭귄	penguin
편의점	convenience store
편지	letter
포도	grapes
프랑스	France
피자	pizza
필리핀	Philippines
필리핀 사람	Filipino person
필요없다	to not need
필요하다	to need
하나	1, one
하늘색	sky blue (light blue)
하다	to do
하마	hippo
하얗다	white
하지만	but, however
학교	school
학생	student
한국	Korea
한국 사람	Korean person
할머니	grandmother
할아버지	grandfather
핸드폰	cell phone
햄버거	hamburger
호주	Australia
호주 사람	Australian person
호텔	hotel
화요일	Tuesday
화장실	bathroom
쉬다	to take a break
희다	white
흰색	white

SOUTH KOREA 대한민국
Provinces & Major Cities Map

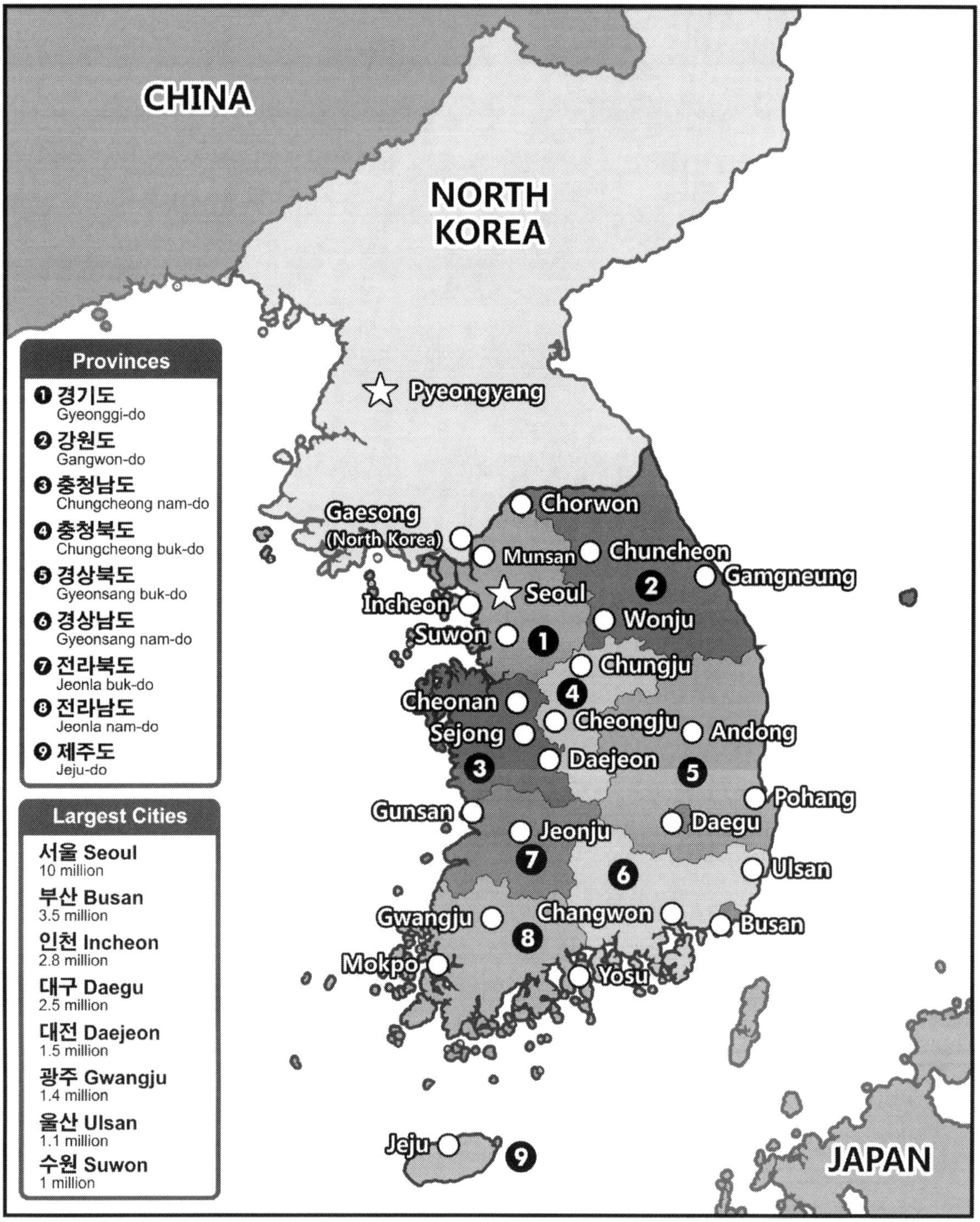
CHINA
NORTH KOREA
Pyeongyang
Provinces
❶ 경기도 Gyeonggi-do
❷ 강원도 Gangwon-do
❸ 충청남도 Chungcheong nam-do
❹ 충청북도 Chungcheong buk-do
❺ 경상북도 Gyeonsang buk-do
❻ 경상남도 Gyeonsang nam-do
❼ 전라북도 Jeonla buk-do
❽ 전라남도 Jeonla nam-do
❾ 제주도 Jeju-do
Largest Cities
서울 Seoul 10 million
부산 Busan 3.5 million
인천 Incheon 2.8 million
대구 Daegu 2.5 million
대전 Daejeon 1.5 million
광주 Gwangju 1.4 million
울산 Ulsan 1.1 million
수원 Suwon 1 million
Chorwon
Gaesong (North Korea)
Munsan
Chuncheon
Gamgneung
Incheon
Seoul
Wonju
Suwon
Chungju
Cheonan
Cheongju
Sejong
Andong
Daejeon
Pohang
Gunsan
Jeonju
Daegu
Ulsan
Gwangju
Changwon
Busan
Mokpo
Yosu
Jeju
JAPAN

HANGUL CHARACTER NAME CHART

Romanization	g/k	n	d/t	r/l	m	b/p	s
hangul consonants	ㄱ	ㄴ	ㄷ	ㄹ	ㅁ	ㅂ	ㅅ
name	기역	니은	디귿	리을	미음	비읍	시옷

Romanization	null/ng	j	ch	k	t	p	h
hangul consonants	ㅇ	ㅈ	ㅊ	ㅋ	ㅌ	ㅍ	ㅎ
name	이응	지읒	치읓	키읔	티읕	피읖	히읗

Romanization	pp	jj	dd	kk	ss
hangul consonants	ㅃ	ㅉ	ㄸ	ㄲ	ㅆ
name	쌍비읍	쌍지읒	쌍디귿	쌍기역	쌍시옷

Romanization	a	ya	eo	yeo	o	yo	u
hangul vowels	ㅏ	ㅑ	ㅓ	ㅕ	ㅗ	ㅛ	ㅜ
name	아	야	어	여	오	요	우

Romanization	yu	eu	i	ae	e	yo	u
hangul vowels	ㅠ	ㅡ	ㅣ	ㅐ	ㅔ	ㅒ	ㅖ
name	유	으	이	아이	어이	야이	여이

Romanization	wa	wae	oe	wo	we	wi	ui
hangul vowels	ㅘ	ㅙ	ㅚ	ㅝ	ㅞ	ㅟ	ㅢ
name	와	왜	외	워	웨	위	의

Cut out for reference.

Cut out for reference.

Special Thanks!

Writing a book, especially a text book, is a daunting task. Without dedicated book reviewers and people to bounce questions off of, it would be even more difficult! We would like to thank all the people that have made this book possible!

김 인종 (Injong Kim)
임 이랑 (Leerang Lim)
김 석진 (SeokJin Kim)
박 혜지 (Hyeji Bella Park)
Frank Lin
Jesse Goodburne
Justin McGowan
Tina Chen
Kathleen Nash
Adan Zurita Pardo
Mitchell Waybright
Yukari Takenaka

❑ Special Thanks to reddit.com/r/korean reviewers!

Before "Korean From Zero!" was released we asked the active members of the reddit.com Korean learning subreddit to help us do a final proofread of the pre-release candidate of the book. They did not let us down! Thank you so much! (listed in alphabetical order)

Top Reviewers

cmfoo
Miguel Angel Castiblanco
Nofap9001
Patrick Joseph Donnelly
Prapon Homvech
shes-fresh-to-death
Wilma Bainbridge
Josh Foote

Other Reviewers

beamingontheinside
BOLDtv
booyah2
Brad Willard
cheesewrangler
Chris Morlang
crozbrobro
daijobu
FloydMontel
Fragatta
hardmodethardus
Kendall Willets
kitchenmaniac111
losingthefight
loungefi
Melvin8
Michael J. Rasicci
piruli3
Ponytron200
Rachel Best
Tatyana Mohr
tooshorthair
vicereversa

Section Reference Guide

Other From Zero! Books

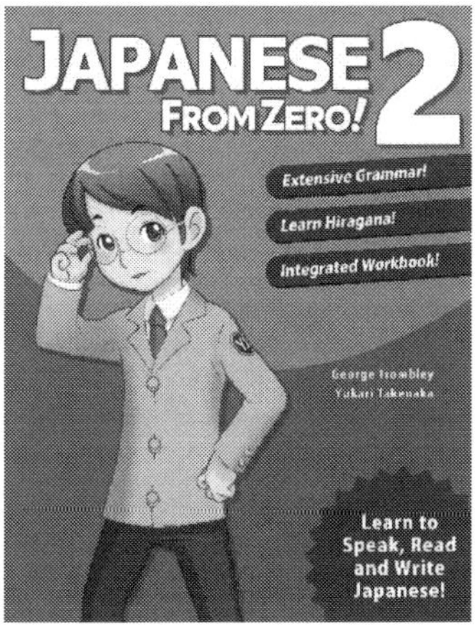

Made in the USA
Las Vegas, NV
03 January 2024

83852290R00197